Affiliate Marketing Crash Course

The Complete Step-By-Step Guide for Beginners to Generate Passive Income by Selling Other People's Products | Includes Most Profitable Niches

Robert McDay

Book 1: Affiliate Marketing for Beginners

Introduction

Affiliate marketing is a system that allows companies to effectively sponsor their products and services using partners and affiliate resources. This powerful tool in today's online business world allows you to increase your audience reach and achieve higher sales rates.

Affiliate marketing is a system based on cooperation between companies, where one party (the partner) advertises and promotes the goods or services of the other party in exchange for a commission or other form of payment. The idea of its creation originated in the 1990s and was a response to the need to attract customers in the growing online business effectively.

The basic principle of affiliate marketing is a mutually beneficial partnership where each party benefits from cooperation. Partners can differ from bloggers, website owners, social media influencers, partner companies, etc. They use their resources and distribution channels to reach the target audience and advertise products or services.

The advantages of this promotion system are obvious. Firstly, this is an effective way to increase your audience's reach and attract new customers. Partners have an audience already interested in their content and can successfully recommend products or services to their subscribers. Secondly, it allows you to reduce advertising costs since partners work on a commission basis.

The key elements of such marketing are an affiliate program, unique links or promotional codes, and a sales and payout tracking system. The program provides partners with the tools and resources to advertise products or services effectively. Unique links and promo codes allow you to track the sales that have occurred due to the efforts of each of them individually.

Through affiliate marketing, companies can achieve greater success in a competitive online environment by attracting and retaining new customers. Let's consider how this system works and the stages of cooperation between businesses and affiliates.

Chapter 1: Understanding the Basics

What is affiliate marketing?

Think of affiliate marketing in the same light as an independent brand seller. Your task is to attract people to the product to sell it. However, the product is not made by you. There are 3 key roles in affiliate marketing:

1. Branches

This is the role that you, as a marketing partner, must fulfill. Your task is to convince people that the product is worth buying. When someone devours your presentation and buys the product, you will receive a commission from the seller. It's important that you offer potential customers useful information to help them evaluate products for purchase.

2. Merchants

These are the guys who have a product that they want people to buy. However, their interest lies in creating the best product and supporting their customers. To attract more customers, they turn to partners who will promote products on their behalf.

3. Clients

Aside from affiliates and merchants, the rest of the online population is potential customers. As customers, they have needs or interests. When trying to find products that meet these needs, they need more information than what's usually offered in flyers.

While the seller and buyer roles are fairly simple, your job as an affiliate is a bit more complex. This is partly because there are many affiliate marketers out there.

Your success largely depends on how well you attract (and convince) your audience.

Just the way it's done, the magic happens. Affiliate marketers can use several methods. For example, you can start a simple blog with affiliate links embedded in it. Or perhaps create an e-book, do a live presentation, or create podcasts and videos.

In addition to the form or medium of your communication, you also need to decide what tone you want to use for your audience.

Are you going to shower them with unicorns and sunshine about the product?

Different Approaches to Affiliate Marketing Business

Influence model

Influencers are people who can attract the attention of a wide audience. They build large groups of loyal followers and can sway them towards certain opinions or even products (hence the term "influential").

Who are the influential people:

- Bloggers
- YouTubers
- Podcasters
- Social media users

Based on their popularity, influencers will try products and present them to their audience in different ways. Some may offer unbiased opinions, but others may directly promote, demonstrate usage patterns, or use any other means to raise audience awareness.

In these situations, they will give affiliate links for their subscribers to purchase products. Every time a purchase is made, the influencer will earn a commission from the brand selling it.

Influencers come in various flavors; you might be shocked by the options.

Benefits of the Influence Model

The beauty of influencers is that they don't have to do anything special. People love (or hate) and follow them naturally.

Advertisers are very fond of influencers because of their large followings. They are often versatile and can meet the needs of various brand profiles. Best of all, they have so much attention that whatever they offer or promote is instantly in the spotlight.

Despite their huge popularity, influencers are often in danger of a steep fall. Their worst nightmare is waking up one day and finding that they are a thing of the past and no longer trending. After all, the audience is fickle.

In addition to this, due to mass tracking and scrutiny, small incidents can quickly escalate into major ones. Promoting a "bad" product can cause a massive and immediate reaction from an angry audience.

Niche-driven model

Affiliate marketers with a more precise strategy will aim to build a small but targeted audience in a specific niche. As with influencers, the choice of platform can vary. However, as a rule, they do not.

Specialized affiliates:

- Bloggers
- Site owners
- Niche market experts
- Techies

This is the most common affiliate marketing business model - you build a website, blog, or YouTube channel around a niche. Your goal is to get the attention of a certain group of people.

While the numbers may seem low at first glance compared to the influencer model, those most interested in your niche will likely buy what you recommend; however, niche marketers are not necessarily separate from influencers, especially among more popular food niches affiliate marketing, with examples.

Currently, the digital marketing ecosystem has various tools and strategies, ranging from classic SMS marketing to the innovation of streaming marketing. Each strategy has specific characteristics that allow traders to adapt to different audiences. Allowing in this way, expand the scope of the business and improve the relations between the company and its consumers.

On the other hand, some strategies can benefit both parties, merchants, and consumers, as is the case with. This is one of the best-known and most used marketing strategies in the digital ecosystem, taking the Amazon affiliate program as an example. According to Statista, an investment of around $8.2 million (the equivalent of €7.3 million) is expected in this type of marketing, only in the United States. Considering the importance of affiliate marketing, we will explain what it is about and its different types.

What is affiliate marketing, and what are its types

Affiliate marketing is a marketing strategy that takes advantage of the user community loyal to a business or brand to attract new users. That is, it consists of users promoting the services or products of a brand in exchange for receiving a commission. Said commission can be generated from new registrations that have been referred, purchases made through an affiliate link, or simply filling out a form.

In any case, the basic idea of this strategy is that users who have interacted with the business help generate greater attraction towards it, which allows businesses to generate greater visibility and get qualified customers with larger investments. While at the same time, affiliate users can generate passive income for their benefit.

In addition to the mutual benefit that affiliate marketing presents, another of its most attractive aspects is accessibility. Since it can be incorporated into any digital medium, be it a social network blog or website, just by integrating the affiliate link.

Now, depending on the strategy they use, there are 6 different types of affiliate marketing, which are the following:

1. Niche Pages

Affiliate marketing on niche pages refers to websites promoting a particular product or service. These sites often feature informative content and reviews regarding the products they promote, helping consumers to decide on them.

An example of niche pages is the Review affiliate program, a review platform for eCommerce. This program, eCommerce, creates a collection of opinions about products and services, offering different means for users to leave their reviews. Review is part of Google's official list of external aggregators; it takes these reviews as a reference, filters them, and makes them public as if they were the search engine's own. It also helps increase website visits and trust, which improves conversion rates. In addition, it helps to improve the reputation and positioning of the site in searches and social networks.

2. Cashback

Cashback is a strategy based on a database of subscribers with whom a commission is shared according to the actions carried out. Users who purchase or order on the affiliated platform will receive a percentage of the payment. In these cases, the commission can be given as redeemable points, a balance for future purchases on the site, or simply as a percentage of what you have paid.

An example of this typology is the Consent website. This cashback platform offers different ways to earn money from home by taking surveys or buying in the stores it offers to earn a percentage of the purchase.

3. Affiliates through search engines

In this case, the affiliated users promote the products or services working on the specific keywords through Google AdWords. In this way, they can create qualified traffic to the website from different search engines such as Google, Yahoo, or Bing.

4. Email Marketing

In this strategy, the key is good segmentation by the advertiser since a list of subscribers is used for the promotion. It consists of sending campaigns via email to an audience with specific and well-defined interests.

Mailchimp or Mittum, for example, are platforms designed to manage this type of campaign, which generally has CPM (Cost per thousand impressions) commissions.

5. Co-registration

Co-registration is a strategy that takes user databases on specific topics, products, or brands to send you promotions, offers, or images of a related product or brand. To do this, users must authorize the use of data for any sponsored advertiser at the time of their subscription. Among the platforms to promote this type of campaign, we have Coreregistros, which has rental and database capture services.

6. Affiliate networks

Affiliate networks are intermediary platforms that connect affiliate companies with users interested in affiliate marketing. In addition to serving as intermediaries, these networks offer both parties the necessary tools and technologies to carry out their campaigns. Awin is one of the best-known platforms, with 20 years in the market.

Affiliate program management

Companies typically run their affiliate programs in-house or partner with an affiliate management agency to manage the day-to-day requirements of an effective program. There are also brands, particularly enterprise brands, that take a "hybrid" approach to their program management, where they oversee internal elements and partner with an agency to manage the day-to-day aspects.

Internal affiliate program management tends to work best for:

- Companies that have intentionally chosen to run a small, private affiliate marketing program with only a few select partners. An in-house manager can usually manage this type of affiliate program without much difficulty.
- Companies are not looking to grow their program. Partnering with an affiliate agency is an investment; if a company doesn't invest in your program, the expense may not be worth it.
- Affiliate agency program management usually works best for:
- Businesses (typically growing) that lack the internal resources, industry and operational experience, platforms, and affiliate associations to run their affiliate program effectively.
- Hybrid affiliate program management (internal + agency) usually works best for:
- Business brands need a large team to manage their program.
- Brands that want to use an agency for specific purposes or to expand their geographic presence strategically.

How affiliate marketing works

Affiliate marketing is an effective system that allows companies to expand their audience and increase sales by collaborating with partners and affiliate resources. Let's see how this process works:

1. Establishing partnerships. The company and affiliates enter into a cooperation agreement. It defines the terms and conditions of the partnership, including the commission amount or other payment forms.
2. Providing unique links or promo codes. The company provides partners with individual links or promotional codes, through which you can track their activity and mark sales made thanks to their efforts.
3. Product advertising. Partners use their distribution channels (websites, blogs, or social media) to advertise the company's products or services. They create content that includes links or promo codes to engage their audience.
4. Attracting clients. The partner recommends the company's products or services to their audience. When customers follow a unique link or use a promotional code, the company tracks these actions and associates them with the affiliate.
5. Commission payments. When a client purchases using an affiliate link or promotional code, the affiliate receives a commission or other payment, according to the terms of cooperation.
6. Tracking and analysis of results. The company uses special tools and software to track the sales generated by affiliates and analyze the effectiveness of the affiliate program. This allows you to optimize your strategy and make informed decisions.

Affiliate marketing enables companies to effectively expand their audience and attract new customers and partners to receive an additional source of income for promoting products or services. This mutually beneficial approach allows for long-term partnerships and shared success.

Key elements

The effectiveness and success of affiliate marketing is provided by several of its key elements:

- Affiliate program. The basis of affiliate marketing is that the company has a special program. It details the tools, resources, and rules for working with partners. In addition, it determines the size of commission rates, ways to track sales, and other conditions for cooperation.
- Unique links or promo codes. They identify the partner's contribution to sales. When customers purchase these links or promo codes, the system tracks their activity and associates it with a specific affiliate.
- Tracking and analysis system. It is necessary for the effective management of the affiliate program. Such a system allows the company to control the sales attracted by partners and analyze the performance of each affiliate. This allows you to make informed decisions and optimize your strategy.
- Partner training and support. The company should help them understand the program, master the tools and learn about promotion strategies. Constant support allows you to answer partners' questions, quickly solve emerging problems and maintain long-term fruitful relationships.
- Motivation and reward. These elements are among the most important. The company may offer various forms of remuneration: commissions, bonuses, or special statuses. Motivation encourages affiliates to work more actively and achieve high results.
- Mutual benefit and trust. The basis of affiliate marketing is a mutually beneficial relationship and mutual trust between the company and its partners. The business provides quality products or services; its affiliates recommend them to their audience. Both parties benefit by meeting customer needs and achieving their goals.

Understanding and considering these key elements will allow the company to build a successful affiliate program and achieve high results in promoting its products and services.

Effective Strategies

Affiliate marketing success depends on identifying the right approaches to implement it. Here are some of the most successful strategies that can bring you positive results:

- Selecting suitable partners. Define your target audience and look for affiliates who are similar or cross with it. This will help increase the likelihood of attracting interested people who can later become your customers.
- The quality of content and advertising materials. Provide partners with high-quality and compelling content for them to use in promotional materials. These can be reviews, videos, articles, or banners. Content should be informative, persuasive, and catchy with the target audience.
- Individual offers and promotions. Create unique marketing offers and promotions for customers who click on affiliate links or use promo codes. They will encourage customers to buy and thus increase the effectiveness of the affiliate program.
- Motivation system. Its implementation will support the activity of existing partners and attract new ones. This can be an increased commission for completing a certain amount of sales, bonuses for reaching goals, or prizes for the most successful affiliates.
- Close cooperation with partners. Maintain regular communication with them, and provide them with prompt feedback and support. Exchange of experience, joint action planning, and training help to strengthen partnerships and achieve better results.
- Analysis and optimization. Constantly analyze the data and results of the affiliate program. Evaluate the effectiveness of different affiliates, promotion channels, and offered conditions. This will help to identify all the strengths and weaknesses of the strategy and make appropriate adjustments to optimize results.

Choosing and applying the right affiliate marketing strategies allows companies to expand their audience, increase sales, and establish long-term and successful partnerships.

Examples of Successful Affiliate Marketing

The effectiveness of the affiliate marketing system is illustrated by several examples demonstrating its success:

- The partnership between a company and a blogger. Many merchandise manufacturers are partnering with popular influencers. Bloggers talk about products, share their experiences, and recommend them to their audience. This allows manufacturers to achieve greater reach and trust from potential customers.
- Network affiliate programs. Large companies create affiliate programs allowing other organizations and entrepreneurs to promote their products and earn commissions for successful sales. Such programs exist in various industries, including tourism, finance, and information technology.
- Joint promotions and discounts. Brands can partner with other companies to run promotions together and offer discounts to customers. For example, a restaurant may partner with a food delivery service to provide joint packages or special offers. This helps to increase the mutual interest of customers of both businesses and attract new customers.

Successful examples of affiliate marketing confirm that cooperation and mutually beneficial relationships among companies and their partners can be effective for all parties. They allow companies to expand their audience, increase sales and achieve greater market power.

Amazon Program

Amazon's affiliate program, Amazon Associates, is one of the most popular and successful worldwide. It allows members to earn commissions by recommending products featured on the Amazon platform.

One of the benefits of the Amazon affiliate program is ease of use. Registration in the program is free and takes a little time. Partners are provided with tools and reports to track sales and monitor the effectiveness of their efforts. Amazon Associates also offers a variety of reward models, including sales-based commissions and fixed amounts for referring new customers or signing up for Prime. This allows affiliates to choose the most profitable strategy for monetizing their traffic.

The Amazon Affiliate Program is essential for many entrepreneurs, bloggers, and website owners. It allows them to generate additional income and expand their marketing opportunities.

The success of fashion bloggers

Fashion bloggers are one of the most successful affiliate marketing participants. They create unique content about fashion, style, and accessories, attracting a large audience of their fans. Here are a few reasons why these influencers are successful in affiliate marketing:

- Authority and influence. Fashion bloggers create personal brands and develop their fashion expertise. Followers trust their opinions and recommendations, making them influencers in the fashion industry.
- Visual content. Fashion bloggers extensively use visual content, including photos and videos, to showcase trending outfits, accessories, and looks. It draws attention and inspires their audience.
- Brand collaboration. Fashion bloggers establish partnerships with various fashion brands. Influencers advertise their products and services through their platforms through links and promo codes so followers can easily purchase the featured items.
- Personalization and relevance. Fashion bloggers are sensitive to their audience and offer products that match their interests and style. They create content that inspires and helps subscribers find their desired style and look.
- Building a community. Fashion bloggers actively interact with their audience, creating a community of people passionate about fashion. They actively communicate with their fans: maintain a dialogue, and answer questions. This enhances their influence and brand appeal.
- The success of fashion bloggers in affiliate marketing is due to their uniqueness, authority, and ability to inspire and influence their audience. This makes them valuable partners for fashion brands looking to grab and hold consumers' attention.

Affiliate Marketing Success Isn't Just Single Campaigns

With all this noise around achieving success, it can be easy to succumb to the lure of affiliate marketing. If this is what you want, you must know that success is achieved over time despite the potential. This is especially true when it comes to making money from affiliate marketing.

You cannot spend X hours on it and then walk away to dump money for the rest of your life. Affiliate marketing is more than a full-time job; to be truly successful, be prepared to put in long hours of hard work.

Apart from this, you also need to take into account a few more things before you start:

- Making the Right Choice

Industry Fit - While it's important to pursue what you're truly passionate about, remember that not every industry has the same potential. Ideally, choose one with an established ecosystem of established brands and demand - plus still growing.

Affiliate - By affiliate, I mean brands, which is an area that affiliate marketers should approach cautiously. Brands are not always your friend and may sometimes try to deceive you about your fair share of income. Choose the right partners and work closely with those you choose.

Content Approach - Decide which platform you will live on or die on. Only try to gain a foothold on some or even a few. This is a sure recipe for a broken heart. Not all platforms suit different approaches, so think carefully about yours.

Marketing Angle - Decide how you are going to market your content. Will you go to the golden school and rely on yours? Or are you ready to invest and invest in contextual and social media advertising? I recommend that you consider a holistic approach.

- Deliver value to your users.

Remember that you need subscribers, viewers, or readers regardless of your platforms, models, or choices. They are your key source of income, and the only way to attract and retain them is to offer them real value.

This does not mean you give them a permanent freebie or something like that, but you deliver something to them. If you are an artist, entertain them. If they want to see food culture, explore and show them. If they are in business, show them how to simplify solutions or solve problems.

Take, for example, TripAdvisor. A big part of their success is that they offer a huge amount of useful information, such as guides and tips from those who have experienced these places. The value is unimaginable.

- Places to join affiliate programs

If you're ready to start making money, there are two main types of places you can look to. The first and most direct are brands that have affiliate programs. For example, many software publishers will have affiliate programs such as.

For those who want to work with larger brands, it would be better to look for affiliate networks. Among them are many big names such as ShareASale and more.

- Overcoming problems and obstacles

While developing an affiliate marketing system, you may need some help. However, they can be solved by choosing the right strategies and approaches. Let's take a look at a few common obstacles and how to overcome them:

- Need for more interaction with partners. For a successful partnership, it is important to maintain regular and open communication with affiliates. This helps to resolve issues, clarify goals and expectations, and provide mutual support. Regular meetings, feedback, and exchange of experience contribute to strengthening relations.
- Target audience mismatch. If the partners do not match the company's target audience, the affiliate program's results may not be sufficient. Choosing affiliates carefully, considering their audience and interests, is important to ensure a more accurate match and attract the right customers.
- Problems with training and partner support. Some affiliates may experience difficulty using the program or require additional training. Providing access to training materials, instructions, and personal support helps partners better understand the process and increase efficiency.
- Lack of motivation among partners. If affiliates are motivated to achieve results, their activity and productivity may stay the same. Creating incentives (increased commission rates, goal achievement bonuses, or contests) helps keep interest and motivation going.
- Opacity and insufficient tracking. It is important to provide partners with access to a reliable tracking system that will allow them to see the results of their work and commissions earned. This approach creates trust and transparency in dealing with them.
- Solving these problems requires attentiveness, proper communication, and an understanding affiliates' needs. Successfully overcoming obstacles contributes to the development of a productive affiliate program.

Future trends

Affiliate marketing continues to change and adapt to the changing business environment. Here are a few key trends that will come to this area in the future:

- Growing partnerships with niche influencers. Instead of partnering with big bloggers and celebrities, companies increasingly focus on niche influencers. They have a narrower but more loyal audience, thanks to which the promotion of products and services is carried out more accurately and purposefully.
- Integration with influencer marketing. Affiliate and influencer marketing are increasingly merging, creating a synergy in promotion. Companies will actively partner with influencers to attract more customers and build long-term, rewarding relationships.
- Automation and the use of technology. Technological progress has an impact on many areas of business. Affiliate marketing is no exception. Thanks to it, it has become more and more

automated and efficient. Using algorithms, artificial intelligence, and analytics allows companies to track results better and make more informed decisions.

- Geographic expansion. With the development of the Internet and globalization, companies are increasingly looking to establish partnerships outside their region. By expanding the program's geographical scope, they can scale their business to new markets and attract more customers.

- Development of interaction with social media platforms. Social networks will continue to be a powerful tool for affiliate marketing. Companies will actively use popular platforms such as Instagram, YouTube, and TikTok to establish partnerships and promote their products and brand.

- Future trends in affiliate marketing point to the constant development and adaptation of this system to changing business and market requirements. The introduction of new approaches and the use of modern technologies will help companies establish effective partnerships and achieve success.

Chapter 2: How to Choose the Right Affiliate Networks

What to look for when choosing a PP

Choosing an affiliate program is an important step in your internet marketing career. Make sure you choose an AP that suits your interests and skills.

The principle of operation of the software

The principle of affiliate programs is that you promote products or services of partner companies and receive commissions from sales. The partnership is done through affiliate links or codes that track the sales made by your customers.

The PP process looks like this:

- You choose an affiliate program and register for it.
- Get a unique affiliate link or code.
- Place this link or code on your website, blog, social networks, or other places where it can attract leads (target customers).
- Leads follow your link and purchase (order a service) from a partner company.
- You receive a commission on the sale.

It is important to remember that successful work in the PP depends on how effectively you will sponsor the products or services of the partner company. Use marketing methods and tools such as contextual advertising, social networks, and email to increase your income.

Types of affiliate programs

Before choosing an affiliate program, study their types:

1. Cost-per-Sale - an affiliate only receives a commission if the lead buys through your unique affiliate link.
2. Cost-per-Click - payment for each click on its link.
3. Cost-per-Acquisition - payment for each lead who signed up or bought a product through its link.
4. Cost-per-Impression - A reward for every ad or ad is shown, even if the lead doesn't click on the link.
5. Pay-per-Lead - money is paid for each lead, that is, for the contact details of a client who has shown interest in a product or service.
6. Referral PP - commission for attracting new partners to the program.
7. Cost-per-Install - payment is made for each application installation on the device.
8. Cost-per-Subscription - The partner receives a payment for each product or service subscription.

The choice of types of PP depends on your target audience, the product or service you are promoting, and your marketing strategy.

Affiliate program requirements

Most affiliate programs have the following requirements:

- Registration: To participate in the PP, you must create an account.
- Compliance with the rules: You must comply with the rules of the TPP, which govern how you can promote the company's products or services. Some companies may prohibit certain marketing methods, such as spam or unfair practices.
- Quality of traffic: Affiliate companies want to receive only quality traffic that leads to sales. Therefore, your website or blog should be related to the theme of the product or service.
- Affiliate Link Availability: You must ensure your link is available for leads and does not violate search engine rules.
- Commission Payments: Affiliate companies may set a minimum commission threshold or require proof of sales before calculating commissions.
- Proper use of materials: if a partner company provides you with marketing materials, you must use them by the rules of the affiliate program, not change them without permission.
- It is important to familiarize yourself with the requirements of an affiliate program before registering it and starting to promote products or services. This will help avoid possible violations to profit from participation in the PP with a guarantee.

Variety of offers and verticals

Offers can be different verticals. A vertical is a category of goods and services that participate in an SP. Consider some verticals and examples of offers:

- E-commerce is the sale of goods. Examples of offers: sale of electronics, clothes, shoes, cosmetics.
- Finance - offers financial services such as loans, insurance, and investments. Examples: credit cards, bank deposits, life insurance, and investment funds.
- Health and beauty - goods and services related to health and beauty. Examples: vitamins, cosmetics, sports nutrition, dietary supplements, and medical center services.
- Home and family - goods and services for home and family. Examples: furniture, household appliances, toys, and travel services.
- Entertainment - products and services related to recreation and entertainment. Examples: tickets for concerts, theatrical performances, cinema, hotels, and computer games.
- Education – products and services related to education. Examples: training courses, textbooks, and online courses.

The abundance of offers in the PP allows you to choose the right offers for your audience and profit more from participating in the program. The more offers, the lower the threshold for joining the affiliate program, and the more opportunities to adapt traffic sources to the offer.

Support

Technical support in affiliate programs is needed so that partners can solve problems that arise and receive assistance. If you are thinking about which affiliate program to choose, pay attention to the features of the technical support work:

- 24/7 support - companies provide technical support around the clock, seven days a week.
- Communication channels - partner companies provide different communication channels for technical support: e-mail, phone, chat, in instant messengers.
- Training and Resources - PPs provide training materials and resources for partners that help them better understand the terms of offers and promotion methods.
- Tracking system - Partner companies provide a sales and commission tracking system to help partners track revenue and resolve issues.
- Regular contact - companies maintain regular contact with partners to learn about problems and suggestions for improving the SP.

- The more attentive technical support, the more likely partners will effectively promote the partner company's products and generate sales.

Reviews

Affiliate program reviews are important for attracting new partners and retaining current ones. Suppose a partner site responds to reviews, improves the site or application's functionality, resolves disputes, monitors and punishes the authors of dishonest offers. In that case, this PP can be considered for making money.

How to earn first money on PP

You must comply with its conditions and choose an offer to earn the first money on the PP. Here are some tips for making money on PP for beginners:

- Choose an offer that matches your topic and interests. This will help you promote products and services more effectively.
- Attract the target audience to your website or social media pages using marketing methods such as SEO, contextual advertising, and social advertising.
- Track the results of your work. Use tracking tools to understand what products or services attract more customers and how to improve your work.
- Participate in training programs: Many companies provide educational materials for their users: about offers, about email marketing methods.

Making money from affiliate programs can be lucrative but takes time and effort. The best offers for affiliate earnings are financial (banking). Their consumers are a wide audience. For other verticals (goods, health, tourism, etc.), reducing its reduction will require a more thorough audience selection. The PAMPADU affiliate sales network offers to make money on the simplest offers: banking products and insurance. This can be done by a specialist (realtor, banking, or insurance agent) and a web admin - someone who only knows how to create websites and set up advertising.

A few words about the best geos from Adcombo

If we talk about the lead gen, then the USA, Thailand, and Indonesia.

If mobile content is Eastern Europe.

I always recommend that beginners start with offers with subscriptions, where advertisers do not set restrictions on the mobile operator and pay for all users - solvent and not. This helps to test various approaches on a budget, identify working ones, and then scale.

A few words about the best geos from Natifico

Generally, it is the USA, Europe, and several Asian countries.

For sweeps, America is the number one country. Moreover, almost all verticals visit this GEO. The population and the traffic itself are conducive to this. If suddenly the traffic on such a GEO does not convert, then most likely, something is wrong with the bundle itself, and we recommend that you carefully double-check it before relaunching the campaign.

Examples of successful Sweepstake offers from Mobidea

First offer

South Africa (or South Africa) is a country that works well for Mobidea's offers. Below is an example of an offer where the user signs up to win some money. As you can see, this offer converts with two clicks.

Sometimes, especially in Africa and Asia, offers are not classic CPLs but a short funnel. To subscribe, the user must tick the checkbox and agree to the terms.

You can test direct links for such offers, but I suggest split testing with and without a pre-lander to see which works best.

Like some other African GEOs, South Africa has strict rules regarding banners and landings. Here you will not be able to place text on the banner that the user has won something; you will need to dodge and hint at a chance to win.

Talk to your manager about what creatives you can use.

Second offer

Some Asian countries perform particularly well with mobile data. They have fewer restrictions on what you can show on creative and landing. Geo examples are visible on the screen; iPhone plays the offer.

The advantage of the offer below is that there are no such restrictions, and you can place bolder approaches on the creative.

Mobile traffic, in general, performs much better for Sweepstakes. For Mobidea, mobile traffic generates the majority of its revenue.

For now, that's all about traffic sources, the best products, and GEOs for Sweepstakes. But that's only part of what we talked about with Francisco. In the next part, we will focus on how to choose the best offer and what mistakes prevent you from profiting from push ad sweeps.

Sweepstakes in 2023. How to choose an offer?

We continue to discuss Sweepstakes in 2020. Let's talk about how to choose the best offer and what mistakes prevent you from profiting from sweepstakes.

We continue to discuss Sweepstakes in 2023. This is the second part of the conversation with Francisco Guerreiro, affiliate manager of Mobidea. In it, we will focus on how to choose the best offer and what mistakes prevent you from profiting from sweepstakes.

Sweepstakes 2023: how to choose the best offer?

Good offers, like good wine, never stand out in plain sight. To get something worth talking to your manager.

Many affiliate programs save the best offers for trusted (and often more experienced) arbitrageurs. The better the offer, the more pitfalls can be in its launch. These can be restrictions on the type of traffic, the quality of leads, or strict requirements for creatives. The manager must understand that you know about working with such offers.

In my experience, a manager needs time to see how you work and if you can be trusted with more difficult offers.

Try to find interesting products to promote.

See what the affiliate program has "prize" options. Users are already a little tired of the usual iPhone pranks, especially in Tier 1 countries - they have already seen all this more than once. Try something else: cash prizes and gift cards convert especially well now.

Evaluate how the offer type works on the selected GEO.

Remember that CC submission works very well in Tier 1 countries such as Scandinavian countries, France, and the Baltics.

DOI and SOI perform well in Tier 1 countries such as Spain, Italy, Portugal, the US, and the UK.

As for, you can look towards Asian countries, where there is less regulation.

Discuss with the manager what kind of traffic is best for the offer.

In Mobidea, pushes, especially for mobile devices, have more potential for sweeps than pops. Internal statistics show that push ads provide higher quality and user engagement. The novelty of the format plays its role. Compared to push notifications, pop audiences are still less sensitive to ads.

What Mistakes Prevent Profits on Sweepstakes

- Do not use pre-landers.

With pre-landers, it is possible to create such conditions when a person is sufficiently involved in interacting with the page. He will feel sorry for the achievements there (a small win in the wheel of fortune, answers to questions) and the time spent. A user is more likely to leave their data that way than if you direct them to a data entry page.

Exception: offers where the subscription is made in one or two clicks.

In such offers, the user needs to click on the checkbox with the word "Accept" and agree to the terms of the agreement. Many people who install programs, games, or the like don't read what they "accept." In this case, you can test direct links.

To think that the payout is the most important thing in the offer.

Most often, this applies to beginners. They see the same offer in affiliate networks with different payouts and think the payout is everything. This needs to be corrected! More importantly, how much you spend per click and how much income you get.

The same offer can have a payout of $4.60. At the same time, an offer for 4 will receive 1 conversion and 60 - 10 conversions with the same traffic. As a result, an offer with a payout of 60 cents will be more profitable.

The only thing that can prove that a proposal works is a test.

- Poor postback setup.

Sounds so obvious, but it's a common problem! Many affiliates carelessly set up click IDs, and a real integration must be made.

Please ensure your postbacks are set up correctly and convey as much useful information as possible.

- Test and conclude a small volume of clicks.

Some arbitrageurs buy some traffic from the source, wait to see the results, and refuse the offer.

If you buy traffic in a grid with more than 50 sources and your offer gets 50-100 clicks, that means 1-2 clicks from the source on average. And this is just a drop in the ocean for decision-making.

You don't have to be a millionaire; tests need a budget. Start small, but don't let it be 100 clicks from a large ad grid.

Yes, you will have cases when money is spent without profit. This is the daily pain of affiliates. Your best bet is to set a budget for each test and evaluate its effectiveness.

- Antivirus/Utilities/VPN

This niche includes various products to improve the performance and security of devices.

Vertical and its products are in demand all year round; there is no reference to the season. And after the pandemic's start, such offers experienced an incredible surge in popularity. People began to spend all their time at home using home gadgets. At the same time, home computers are often less protected than workers, which the employer cares about.

Security software can be promoted to the widest possible audience since everyone today uses some device, and often more than one.

Vertical products are designed for mobile and computers, Android and iOS.

The vertical works especially well with push notifications, as they are similar to reminders from the operating system. Use this to get your first conversions.

How to Use a VPN for Affiliate Marketing

Now proxies and VPN services are becoming more relevant for affiliates.

This topic will analyze how to use proxy and VPN services in affiliate marketing.

The arbitrator now clearly needs an extra pair of hands to help. After all, he must be able to effectively promote goods and services and also overcome many obstacles in the form of blocked Internet resources and banned accounts.

In this topic, we propose discussing proxies and VPN services and why they are needed in affiliate marketing.

What is a proxy?

When you proceed connecting to the Internet, your device is assigned a unique address (IP address). You can get information about the user who logged into the network by IP address. You can determine its location, provider, last name and first name, phone number, and address.

Proxies exist to help you remain anonymous and hide your IP address. They replace your IP address with a different one using a proxy server.

How Proxy Servers Work

Your computer or any other device can connect to the proxy server, receives an anonymous IP address, and accesses the necessary resource.

A proxy server is a computer that works as an intermediary, an intermediate link between the user and the server of the required resource. When using a proxy server, all the sites you visit see only your proxy server.

For example, if you bought a German proxy, then you will be identified on the network as a user from Germany.

This scheme allows you to remain anonymous, access blocked sites, and use special programs and online services for parsing, mailing, farming, and more.

What is a VPN, and how does it work

VPN (Virtual Private Network) consists in a virtual private network that ensures your online privacy. It sounds almost like a proxy, but there is a difference.

What is the difference between a VPN and a proxy?

Once your computer is connected to the VPN, it protects all your network traffic down to the operating system level, ensuring it is completely anonymous and secure.

A proxy server can only forward web requests. Unlike VPN, you do not connect to the network but pass your Internet connection through a proxy server.

In addition, the VPN uses end-to-end encryption. Data is completely secure from the entry point to the exit point. Neither cyber criminals nor competitors will be able to intercept such information.

Thus, VPN protection is more serious, while proxies use less secure technology. Of the cons of a VPN, it is worth noting that it is more expensive, and the connection with a VPN is usually slower than with a proxy.

How to Use Proxies and VPNs in Affiliate Marketing

A proxy server and a VPN are essential tools if your business is related to promoting goods and services.

What to choose, use proxy or VPN in affiliate marketing?

Let's examine why proxies and VPNs are needed in affiliate marketing, what they do, and how affiliates can use VPNs.

Security, speed, espionage

- To ensure anonymity

Proxies and VPNs keep you anonymous. Any of your activity on the Internet: from surfing, farming accounts, parsing, and mailings to working with various trading platforms, can be hidden using a proxy and VPN.

- For security

A proxy server and VPN increase the connection's security, protect a working computer from scammers and hackers, and enable access to even unsafe sites.

- To improve the connection speed

Connecting a proxy significantly increases the connection speed with various web resources, which is important in traffic arbitration.

- For advanced espionage

You can access a proxy server to sponsor on a specific website for a defined and specific GEO. You will be able to see what ads are currently being shown on the site for users of that GEO, where those ads are placed, which landing pages are linked to, and more.

For an advertising campaign

- To work with offers of various GEOs

A VPN helps affiliate marketers work with various GEO offers.

Before launching an offer, you will want to see the offer website to get acquainted with the product or service, product benefits, promotions, discounts, etc. Moreover, this page must be seen through the eyes of the GEO user that your campaign will target.

If you are in Poland and the campaign is created for Germany, the affiliate network will redirect you to a page intended for Poles unless the offer is multilingual. Otherwise, you will not get to the offer page.

- To set up, test, optimize, and scale various GEO campaigns

How to use a VPN in the field of affiliate marketing when creating, testing, and then optimizing a campaign?

When the company is set up, with the help of a VPN, you have to test all the way a user must go by clicking on your banner. You need to ensure that from the banner, it gets to the landing page.

With a proxy, you can check if your Argentina campaign is set up correctly if you're in Turkey.

A proxy server is also useful for testing, optimizing, and scaling a campaign for a specific GEO.

To bypass bans and anti-fraud systems

- To bypass restrictions

A proxy will make it possible to visit web resources that are blocked or just inaccessible in certain countries. For example, the well-known blocking of Telegram in the Russian Federation led to users using a proxy to access the messenger.

Each traffic source has certain rules. If you voluntarily or unwittingly violate them, for example, by advertising a prohibited product or choosing the wrong advertising format, your account will be banned. The proxy server will allow you to create a new account for the desired website.

- To bypass anti-fraud systems

Proxies are especially relevant for working with Facebook and Google Ads. Each account of these traffic sources requires its IP address. Accounts that were registered from the same IP address get banned very quickly.

Proxy servers are required to mass register accounts in other social networks and instant messengers.

Overview of proxy services for affiliates

1. AstroProxy

This is a large premium network. AstroProxy offers hundreds of thousands of residential addresses of any GEO, free test, and money back.

Advantages:

- Instantly create an order and get a proxy around the clock.
- Detailed FAQ.
- A detailed description of all types of proxy networks.
- Many GEOs are available, including Tier 1.
- Expert support and free test.
- Discounts for large volumes.
- All proxies in one single panel, flexible configuration for any software and task.
- Possibility of grouping by various parameters.
- 100% compatible with most programs.

2. I proxy. Online.

The service offers private mobile proxies on Android. There are all necessary functions for management.

Advantages:

- Remote change of IP address + change of IP by following the link.
- High speed.
- Maximum control.
- Automatic change of IP address.
- Telegram bot for notifications and managing IP address changes.
- Support for SOCKS5 and HTTP proxies.
- Possibility to create several proxy accesses on one phone.
- Unlimited traffic.

3. 911 S5

residential proxies. IP addresses in over 190 countries.

Advantages:

- Access IP addresses by country, state, city, IP address range, ZIP, ISP, etc.
- Free software.
- Supports all Windows operating systems.
- Lifetime validity.
- Secure encryption and anonymity.
- Sales analytics.
- Brand protection.
- Self-test.

4. Proxy.io

Elite proxies with high speed and high uptime.

Advantages:

- Support 24/7.
- Multiple payment gateways and 50 payment methods.
- Individual IPv4 proxies.

- Shared IPv4 proxy.
- Individual IPv6 proxies.
- A new generation of IP addresses.
- Automatic issuance of orders.
- Affiliate program.
- The ability to return the proxy within 24 hours.
- HTTP and SOCKS protocols.
- Authorization by IP address.

VPN Review for Affiliates

1. Netmap

Popular VPN provider has a large arsenal of servers around the world.

Possibilities:

- The high degree of traffic encryption.
- No logging.
- High connection speed.
- Suitable for all platforms and operating systems.
- 24/7 support.
- Affiliate program.

2. ExpressVPN

The service is considered one of the recognized leaders.

Possibilities:

- Private web surfing.
- Website unblocking.
- Unlimited streaming.
- IP masking.
- 160 VPN server locations.
- The best encryption methods.
- VPN speed test.
- Private DNS servers.
- No logging of browsing and connection history.

3. Free Avira Phantom VPN

Cheap and secure access to websites and services with full personal data protection.

Possibilities:

- Anonymous web browsing.
- Secure connection.
- Access to blocked websites
- Support for multiple devices.
- Streaming.
- Confidentiality.
- Access to censored social networks.
- Finding better deals on the market, such as cheaper airfare.

4.   IPVanish

VPN offers secure access and high speeds.

Possibilities:

- No logging.
- Decent protocols, secure service.
- Very comfortable speeds.
- Useful connection map.
- You can access Netflix content.

How does VPN help affiliate marketers? Life would be much more difficult without them.

Proxy servers and VPNs are essential tools for affiliates. They provide anonymity, security, and confidentiality of data, making it possible to bypass blocking and minimize account bans in traffic sources.

And without a good traffic source, there will be no launch of advertising campaigns.

5.   Finance and crypto

Finance and cryptocurrencies are very popular right now. The passive income idea they are often promoted sells well. People always want to earn extra money, and these offers give hope to get rich without doing anything.

The financial vertical covers all money-related offers: from credit cards to investment services.

The crypto vertical is also more complex. It is much broader than it seems at first glance. The vertical consists of various offers, from learning blockchain technology to auto trading (when the broker-provided robot will do all the work for the client).

To get started in this niche, you need to understand the topic or be willing to learn it. At the same time, offers usually have higher rates than most other niches. But it will not be possible to find your client right away, so the vertical is not the easiest for beginners with small budgets.

6.   Dating

You only need to promote dating sites among users and receive money for registration. Often you can get additional commission for premium accounts or paid subscriptions that increase profits.

But promoting such offers takes much work. It is important to understand who your client is and their needs: sometimes they are just acquaintances, and sometimes they are adults' needs that must be presented carefully so that advertising materials are not rejected for moderation.

The format of push notifications, similar to messages from instant messengers, has proven great for dating. It is actively used in this niche and gets good results.

Chapter 4: Setting Up Your First Affiliate Marketing Website

Affiliate marketing can be rewarding to make money online. This is a fantastic strategy for creating a steady stream of passive income and expanding your financial horizons. But how do you create affiliate marketing websites?

Despite the simplicity of the idea, building an affiliate marketing website takes significant time, work, and commitment.

Much work is happening in the background, from choosing a niche to joining relevant affiliate networks and building a website and email list.

The following are helpful tips and tricks on how to build successful affiliate marketing websites.

1.   Choose a Niche

You can spend many hours trying to find the perfect niche or start with the one that interests you.

2. Choose a Reputable Affiliate Program

Once you have chosen a theme, you must find available affiliate programs. Now you can go a little deeper into the specifics of affiliate marketing.

3. Choose the best domain name.

Users enter your website's domain name to access it. Getting them to visit your site is the only thing they type into their browser.

Use the ".com" extension if possible, mainly because it's easier to remember. Be concise and to the point when choosing a reliable domain name registrar. Please note that the domain name must not contain special characters.

4. Choose a web host and website builder.

Hosting is where all the files are stored, including pages, content, images, videos, and more, while the domain name is the URL of your website. Hosting and domain management go hand in hand.

Your site's performance can be improved by choosing the best hosting company.

5. Pick a Theme and Plugins for Your Affiliate Site

After installing WordPress, you must install the theme and a few required plugins for your affiliate site.

The theme determines the whole look and feel of your site. It usually includes default options for your logo, color scheme, and typography that affect how your website looks and functions.

6. Write content for your specific niche.

Now it is the time to start producing content. Blogging about topics that you find interesting and enjoyable is a great way to create content for your website. You can use your blog to write how-to articles and other interesting content to keep your visitors interested.

7. Create a mailing list.

Are you aware that an email marketing campaign can provide a return on investment of up to 360%? This equals $36 for every dollar spent.

It takes some time to create a list, but the effort is worth it. You gain loyal customers by consistently providing helpful content and growing your list.

8. Promote your content on social media.

We assume that your target audience visits one of the social networks since they are used by more than 50% of the world's population.

This is one of the many excuses for you to sponsor your work on social media!

Building a user base that does interact with your material can take some time, just like email marketing. However, it is worth investing in, given its potential reach.

9. Focus and work on perfection for your SEO site.

Successful online businesses have relied on search engine optimization (SEO) for years. This helps search engines find and rank your site in the SERPs.

Create your website

If not, it's time to put your research into action. If you've never built a website before, you need to know that if you want to make money from it, your site must be hosted on a web server, giving you complete freedom. Settings.

There are a few steps you need to follow to set up your site properly:

1. Choose a domain name

A domain name is just a more difficult way of saying the name of a website.

- • My top tips for choosing a name:
- • Choose an easy-to-remember name
- • Simplifying spelling
- • Keep it short
- • Choose a name that applies to you and what you want to write

2. Choose the right platform

WordPress.org is the most popular web platform in the world. It's free and extremely flexible and is what I use for Gathering Dreams.

Although WordPress.org is free, you need to host your files on a server. This option has a cost, but you can only apply for some affiliate programs if you set up the site correctly.

3. Buy hosting for your website.

I use Bluehost as my hosting provider (a company that will store all your files on an online server!).

Select your package by clicking the green "Get Started Now" button.

4. Install WordPress

Once you've set up your hosting, you must install WordPress. If you're using Bluehost as your host, you can install WordPress with one click, meaning it only takes a few minutes to install WordPress and get it ready to migrate to your website!

5. Choose a theme

The WordPress theme will provide all the styling you need for your website.

It includes:

- • scheme
- • Banner
- • Font style
- • widget layout
- • navigation menu

There are many free themes and some beautiful ones for a fee.

Find the best affiliate marketing programs for beginners

Once you have chosen on which niche you want to focus, you must determine the most effective affiliate marketing programs and products you want to promote.

Selecting the ideal programs will take some time, but be bold and invest in the process, as it can make or break your affiliate strategy.

There are two different kinds of affiliate programs that you can participate in:

- • Affiliate Networks: Publishers of affiliate network groups with affiliate programs on the same website (such as Awin). If accepted into an affiliate network, finding and applying to different affiliate programs and tracking offers and conversions will be easier.
- • Custom Affiliate Programs: Some companies offer their affiliate platform, and you must apply separately for each company (e.g., Junkie Survey).

What You Need to Know Before Applying for Any Affiliate Marketing Program

1. You must have content on your site, and sometimes you will be rejected!

To join an affiliate program, you must follow the application process. This usually requires you to enter information about your website, your location, your site traffic, etc.

Depending on the specific requirements, you may be denied. The trick is to ensure you have at least 5-15 articles on your site and make sure your site looks good and legit. And if you get denied an affiliate program, try looking for an email contact and ask why you were rejected. You may only need to improve a few messages or get more traffic from a particular location.

Don't be discouraged! It's okay to get rejected from time to time!

I know I have applied for many affiliate programs, and not all of my applications have succeeded!

2. There is a minimum payout limit you need to reach before getting paid

The majority of affiliate programs have a minimum payout threshold. It might be as little as $10, but it could also be $100. So don't get too excited after making your first sale. It took me a few months to get my $1.30 from Amazon!

Be sure to check the minimum threshold for each of your affiliate programs.

3. It can take up to three months to receive payments. Some affiliate programs only pay 15 days after the end of the month, but the majority of affiliate programs will take between 30 days and three months to pay you. This is usually because they must verify the sale and sometimes offer a 30-day return. If someone decides to cancel the purchase and request a refund, the commission will be forfeited.
4. Check how much commission you will receive.

Every affiliate program is different. Sometimes you will be paid a fixed amount based on someone signing up for the service; other times, you will earn a flat commission on sales.

Ensure you know exactly how much money you can make with each partner - this will give you an idea of how profitable the program can be. And remember that every small amount adds up.

As great as receiving a $100 commission for a $250 product recommendation, your readers are likelier to purchase a free app subscription and get paid $2.

5. Keep an eye on your partners. It can be overwhelming

To apply for affiliate programs, especially at the beginning. Keep a list of all the programs you have applied for and whether you were accepted or rejected.

5 Best Affiliate Marketing Plugins and Tools for WordPress

Want to easily manage and track all your affiliate campaigns and links from one place? Check out our complete list of the top 5 affiliates and tools that can help you create, manage, organize, and monitor the effectiveness of your affiliate campaigns with ease.

You no longer need to install dozens of different WordPress plugins and tools to manage various aspects of your affiliate marketing campaigns. You will get all the features and functionality necessary to create and track your campaigns with the affiliate marketing plugins mentioned in this topic. You can also effortlessly monetize your site with affiliate marketing and get the best results.

Easily Manage Your Campaigns With Top 5 Affiliate Marketing Plugins

Before we get to our final list, let's take a quick look at the features that an ideal affiliate marketing tool should allow you to:

- Create and shorten easy-to-share affiliate links in a few steps
- Manage more URLs easily
- Redirect affiliate links based on redirect type
- Track the performance of all your affiliate campaigns
- Provide you with full, detailed reports and more.

Look at the best available affiliate marketing tools and plugins to help you grow your business.

1. Track affiliate link analytics in detail with BetterLinks

First, we have one of the plugins for the WordPress community -BetterLinks, the simplest link management solution. This versatile tool can help you create short, custom URLs for your affiliate campaigns, redirect them, manage them from one place, and track them with multiple analytics systems.

BetterLinks also helps reduce link load times with optimized queries, track marketing campaigns with UTM Builder, prevent bot traffic and clicks with Bot Blocker, and check for broken links - all within the plugin's user interface.

You'll get an advanced tool with the free version of BetterLinks, which will provide you with detailed data on the performance of your links and help you better manage your campaigns. It allows you to check the performance of each campaign link by measuring click-through rates and provides you with analytics data such as link name, referrer, destination URLs, and more.

But for more information, BetterLinks PRO allows you to connect analytics with just a few clicks on the user interface or easily generate UTM code that you can use to track your links and marketing campaigns with customizable parameters.

To take it one step further, PRO gives you an easy process to perform a split and see how your offer pages perform. You can view and analyze the results with the built-in BetterLinks analytics tool mentioned above and see each offer page's conversion rates and other reports in a beautiful graphical format.

And finally, you can easily improve your affiliate link management routines and make them more successful by using the BetterLinks premium redirect feature, which comes in many different types.

- Dynamic redirect based on geolocation
- Dynamic redirect based on devices
- Dynamic redirect based on time

To top it all off, this affiliate marketing plugin allows you to manage all your affiliate marketing links with your team, allowing you to set individual permissions for different user roles and grant them access to various BetterLinks features.

2. Use the unique features of Pretty Links to build and track affiliate links

With over300,000+ activated installs, the next best plugin for affiliate marketing in the WordPress community is. This very popular marketing tool can also make it easy to compress, customize, track, manage, and share the URLs of any website.

One of its main advantages is the unique feature that allows users and affiliate marketers like you to shorten any link on the site. Using the domain name of your choice. But most importantly, you can easily track all the links of your affiliate campaign and monitor the performance of campaigns with a full detailed report.

Its main features allow you to track the total and unique clicks on a link and create a customizable graph of clicks per day reporting interface. You can also view detailed click information, including IP address, browser, operating system, and referring site - all important data needed to understand your marketing campaigns' performance. You can also download this reporting data as CSV files, pass custom parameters to your scripts through this plugin, and still have full traceability.

Among many other outstanding features, you can create follow/no links on the pointer, enable per-link on/off track, redirect URLs using 301, 302, and 307 redirect types, and more.

3. Hiding and managing affiliate campaign links with ThirstyAffiliates

Next on our list, we haveThirstwhich gives bloggers and marketers a complete opportunity to monetize their WordPress website through affiliate marketing and comprises a huge community of 40,000 WordPress users.

As you can tell from the name, this affiliate marketing plugin has been designed to help you easily manage your affiliate campaigns and links using all the essential features. This very simple plugin allows you to easily search for affiliate links you have created earlier by name in a few clicks.

This helps you add click tracking to your links to keep track of every click and comes with a built-in reporting system. This allows you to learn how many clicks your affiliate links have and what's popular on your site over time.

ThirstyAffiliates PROadds a ton of extra features to make it easier for any advanced affiliate marketers and bloggers who want to automate parts of their affiliate marketing:

- Use keyword auto links to increase your affiliate income by linking in an automatic way affiliate links to keywords on your site.
- Get amazing advanced reports such as category performance, 24-hour performance, geolocation reports, and more that can be easily created with a few clicks.
- Geo-target visitors based on their country of origin and redirect them to geographically relevant affiliate URLs.
- Import and export affiliate links via CSV file type.
- Automatically examines your affiliate links for 404 or broken links and notifies you of problems.
4. Manage your affiliate programs with ease with Affiliates Manager

Affiliate Manager(also known as WP Affiliate Manager) is another great affiliate marketing plugin you can look into if you want to run your affiliate program for your WordPress website and hire other people to promote your products. This popular affiliate management system allows you to sign new affiliates and streamline the process with simple steps.

With this WordPress plugin, you can control everything from affiliate signups to individual commissions and bulk payouts via PayPal.What's more, it allows you to track unlimited affiliates in real time, create banner ads and creative content for your affiliates, integrate the plugin into MailChimp and WooCommerce, track ad impressions and customize affiliate messages, and more.

Affiliates Manager allows you to choose whether to pay your affiliates a flat rate per order or a percentage of each order they initiate. Each of your partners can beset their payout amount individually and make manual adjustments if needed.

To top it off, the Manager is translation ready. You can translate the plugin into your native language quite easily to make navigating and connecting with partners worldwide easier.

5. Get a Solution to Track All Aspects of Your AffiliateWP Campaigns

Program is a complete affiliate management system that provides simple procedures to manage your referral programs and track them at a glance with detailed reports, real-time charts, and an advanced affiliate dashboard to organize your affiliate programs.

It is a commonly used affiliate marketing plugin that helps you set up and manage all the steps of your affiliate marketing campaigns. It comes with full integration with all major WordPress eCommerce and membership plugins.

AffiliateWP also includes adding other affiliates and translations to your programs manually. You can easily set commission percentages, cookie duration, affiliate pages, and more.

And that concludes our definitive list of the top 5 affiliate marketing plugins and tools for WordPress to help you easily manage all aspects of your campaigns and programs.

Bonus: Boost Sales and Engagement with Leading Marketing Trends

While you're at it, if you want to increase the conversion rate for your business or marketing campaigns and boost engagement rates dramatically, you can also look at our top list. This topic will provide insight into all the major trends to keep an eye on and instantly engage your audience and potential customers.

Chapter 5: Basics of Search Engine Optimization (SEO)

Some people think that SEO is separate from affiliate marketing. This is rather unusual.

This applied to me. The main reason why many advertising and online affiliate marketing agencies do not like to focus on search engine optimization is that they do not fully understand search engine optimization and do not understand how to implement a very effective SEO campaign. Instead of admitting their lack of knowledge, they like to focus on Internet marketing techniques they understand well.

Search Engine Optimization Benefits

Research by MarketingSherpa shows that clicks on top organic positions take 20% of the time, and clicks on top paying ad positions take 10% of the time. However, if your site has the best organic and paid ad positions, links to your site are clicked 60% of the time. This is a unique situation: $10 + 20 = 60$.

Affiliate marketers need to gain more understanding of search engine optimization. Having a well-built and user-friendly affiliate website can lower your advertising costs.

Partners: friend or foe of the Internet search engine?

More often than not, affiliate entrepreneurs or marketers are dangerous to search engines like Google. One day I thought about internet affiliate marketing junk e-mail. In the mail, I think of the logins of all Amazon affiliates. People can be pretty ugly on internet sites.

However, most of the websites I have seen are affiliate websites. For example, one customer does not sell directly to the customer. The website offers information about the organization and its products, but customers need help to purchase something from it. They need to go to a joint venture partner to buy them. In such cases, joining a corporate partner is better for that client. The subsidiary is usually located close to the client, allowing the client to have personalized and fast product delivery.

A client's affiliate program search engine optimization plan aims to provide unique content to search engines without using them. In addition, almost all clients do not want a corporate website to work for a too-conscientious partner or for the entire affiliate network to get in trouble. Everyone should benefit: customers, organization website, and affiliate marketing.

Affiliate SEO and Search Marketing Plans

Affiliate management is key to an effective SEO/search engine marketing plan. Many companies turn to affiliate management for further consideration, often getting in the way of the corporation.

I'm helping a non-profit organization freeze in the search engines. Unfortunately, helping websites hang is a normal part of SEO work. The company itself did not spam Google. The site is easy to use, and the organization is a well-established brand. You will find no technical reason why a website should not be included in the Google index. However, after looking into the reasons for Google's punishment, we discovered a problem: Affiliate marketers have fled.

As part of an online affiliate marketing search engine optimization plan, companies must explain the importance of offering unique content by adding corporate content. For example, effective information architecture is an important element of engine optimization. Is there a grouping and classification of affiliate marketers that goes beyond the organization of a corporate website? Some products sell better in regional markets than others. An affiliate site might focus on the best retail because of its region.

I have seen that cross-links to regional partner sites (internal, page links) depend on the region. Affiliate marketers provide unique commercial search engine insights with a 100% user-friendly smell of knowledge by demonstrating a distinctive cross-link structure.

In addition, FAQs, customer support, or help desks may be unique to each partner site. Many affiliate marketers work directly with clients. What questions do clients often ask? Getting these questions and answers in the FAQ, customer support, or help section provides unique content for customers and search engines like Google.

Finally, one of the biggest mistakes I see with affiliate websites and companies is forcing affiliate marketers to use the exact wording of the printed catalog. Print copying works great inside printed publications; it Doesn't always work with the website. Because affiliate marketers are often familiar with their customers, they must be able to change product definitions without deviating from the corporate branding message.

Finish result? Affiliate sites are fearless in duplicating content from search results, and customers can quickly and easily find what they are trying to find.

In conclusion, while unsolicited online affiliate marketing is a big problem for these commercial web search engines, Internet search engine representatives want to include affiliate search results (both paid and organic), especially if the content and content organization is unique. Users appreciate content tailored to their individual needs.

The power of affiliate marketing to increase income is no secret. But while this key branch of digital marketing is rife with potential rewards, many brands or marketers fail to make an impact.

Combining your affiliate marketing strategy and SEO can seem challenging, but once you get started, the link between the two elements will become clear. To guide you to affiliate marketing SEO success, here we explore practical ways you can combine your affiliate and search engine optimization strategies.

The Importance of SEO in Affiliate Marketing

The importance of SEO in Affiliate Marketing. In this chapter, we will explain SEO's important role in Affiliation.

Occupying the top positions in search sites is one of the biggest goals of those who work with online sales or generate traffic on the web, and that is no coincidence!

The first results that appear in the organic search on Google receive 33% of the traffic for that search, and those that occupy the second position receive 18%, while the third ones get 12% of the clicks.

In principle, it is about attracting more traffic to your website, reinforcing your authority on the subject, and increasing your chances of sales.

But do you know what it takes to appear #1 in Google search results?

In this topic, we will show you how an Affiliate can use SEO to increase their ranking and achieve better and better results.

What is SEO, and why is it important in Affiliate Marketing?

It is a set of strategies to get better the positioning of a page in the results of different organic search engines.

With the emergence of the new generation of search mechanisms and the evolution of their relevance algorithms, the need for pages to adapt to their demands to obtain more traffic also grew.

SEO work then appears to qualify, measure and guarantee page visibility for entrepreneurs and businesses.

That is why it is so important, because thanks to SEO, we will have more relevance and visibility in Google and, therefore, more traffic on our website.

Before you know all the information, we want to mention that organic positioning is divided into Seo On Page and Seo Off Page.

In this content, you will find specific information about Seo On Page.

On-page SEO

SEO on page encompasses the factors that depend only on your actions for optimization.

Using these techniques, you will improve your SEO; you will climb positions and increase traffic and, with it, the sales on your page.

These are the elements that must be observed:

- Content

This is one of the three most important factors of an SEO strategy.

Invest in complete, organized, and exclusive content. Your followers will thank you.

Only then will you be able to stand out among so many other existing pages on the Internet, occupy the top positions in Google, and accelerate your online sales?

- Titles

For good SEO on your website, you should pay attention to two types of titles.

The SEO title is the first thing the user sees when searching. For them to be interested in your content, that title must be attractive to whoever is looking for it.

To create a good SEO title, it is important to capture it as a summary of the main idea of your content.

This way, the user can immediately realize what he will find on your website and define whether it is worth accessing.

The ideal title should contain 55 to 65 characters, and the keyword must be included, preferably at the beginning of the title.

- scannability

When accessing a page, it is almost instinctive to look at the content in a general way to determine if we will consume it.

Poorly organized content negatively affects the user experience and can drive away potential customers.

To improve the scannability of your page, there are a few techniques that can be used.

The proper use of headings and subheadings and the inclusion of markers facilitate the segmentation of the text and make reading more fluid.

- site speed

We all know how boring waiting for a page to load is.

To avoid a negative user experience, constantly check and improve the loading speed of your page.

You can use Google Page Speed Insights to analyze content and see what can be optimized.

- alt text

Alt text (Alternative Text) consists in the text that describes the images on your page.

To elaborate, you must create a brief but complete description of what is shown in the image in question.

Paying attention to this resource is important since it is only through this that Google locates the visual content of a page. With this description, the search engine can show your page to users when they search for similar images.

- Url address

The URL is the unique address of your page.

For it to also work as an attraction for users, you must carefully craft the text you will use.

Long addresses need to be more aesthetically pleasing and can impair the understanding of the page's topic.

- The importance of internal links

Internal links are those that basically direct visitors to other content within your page.

By adding them, you increase the chances that users will stay on your site longer, strengthen other articles, and maintain the good structure of your page.

Affiliate Marketing Trends To Get Ahead

Affiliate marketing is a profitable business but also a competitive one. By following these trends, stay ahead of the game.

Affiliate marketing can help you stay ahead of your marketing efforts. Whether you need more sales, attention, or satisfied customers, developing and optimizing your affiliate programs is critical to improving business performance.

Affiliate marketing will face significant changes in 2023, from the popularity of micro-influencers to trend-setting green products and services.

You will notice that successful companies use this type of marketing, promoting their brands according to what is happening in the market or their particular niche. This is a great opportunity to review your affiliate marketing budgets and dedicate some time to research!

f you are in the affiliate marketing business or know someone on the job, remember that 2023 will bring new trends that will modify the current landscape. Partnerships should provide customers with quality content and boost online sales.

So what are the upcoming trends in affiliate marketing for 2023? Are there entirely new ventures, or should marketers emphasize existing practices?

Finally, with the new year approaching, how can you take the latest topics among affiliate marketers and capitalize on the new wave of affiliate marketers to attract more customers, earn more commissions, and generate higher profits?

- Optimized for Voice Search
- Increasing Link Building & Co-Marketing
- No Cookies
- Turning Into the Metaverse
- Virtual & Live Shopping
- Constant Attention to Micro-Influencers
- Trending Industries: Green Foods & SaaS
- Use Cross-Device Tracking
- More Coupons & Cashback
- Social Selling Continues to Grow
- Did Someone Say About Crypto Affiliate Marketing?
- Emphasis on Social Proof

1. Optimization For Voice Search

The rising popularity of voice assistants is shaping our daily habits—more than 42.1% of the US population had them in 2022. They help with purchasing decisions, weather reports, and the overall user experience of new gadgets.

Therefore, you must consider that your customers use them daily, and you must cater to their needs accordingly. This is one of the biggest affiliate marketing trends in 2023. Who wouldn't want to reach half the US population and make them their customers?

You should adjust your marketing strategies to match the voice search feature with your partner products or services.

You will offer your customers convenience and ease of access by having them add items to their cart with their voice.

Be sure to include long-tail keywords so people can find your business and place an order! Standard SEO practices are essential to improve your store's search rankings. Ensure you're posting original content, and start posting blog posts that match your niche!

You can even try guest posting to get a lot of organic traffic and help your affiliate marketing meet new challenges. This is a great way to meet other content creators and build long-term partnerships.

Affiliate marketers should watch for voice assistants, which will become the norm in many homes and can be a great tool to reach more customers. A wider audience can become a bigger customer base if you post authentic content!

2. Increasing Link Building & Comarketing

What should affiliate marketers look out for next? It's accelerated link-building and co-marketing! If this sounds a bit complicated, let's break it down into two parts since it closely relates to search engine marketing.

Link building is the action of getting links back to your site from other sites to rank higher on search engines like Google. These can be affiliate links or sources to landing pages.

This will help with organic traffic to your site.

This is closely related to, and you should already know the basics as an affiliate marketer. However, you can always consult a specialist or read more about it! This is one of the best affiliate marketing tools to increase your customer base.

Search engines underwent major upgrades in 2022; for example, Google had ten algorithm updates, which will likely roll over into the next year as they become more advanced and "smarter." Such failures should reflect your advertising strategy and necessary changes.

On the other hand, co-marketing is a collaboration with other brands through which you promote each other's business interchangeably. This includes creating collaborative content, hosting live sessions, organizing product update announcements, and more!

Affiliate marketers can benefit from co-marketing as they can reach new target audiences, gain attention and increase sales. This is a great way to connect with content creators and establish your name in the affiliate industry!

3. No Cookies

Don't be discouraged if you see the next trend is "no cookies" - we're not discussing yummy treats.

Cookies are basically small text files saved on your computer to track your behavior and preferences when you visit websites.

You may have noticed the third-party cookie banner that appears whenever you visit a new website. Usually, I click "Accept" and move on with my life, but this little banner has much power. Essentially, you are giving the website permission to collect data about you.

We understand this is an integral part of affiliate marketing, but we must be more creative in understanding customers. People are too aware of privacy issues, and many browsers have started restricting the use of cookies. The era of a "cookie-free future" has arrived.

Suppose cookies are essential for your business as an affiliate marketing. In that case, you can use alternatives such as browser footprints or link-based tracking to see what your customers like and monitor affiliate traffic.

This is one of the biggest changes in e-commerce in the last few years.

In addition, the affiliate marketing niche must comply with data usage regulations, so check out the GDPR and CCPA! It has changed over the past few years, so it must be updated to run affiliate marketing campaigns successfully.

4. Turn Into the Metaverse

Affiliate marketers can use the Metaverse, a virtual world accessible via the Internet, to interact with users and organize activities in the digital space to reach more customers.

It is great for contextual targeting and increasing sales in affiliate marketing.

How can you incorporate such exploration of the virtual world into your affiliate marketing strategy? You need to get your creative juices flowing! This can help you acquire new customers, close online sales, and develop your advertising strategy.

A virtual storefront or event participation can increase the level of your brand awareness. Inside the metaverse, you can even run virtual marketing campaigns with influencers! This is a real-world simulation with a global audience full of potential customers.

Marketing partners can stay on top of their game and reach more customers by keeping up with the cutting edge of technology. The Metaverse is a great example of the changing affiliate marketing landscape, and 2023 is the time to experiment with your strategies.

5. Virtual & Live Shopping

Another trend that affiliate marketers should look forward to in 2023 is virtual and live shopping. Who has yet to make an online purchase in the past six months? Virtual shopping saves many people during the holiday hustle and bustle when shopping for gifts or even during peak hours.

Online stores are accessible and easy to navigate, so it's no surprise that people often prefer them over physical stores. Virtual shopping allows shoppers to shop online just like in a brick-and-mortar store.

This is e-commerce with a human touch.

Moreover, the retail e-commerce niche is huge. In 2021, its sales reached.

These numbers open up opportunities for affiliate marketers to partner with brands and retailers in the online shopping category. Why? This is a great way to increase sales and reach a wider audience.

But what is live shopping? Live shopping is live shopping. This is becoming increasingly popular because buyers can ask questions about the product during the live stream. Involvement and interaction in fashion.

Another benefit of affiliate marketing through live streaming is that most live streaming happens through social media platforms (such as YouTube or Instagram). This way, you bring your product to people, making it easier for them to buy.

Even high-end luxury brands such as Prada have online stores that offer a variety of makeup kits, clothing, and accessories. That's how you know affiliate marketers need to pay attention to the changing buying habits of their customers.

6. Constant Attention to Micro-Influencers

To increase sales in the affiliate marketing industry, consider hiring micro-influencers to promote your business.

Although these influences have few fans, they have the two most important things for an interested audience – trust and reputation.

Micro-influencers gain the trust of their audience by responding to their wants and needs through content. Because micro-influencers focus on daily content, many people find it interesting and easy to follow. This builds trust between the influencer and the viewer.

Marketing partners should accept to work with micro-influencers if their number of followers is small. Usually, their engagement rates are excellent, and this rate can positively influence the success of affiliate marketing campaigns.

Hence, such influencers are more likely to promote products successfully. Although their audience is relatively small, they are much more interested in quality content. That's the reason why influencer marketing will be a big trend in 2023.

In 2023, the influencer industry will constantly grow, and affiliate marketers can then benefit from taking the less-traveled path when hiring promoters. Collaborating with micro-influencers is cost-effective and can deliver great results through authenticity!

7. Trending Industries: Green Foods & SaaS

Another trend that affiliate marketers should look forward to in 2023 is the growing demand for green products and SaaS (software as a service). Artificial intelligence will also be popular, but it's a long story.

We have seen the impact of climate change on media coverage and how it affects our ecosystems, everyday life, and shopping habits. More people choose sustainable products because of sustainability and the conscious decision to buy from socially responsible brands.

In addition, SaaS companies often offer solutions when promoting their services. This may include paperless initiatives, remote work, and digital tools. And these solutions are just the tip of the SaaS iceberg.

Affiliate marketing campaigns can take advantage from subscription-based SaaS products as they provide longevity. Most customers don't cancel their subscriptions even if they don't like a product, and marketers can negotiate great deals with these companies to stay on top of trends.

8. Use Cross-Device Tracking

In the early 2000s, people were extremely excited about mobile devices because they made communication easier. Back then, we had Wi-Fi and available internet wherever we went.

In 2023, smartphones, laptops, and smartwatches will define the affiliate marketing industry.

As a marketing partner, consider that your customers use several smart devices throughout the day, and they may switch between them as they navigate the web. You need to implement cross-device tracking to understand their behavior and preferences!

The popularity of desktop devices has declined as mobile users have taken over the business. This is why organic mobile traffic is one of the trends for affiliate marketers. Various analytics tools, such as affiliate marketers, can easily track customer behavior.

Cross-device tracking works even when cookies are disabled, making it easier to identify your marketing efforts and reach your desired audience. Take advantage of this affiliate marketing trend that can be critical to your affiliate marketing success!

9. More Coupons & Cashback

Did you know that in 1887 Coca-Cola issued the first coupon? And in 2022, the value of a redeemed digital coupon was about $91 billion!

Some people consider "old school" coupons. However, they do wonders for companies by maintaining relationships with their regular customers and increasing the conversion rate of new customers! In addition, it is useful for customer experience.

Thanks to technological advances, digital coupons are available to companies that can utilize to attract more customers. It is common in applications, programs, and other technology products or services..

Thus, affiliate marketers can use these programs to increase their customer base and earn higher profits. The digital coupon trend is likely to become even more popular in 2023.

Your affiliate strategies can be varied and will help you analyze ways to encourage a user to move to the purchase stage. Cashback is an effective advertising player; you can use it on e-commerce sites.

Coupons and cashback programs are integral to retailers encouraging customers to purchase more. Affiliate marketing can also benefit from such schemes! Notably, coupons and cashback can then turn your new customers into regular ones.

Plus, coupons and cashback are a great way to stand out from other affiliate programs. This is a crowded industry; everyone can benefit from cutting-edge solutions that offer tangible customer benefits!

10. Social Selling Continues to Grow

In addition to the many algorithm changes that have taken place in recent years, social media platforms do offer a marketplace for your favorite brands. Thus social selling was born, emphasizing higher conversion rates and a new advertising strategy.

Social platforms such as Facebook, Instagram, and even LinkedIn can direct you to a company you can purchase products from.

People use social media as a research tool to see if online purchases won't match their needs.

In addition, social media platforms make placing orders in digital stores easier. Companies can customize their social media sales profiles to include immediate purchases, PayPal integration, and better ways to retain users.

In 2023, the affiliate marketing landscape must embrace social selling to reach new global audiences. Social selling is one of the biggest trends for marketers in 2023.

Social selling can be a really fun niche to dive into as it offers an engaging online shopping experience with various product mockups, live commentary, and more! This aspect can be a great way to connect with your customers.

11. Did Someone Say About Crypto Affiliate Marketing?

The current situation in the cryptocurrency market could definitely be better. However, perhaps now is the right time to start building a cryptocurrency affiliate marketing program to get ahead of your competitors!

Effective content creation and audience matching can help your affiliate strategies.

Over the past few years, crypto and blockchain technologies have experienced a boom, and many companies are now integrating cryptocurrency payouts as an option for their customers. Notably, cryptocurrency affiliate marketing programs allow marketers to earn commissions for promoting cryptocurrencies.

It is a diverse marketplace that offers a variety of affiliate marketing methods, including referral programs, bonuses for referring more investors, and more.

In addition, you can learn about the bear market, tokens, and other interesting topics!

In addition, you can promote exchanges, wallets, mining tools, and anything related to crypto. Many more crypto investors and enthusiasts are looking for new crypto affiliate programs.

Time to Refine Your Strategy

As the world changes, affiliate marketing must keep up with digital marketing trends, data usage, and even virtual worlds like the metaverse. However, affiliate marketers can take advantage of the changes and reach even more customers!

For example, customer privacy regulations introduce cookie preferences, but there are several alternative tracking methods, namely cross-device tracking, that allow better tracking of consumer behavior. Cookie-free ads will affect the affiliate network, but it's not the end of the world.

While technology does advance rapidly, affiliate marketers can then improve their SEO knowledge and learn more about the SaaS sector. Many experts argue that this is the future of e-commerce with a high ROI. Also, pay attention to influencer marketing as it will be trending.

In particular, it would be helpful if you learned much information to successfully implement new affiliate marketing strategies.

Trends come and go, but a clear plan for what you want to achieve is critical.

Incorporate one or more aspects into your affiliate marketing strategy and stay ahead of the competition in 2023!

Search Engine Optimization Tips

There is a close relationship between SEO and.

For example, if a site's rating drops, affiliates are often blamed for everything.

The main reason could be a bad backlink reputation.

To avoid this, you must familiarize yourself with the basic SEO best practices.

First, you need to understand how Google ranks websites.

This will help you design your site in a way that meets all of its requirements.

Your site's income will increase, and you can ensure everything is in order with your traffic.

In other words, basic SEO guidelines will help you avoid many online marketing problems.

4 Search Engine Optimization Tips You Should Start Using Right Now:

1. Choose the right keywords

Google is constantly changing niches, domains, and keywords.

Choosing a short and catchy domain name and having a short URL is very important as the Google search engine gives the most importance to the first 5 words.

However, this rule no longer applies to keywords.

After adding, Google introduced Latent Semantic Indexing (LSI), which means that the search engine tries to determine the actual content of an article based on each word you write.

Long tail keywords also go a long way in ranking up!

Instead of competing for "good restaurants," it's better to focus on the long-tail keyword "good Italian restaurants in Brooklyn."

We want to draw your attention to an excellent tool for working with hidden semantic indexing - LSI graph.

How to start working with it?

You must enter your chosen keywords into the LSI graph and wait for the magic!

You should choose a niche that is directly related to what you are promoting. Ideally, this niche should be close to you in spirit.

One of the most important aspects in finding keywords for your site is how you can predict user behavior and, therefore, their query in the search engine so that you are always one step ahead of them.

Let's look at 10 steps that will make your life easier.

10 Steps to Keyword Research

Step 1: Make an Excel file with the following columns: Keyword, Volume, Competition, and Keyword Competition.

Step 2: Enter a general keyword, such as affiliate marketing, into the search bar and check Google's suggested keywords.

Then enter these keywords into the file (choose relevant keywords that suit your site).

The following is an example query (keyword research).

Step 3: Go to and enter your keyword there.

The next step is to assess whether the suggested keywords fit your content.

Yes? It's time to bring them into the Excel file!

You can then repeat the request with other keywords that match your site.

Step 4: Proceed on Google Keyword Planner and enter all the keywords you have on your list. Check out our excellent guide to keyword planning.

Step 5: Download the results from Keyword Planner, which will allow you to see all the results related to the selected keywords, along with the number of searches and competition for the keywords you entered.

Step 6: Clean up Keyword Planner results. Remove all columns except the following: Keyword, Volume, Competition, and Keyword Competition.

Step 7: Remove all keywords that do not fit your site's content.

Step 8: Copy and paste the keywords into the Excel file you created earlier.

Step 9: Remove duplicate keywords.

Step 10: Filter and choose the most suitable.

You have to focus on keywords with high search volume and low competition.

Tip: You can find variations of your keywords on Quora, which will be very useful in your work.

Also, you should pay attention to the new Google artificial intelligence system used with the already-known Google search algorithms.

The main purpose of the system is to provide users with a large number of queries.

RankBrain - an artificial intelligence system - uses complex mathematical processes and an advanced understanding of semantics to understand why and how people search in a search engine.

Then, Google will apply these findings to their search results.

Why is it important?

Because it affects your future SEO strategies!

2. Avoid Content Farms and Low-Quality Content

You might think that much content that doesn't add value to the user is what you should be focusing on. However, it is not!

After numerous algorithm and search engine changes, this strategy can negatively affect your site's search results!

The best way to get high rankings and traffic is high-quality content.

You definitely need to engage your audience and provide them with something of value to them.

You will get many backlinks if you have content that entertains, engages, and engages your reader.

Quality greatly affects the loyalty and trust of your users, so they will be more receptive to the products and services you advertise.

"How can content marketing overtake SEO when the only way to successfully market is SEO?" – Neil Patel

Backlinko's Brian Dean showed that from an SEO standpoint, the ideal article length in 2016 was over 1,500 words, significantly more than the 300 words previously considered long text.

Thus, the focus of 2016 is more detailed articles.

Whatever you do with the length of your videos, posts, and presentations, make sure that it meets the needs of your target audience.

3. Create a mobile version of your site.

In today's world, we no longer have questions about the importance of marketing for mobile users.

More than 80% have smartphones, and approximately 50% of all Internet traffic does come from mobile devices.

That is why having a mobile version of your site is so important.

You can spend little time and money on this, as many different services and templates are available to make your work easier.

For example, WordPress provides several plugins specifically designed for the mobile version of your site.

You can easily check the impression your site makes on mobile devices with the help of several services - for example, the Google service

In addition, with the help of Google PageSpeed Insights, you can solve several problems on your site and increase its speed.

4. Social networks are your true friends.

Social networks occupy a significant place in our lives.

Over 95% of people working in online marketing use social media in their campaigns to advertise a particular brand or communicate with a target audience.

Due to the high interactivity, users get the impression that they are interacting with other people (and not a soulless corporation), and the number of conversions increases significantly.

Has shown that you get higher ad performance than using newsletters and landing pages.

It's very simple!

Many people can view each post on Twitter, Facebook, Instagram, and other social networks.

People can share your post with friends, leave comments and thus promote your post, which greatly increases brand awareness.

If you want to conquer the world of online marketing, social networks are your true friends!

Chapter 6: Case Study: Successful Affiliate Marketing Websites

Successful Affiliate Marketing Strategies

To thrive in a competitive field, it is necessary to employ effective strategies. Below are some of the proven affiliate marketing strategies that can guide you to success:

- Understand your audience. This is the basis of any marketing strategy. Identify your audience, what they need, and how the products or services you promote can meet these needs. Tailor your content and also the marketing messages to resonate with them.
- Promote relevant products. Promote products or services that are important to your audience and your niche. Irrelevant products may not convert, thus hurting your earnings. The credibility of your platform also depends on the relevance of the products you endorse.
- Create high-quality content. High-quality, engaging content is the key to attracting and retaining your audience. Whether blog posts, product reviews, or how-to videos, your content needs to be very informative, fun, and valuable to your audience.
- SEO. Effective search engine optimization (SEO) can help improve your platform's visibility in search engine results, increasing traffic and potential conversions.
- Take advantage of social networks. Social media can be powerful tools for promoting your content and affiliate links. They allow you to get to a larger audience and interact more with them.
- Build email lists. Email marketing allows you to keep direct communication with your audience. You can use it to send personalized content, product recommendations, and exclusive offers.
- Monitoring and analysis. Track your performance through analytics. This can help you understand what's working and what's not, allowing you to refine your strategy accordingly.
- Implementing these affiliate marketing strategies can significantly increase your chances of success. Affiliate marketing requires effort, patience, and continuous learning and adjustment. However, you can turn it into a profitable venture with the right strategies.

Although "Can you make money with affiliate marketing?" may be common among beginners, numerous case studies provide a positive answer. From individual bloggers to corporate giants, many have mastered the art of affiliate marketing and achieved impressive results.

An example of this is the immense success of the Amazon affiliate program. Similarly, fashion blogging provides numerous examples of successful affiliate marketing. In both cases, some of the crucial affiliate marketing tips that contributed to their success included understanding the audience, creating high-quality content, and promoting relevant products. Let's talk about them in more detail.

Amazon affiliate program

The Amazon Affiliate Program, or Amazon Associates, is one of the most recognized and popular affiliate marketing programs worldwide. It allows affiliates to promote millions of products from various categories, making it attractive to many merchants.

One of the key reasons behind the program's popularity is the trust and credibility associated with the Amazon brand. When affiliates promote Amazon products, they take advantage of the company's reputation, which can help increase conversion rates. This is especially advantageous for beginners who still need to establish their mark.

The Amazon Associates program is also known for its friendly interface. It provides detailed performance metrics that allow affiliates to track clicks, sales, and earnings effectively. In addition, Amazon provides various promotional tools, including banner ads and a sidebar for easy link creation.

Despite the relatively low commission rates compared to some other affiliate programs, the wide variety of products and ease of use make the affiliate marketing programs Amazon offers an attractive option for many merchants.

Fashion bloggers, especially on Instagram, have carved out a niche in the affiliate marketing world. The platform's emphasis on visual content has become an ideal place for fashion enthusiasts to showcase their style and promote affiliate products.

Many of these influencers began their journey as hobbyists and have mastered seamlessly integrating Instagram affiliate marketing into their regular content. By promoting products they use and love, they maintain authenticity, which is crucial to building trust with your audience.

Additionally, they have harnessed the power of storytelling to engage their followers. Instead of just showing off a product, they often share personal stories or style tips related to the items they promote. This approach helps drive engagement and increases followers' likelihood to click on affiliate links and purchase. Thus, the success of fashion bloggers underscores the potential of affiliate marketing for Instagram and its power to turn passion into profit.

Overcoming Challenges in Affiliate Marketing

Affiliate marketing, while promising, can present several challenges, particularly for beginners. However, these obstacles can be overcome with the right focus and persistence. Here are some affiliate marketing tips to navigate common pitfalls:

- Selecting the right niche: One of the biggest challenges is identifying the right niche. Selecting a niche that does align with your interests and experience is essential to maintain consistency and provide value to your audience.
- Build trust and authority: Another challenge in affiliate marketing is building trust with your audience. Posting regular, high-quality content and being transparent about affiliate relationships can help build trust and establish your brand as an authority.
- Choosing the Right Affiliate Programs: Not all affiliate programs are created equal. Choosing programs offering reasonable commissions, reliable tracking systems, and timely payments is crucial. Reading reviews and looking for recommendations can be helpful in this process.
- Generate traffic: Your affiliate marketing efforts can only succeed with constant traffic flow. It is essential to employ efficient SEO strategies, social media marketing, and possibly even paid advertising to drive the traffic to your website or social media channels.
- Conversion optimization: Getting traffic is half the battle; the other half is turning that traffic into sales. Good web design, clear calls to action, and engaging content can significantly increase conversion rates.

Affiliate marketing is a journey full of learning and growth. You can overcome challenges and maximize your earning potential by continually testing, learning, and adapting. Remember, the most effective affiliate marketing tips emphasize patience, persistence, and then a commitment to providing value to your audience. With these qualities, you will be well on your way to success.

Future Trends in Affiliate Marketing

As digital landscapes evolve, so does the field of affiliate marketing. Understanding these changes can help merchants adapt their strategies for more significant impact and profit from affiliate marketing. Here are some key trends to watch:

- Increased emphasis on content quality. In the face of increasing competition, content quality will continue to be a significant differentiator. Affiliates that provide valuable, engaging, and audience-specific content will likely outperform those that don't.
- Rise of video and voice search. With the rising popularity of video content, affiliates must optimize their strategies to align with these trends. This could mean creating more video content or optimizing for voice search.
- Greater transparency. As consumers get smarter, they are demanding more transparency from brands. Affiliates must be upfront about their associations to build trust with their audience.
- Personalization and AI. As technology advances, the ability to personalize content based on user behavior will become even more crucial. AI and machine learning-powered tools will play a significant role in this.
- Data privacy regulations. As data privacy laws become stricter, affiliates must ensure their practices comply with these regulations to avoid penalties and maintain trust with their audience.
- Influencer marketing. With the continued rise of social platforms, influencers will play an increasingly vital role in affiliate marketing. Affiliates may need to use influencer associations to reach a larger audience.

Staying on top of these trends and adapting your strategies is one of the best tips for success in affiliate marketing. However, one timeless trend remains the need to learn and adapt continually. As affiliate marketing trends evolve, so must affiliate marketers looking to profit from them. In the ever-changing world of digital marketing, the ability to adjust and innovate is key to long-term success.

By studying these case study examples and applying the lessons learned to your website, you can expect to achieve similar results and increase your commissions as an affiliate marketer.

When you have read these affiliate marketing success case studies, check out this other SEO case study page for facts on how to thrive in organic search engine optimization, this content marketing case study page, digital marketing case studies, email marketing principles, social media case studies, and this PPC case study page if you're excited about paid search advertising strategies.

There is also a complete affiliate marketing SEO strategy guide that you can then follow to get better results.

Affiliate Marketing Case Studies

Case: how an affiliate program was created that helped attract 130,000 new online shoppers in 2022

In October 2021, VkusVill launched its affiliate program for bloggers, opinion leaders, thematic site owners, and ordinary customers ready to recommend the store to their friends. Especially for the launch of this program, PIM Solutions created an individual project based on the PIM.CPA service adapted to the tasks of free delivery by VkusVill. We tell how the development of this platform went and what results were achieved thanks to the launch of the affiliate program.

Why VkusVill needed an affiliate program

VkusVill receives a huge stream of feedback from customers. In 2022 alone, the company's specialists processed over 8 million requests and thousands of reviews on various websites and social networks. The company began to think long ago: if customers are ready to recommend VkusVill, why not support this initiative? As a result, it was decided to create a motivation system for those ready to promote the VkusVill products and services they use.

VkusVilla's partner program was the most convenient and effective tool for working with partner buyers and collecting their feedback. This tool allows you to communicate directly with partners, receive instant feedback from them, track each partner's performance, and quickly pay everyone.

Since the VkusVilla affiliate program involved interaction with many individuals who do not have individual entrepreneurs or self-employment, it was necessary to resolve issues related to the payment of tax deductions by them. This is also why VkusVill turned to PIM Solutions to develop an affiliate program. Its PIM.CPA service develops and implements CPA platforms for large advertisers.

One of the main goals of creating an affiliate program was to motivate buyers to talk more about VkusVill, the opportunity to purchase high-quality products with a pure composition, and that it is always available and always with free delivery. We believe that a personal recommendation or post by an interesting blogger can work effectively and convey information where the user might not pay attention to advertising banners.

It was also important for us to make the program interesting for bloggers with subscribers and our customers who know and love VkusVill and recommend it to their friends and relatives. And here, an important role is played by the opportunity to receive remuneration in a format convenient for the participant, even if he still needs to get the status of a self-employed or individual entrepreneur.

We needed a technological solution that would allow us to respond quickly to new tasks and ideas within the program's framework and solve the problem of document flow and payments to partners.

PIM Solutions was the only company ready to completely solve our problems. As a result, we received a CPA platform optimized for us with high-quality and prompt support; we solved the tasks of paying remuneration and optimizing workflow.

How the VkusVilla affiliate program was created

Specialists from VkusVilla and PIM Solutions jointly carried out the development and implementation of the CPA platform. Due to the complexity of the task, not only programmers and marketers worked on it, but also lawyers, financiers, accountants, etc. Thanks to the experience of all participants, the technology of the companies, and the use of their know-how, the CPA platform was launched in just 1.5 months.

What is a CPA platform? From a technical point of view, this is a tracking platform that performs the following functions:

- setting the rules for the advertiser's offers
- billing (statistics calculation)
- antifraud
- creating a dashboard with charts
- feedback system for partners, including the possibility of mass mailings
- mechanisms for tracking the effectiveness of partners and channels for promoting the affiliate program
- partner profile management
- differentiation of rights by roles necessary to maintain business processes on the side of the affiliate marketing department

Thanks to the launch of its platform, VkusVill got the opportunity to work directly with partners and receive direct feedback from them. The advertiser manages joint promotions and monitors each partner's effectiveness, making it possible to motivate partners and get guaranteed results from them. Integration with our loyalty program made paying rewards with VkusVill bonuses possible. The company also has the opportunity to involve its employees in the affiliate program. This proposal found a lively response in the program; more than 3,500 VkusVill employees registered.

PIM Solutions is still actively participating in the work of the VkusVilla affiliate program as a software provider, an operator for interaction with partners, and a tax agent for individual partners. The company is also constantly involved in the functional development of the CPA platform.

The VkusVilla affiliate program is an example of a White Label product created by a company. They can customize very flexibly, creating CPA platforms tailored to the specific needs of advertisers. On the one hand, it took a lot of work for them to develop this specific program since implementing the customer's requirements required much effort; on the other hand, the customer knew exactly what result he wanted to get and communicated his goals. Therefore, creating the platform took a relatively short time, which allowed the affiliate program to be launched quickly.

How does the VkusVilla affiliate program work?

Participants of the program are offered an extremely simple scheme of work. Register on partners.vkusvill.ru, get a personal promotional code, and share it with friends, acquaintances, or subscribers. Affiliates receive 10% for the first online order of the attracted buyer and 10% from each repeated order of this buyer within 90 days from the moment the promotional code is applied. The partner himself chooses how to receive remuneration: bonuses to the VkusVill loyalty card or rubles to a bank card or account.

As expected, two groups became the most active participants in the affiliate program: bloggers and ordinary buyers. For the first category, VkusVill's proposal was especially relevant since the blogging market was in a difficult situation when it was launched. Some popular sites were blocked, and others turned off their advertising inventory, so bloggers actively explored new sites. VkusVill cooperates with bloggers directly and through specialized agencies, ensuring a stable demand for influencer content and payments for cooperation with the brand.

Buyers and employees of VkusVill are also actively involved in distributing promotional codes. They were attracted by the ease of registration and obtaining promotional codes, favorable terms of cooperation (commission not only for the first order but also for subsequent orders within 90 days), quick settlements (earned for the previous month comes to the account in the first half of the next), the ability to calculate income in a special calculator and track statistics. The partner's account displays information about the first and repeated orders of attracted customers, remuneration, payments, banners, and other advertising materials that partners can use.

From April to September 2022, there was a promotion for participants in the VkusVill affiliate program - an increased reward for orders for delivery outside cities - to delivery areas within 4 hours. In the summer of 2022, the delivery area expanded significantly: it included many settlements where delivery was not previously carried out. In many of these areas, VkusVill was the only one who delivered. Bloggers actively covered this action.

In 2022, over 25 thousand participants registered in the affiliate program, which attracted more than 130 thousand new customers. Partners actively discuss promotions, new products, and services, analyze purchases and give feedback. Thus, the program participants made more than 5,000 posts in their groups on social networks in support of the Mango Egypt product alone. Many partners choose to receive rewards on a loyalty card for subsequent payment for purchases because, in VkusVille, you can buy not only products but also beauty and health products, household goods, pet food, and much more.

ROI (return on investment) for this period was 700%. The calculations considered the revenue from the orders of new customers and their subsequent online purchases within 90 days, minus discounts for promotional codes and payments to partners.

Beyond the affiliate program

Working with such many partners, including individuals without sole proprietorship and self-employment, involves a lot of paperwork, tax deductions, and contributions to the Pension Fund. In the VkusVill affiliate program, these processes are automated.

PIM Solutions deals with all document flow with partners; the process is completely transferred to electronic form. When registering in an affiliate program, it is enough for its participants to accept an electronic offer, after which they can immediately start earning.

Also, on the VkusVilla CPA platform, mass work with individuals in 1C has been implemented. Thanks to this, all reports to the tax and Pension Fund are sent promptly and automatically. This functionality was originally built into the platform. In addition, the closing of reporting periods with partners is automated. This is done by signing documents (acts and reports) with an electronic unqualified signature implemented on the PIM.CPA platform.

With automation, it is possible to organize work with many individual partners. Therefore, this option was originally included in the VkusVilla CPA platform. We have taken over all relationships with contractors within the framework of the affiliate program. Thanks to this, our customers can focus on new promotions without being distracted by document flow.

Yulia Pogorelskaya, Project Director, PIM Solutions

The affiliate program has a main offer aimed at attracting new customers. And also, new offers are being tested to promote other useful and convenient services. The program already has a community of tens of affiliates and thousands of loyal and motivated people ready to recommend new services, so its potential is very high.

Of course, VkusVill will continue to launch and develop various thematic areas, and the affiliate program will be one of the main channels for introducing the audience to new products and services.

If we talk about the technical side of the work, then shortly, the PIM.CPA service plans to automate work with advertising data operators. And the VkusVill affiliate program will be one of the first to implement this feature.

The affiliate program is a community of tens of thousands who love VkusVill, talk about our products, receive free home and country delivery, and receive rewards for their recommendations. Many of our members make detailed reviews of their favorite products and new products and share recipes. Our loyal audience's core is active buyers and partners.

VkusVill aims to make wholesome food for a healthy diet accessible to everyone. VkusVill is easy to recommend because our products are tasty, high-quality, and with an honest composition; everyone will find what they need for their taste and tasks. Thanks to the solution from PIM Solutions, more and more people can recommend VkusVill and receive rewards, which means that the number of those who, thanks to the recommendations, have discovered useful VkusVill products is growing.

3 cases: how companies got a steady stream of orders from a new channel

The business is constantly looking for new sources of sales. You can spend a significant part of the advertising budget on experiments but still need to get the desired customers. Now we will tell you about three companies at once that increased their sales by more than 10% due to the experiment with CPA.

CPA or affiliate marketing is a promotion method in which the brand transfers rewards only for selected targeted actions: sales, installs, or leads. A platform for working with partners (web admins) who attract traffic and sales is the affiliate network. For example, the largest affiliate network in Russia, Admitad, unites over 1,700 advertisers and almost 1.2 million web admins.

Traffic is attracted by numerous specialists in setting up contextual and targeted advertising, bloggers, content sites, cashback services, loyalty programs, storefront and coupon sites, and many other sites. Not surprisingly, many brands incorporate affiliate marketing into their order acquisition channels. Admitad shared with us real cases of companies that tried working with CPA and were able to increase the flow of orders greatly.

Goods.ru — strong start and growth on restart

One of the top marketplaces in the CIS discovered a partnership area and decided to refine it after receiving the first results.

Here is the goods.ru affiliate program at Admitad in numbers for the first two years since its launch:

- +407% - growth in the turnover of the goods.ru affiliate program in Russia year on year.
- +434% - increase in the number of goods.ru orders in the affiliate program.
- +1378% - increase in the number of clicks in the affiliate program.

Initially, the marketplace opened an affiliate program in Admitad to attract an audience in bulk. This goal was achieved, but the project team realized that maintaining such a pace requires significant costs, and it is time to set a new goal for the partnership direction.

Therefore, in the second stage of work with the goods.ru partner network, we focused on increasing the flow of new customers. The marketplace has relaunched the offer with additional conditions: flexible rates and a new reward model.

Webmasters were divided into two types, and different awards were established:

Marketing. These are the web admins who increase brand awareness and audience reach. These include content resources, blogs, Youtube channels, etc. This channel is important for establishing "contact" with buyers despite a smaller share of orders.

Closer. These include web admins who encourage the buyer to complete an order - visits from such web admins often end in a purchase, especially if the user sees an additional benefit. These are, for example, coupon sites, cashback services, loyalty programs, etc.

Such flexible conditions and additional rewards were of interest to the webmasters themselves. As a result of the relaunch of the offer, the number of partners directing traffic to goods.ru offers increased from 1500 to 2500. And most importantly, the main goal was achieved: the share of new customers in the CPA channel increased to 20%.

"Cooperation with Admitad helped us to scale our affiliate program and automate the process – now we have hundreds of webmasters working with us. We also use or test technological solutions of the partner network, for example, a mobile SDK or unique promotional codes," says Kirill Lymar, Head of SEO and Affiliate Programs at goods.ru.

Karina's experience is a ticket to thousands of orders

Niche projects can also achieve success in working with CPAs. Practice shows that giant marketplaces and small and medium-sized businesses get interesting results through their affiliate programs. The case of the ticket operator Karabas is an excellent confirmation.

The brand decided to integrate the partnership with Admitad back in 2018. The company then had a lot of plans to test different areas for promotion, but corny "not enough hands." Therefore, it was decided to start working with CPA - this allowed us to work with many traffic channels simultaneously while not risking the budget and other resources.

"Currently, 536 webmasters are connected to the Karabas offer; they bring us about 10% of all leads. Of course, the best way to motivate is a higher rate. We try to motivate them with bonuses but depend heavily on the event organizers. There was a case when the bonus scale was launched in February (low season), and the traffic even increased. It was very amazing. For the rest, for motivation, we try to use individual KPIs and listen to their wishes," the project team shared their impressions.

Telemart - tenth share of orders with CPA

Affiliate marketing works well with individual product categories as well. The example of Telemart, a company that sells computer equipment, accessories, and components, will be very indicative. The brand's original goal was to find new channels to attract customers and try fresh formats. In 2019, more than 250 web admins joined the affiliate program of the online store on Admitad.

Of all types of traffic, Telemart chose social networks (targeted advertising and advertising in communities), YouTube blogs, cashback services, non-branded context, and SEO projects (blogs and storefronts). The project team notes that web admins working with the Adwords system, organic search results, and trading platforms bring them the most sales, and the latter also gives the highest average check. Although YouTube is not one of the top channels, Telemart highlighted a very successful case of working with YouTuber Alex Real - he approached the topic authoritatively and gave excellent results.

"The main thing a store can do to make it easier for a webmaster is to grow independently. Competitive prices, a user-friendly website with a good catalog rubricator, and adaptation to mobile devices — the better the store converts leads into sales, the easier it is to work with it. If the brand is not developed, neither buyers nor webmasters will trust it. For example, we launched an assembler tool (in other words, you can assemble a computer for yourself right on the site) - this is our competitive advantage and an interesting "trick" through which webmasters quite effectively promote computer components," Telemart shared advice.

As a result, the brand not only works with many new traffic channels, but by the end of 2019, it began to receive up to 10% of its leads through affiliate marketing. In 2020, Telemart decided to further increase sales through CPA.

These examples are a great motivator for many brands to try working with an affiliate network. They show that companies decide to take this step. As a result, not only receive a flow of orders but also complete additional goals: expand their reach, increase the influx of new customers, and increase the average bill.

Affiliate Marketing: Examples of the success of this excellent online business

Discover more about affiliate marketing and its advantages to develop your business and go further.

Affiliate marketing is the opportunity of a lifetime! If you have good sales skills and a desire to start a business, working by recommending physical or digital products of others can be a great way to generate income online. We will see affiliate marketing success stories with some practical examples.

The best thing is that you don't need to create a product and take care of everything that implies. With affiliate marketing or affiliate marketing, you can earn money anytime and anywhere, thanks to the references or links published on your blog, social networks, or website.

7 Successful Affiliate Marketing Examples

Still, have questions about Hotmart affiliates? Let's look at 7 examples of successful affiliate marketing that can give you the inspiration you need to start your affiliate career.

1. Laura Montes: digital producer and sociologist helping people explore their sexuality

Laura is a digital entrepreneur offering workshops and face-to-face sessions on sexuality and interpersonal relationships. Motivated to make her work de ella meaningful, Laura joined the Hotmart Producers and Affiliates team to bring her courses to a much larger community, even crossing borders and impacting audiences in different countries.

The Hotmart Affiliate Program allows you to get your content and products to reach many more people in a simple, accessible, and practical way.

In addition to generating income and living doing what you are passionate about, affiliate marketing allows you to transform people's lives so they can feel freer and happier, enjoying their sexuality to the full.

2. Natalia Gómez del Pozuelo: transforms lives by teaching the art of public speaking

Natalia left her corporate life to live what she liked the most: writing. Influenced by her sister, Natalia began to write on her blog on various topics, and that is how she discovered that the issues that most interested her readers were the barriers that arose when speaking in public.

Natalia had worked all her life in communication, marketing, and project management, which gave her enough experience to speak very properly about speaking in public.

Faced with the surprising impact of her content, Natalia joined Hotmart's affiliate marketing team, looking for more practicality and simplicity to sell her materials. And it was just what she found.

Today, Natalia has one of the most visited blogs, and her product is one of the best sellers on the platform.

3. Priscila Heimer teaches people to eat healthily.

Priscila is an adventurous entrepreneur who one day bought Erico Rocha's online course that taught the "Launch Formula," and it was there that her interest in the digital market began.

Interested in creating a quality digital product and changing her life, she bought the online course on creating and launching digital products and knew that this was what she wanted to do. She then decided to talk about something that interested her very much, and that could also greatly impact the lives of others: healthy eating.

A short time later, she created her first product called "Conlasalud," which was a complete success!

When looking for a platform to sell her info products, Priscila met Hotmart. Now she works at her own pace, makes her schedule, and can choose whether to work from home, in a cafe, or a coworking. She can decide when she has vacations and the best she is doing something that makes sense and helps others.

4. Ana Nieto helps authors realize the dream of launching their books

Some people know their passion very early. This is the case of Ana Nieto, who was born knowing her passion for her books. Even when her life de Ella took her down a different path, she found a way to make a living out of her love of literature.

With her knowledge in the area of marketing, Ana saw that the digital market could be a solution for more people to find out about her publications and for her passion to become a real business.

This is how "Succeed with your ebook" was born, published by herself on Amazon. In a short time, it became a best-seller among the more than 200,000 books on the platform.

But Ana needed a tool that would help her manage her entire business in an automated way. That's how she got to know the Hotmart affiliate program. Today she has less work, more clients, more income, and more free time to dedicate to her family.

5. Javier Pastor lives by writing a utopia that has come true

Javier is an entrepreneur who began his career as a copywriter publishing a benchmark post in the sector. From that moment on, he gained so much visibility that he began receiving job proposals for sales pages, emails, and content for major launches.

This is how the idea of "Adopting a copywriter" arose, a methodology to be a professional copywriter and have a stable business without dying trying.

Javier has relied on Hotmart to sell its online courses and teach others to be writers for all sectors, not only because of its platform but also because of its true value and the team behind it. A great example of how affiliate marketing works.

6. Beatriz's Story: a new path to Happiness

Not all success stories have to do with content producers and digital products. Those who buy can also have a better turn in their lives.

That is why today we decided to share the story of Beatriz, a girl who one day, surfing the Internet, set out to look for new professions, and among all the ones she found, there was one that attracted her attention.

It was a virtual assistant course, which became a new change alternative for his life. After asking and meditating on all these questions, Beatriz investigated more about the profession. She came to an online course from one of the leaders in Virtual Assistance, Esther Mayor.

Hand in hand, Beatriz met Esther and the course that changed her life. She can now enjoy more freedom in her work from her, doing what she is passionate about, and managing her time better.

7. Carmen is living her best version.

Carmen suffered from anxiety; she took refuge in food without following a good diet to deal with anxiety. This brought consequences in her daily life from her since she was not the best way to approach the situation.

In that constant search for alternatives, Carmen found the course that would change her life, an example of how affiliate marketing is an example of change.

An online course called "Emotional Nutrition" was created and provided by Fran Sabal, whose methodology, based on good nutrition and mental reprogramming strategies, aims to heal the body and mind to bring out the best in people.

Such was the confidence that Carmen felt in this course that she put aside her doubts and insecurities and decided to invest in it. Through Hotmart, she could work on herself and change the lifestyle she had led up to now.

Chapter 7: Avoiding Common Beginner Mistakes

If you are starting and want to make money online, avoid these affiliate marketing errors.

Affiliate marketing is great, almost 70% of my online business is based on affiliate marketing, and the other 30% is arbitrage and other things.

I know many affiliate marketers make mistakes, myself included, even after all these years.

For example, sometimes, I need to focus on adding a macro to the Paid Traffic Campaign URL; I usually catch the error before it impacts my overall revenue.

And this is important here; you need to quickly catch your affiliate marketing mistakes and fix them before they can negatively affect your earning potential.

Top Affiliate Marketing Mistakes Newbies Make

I wrote them in no particular order when they came to me, but they are all equally important. Your earnings will suffer by not finding affiliate marketing mistakes early.

1. Choosing the wrong niche

Okay, so that's clear right from the start. You made a mistake and mishandled your niche research, and now you're stuck.

You need to figure out what to write, and your content needs to get traffic; the products you promote need to sell more.

The niche you thought was great has almost no search results, and because you have yet to bother to do your research, all the content you've written barely gets any traffic.

Another problem is that some people (myself included) don't like or need to learn how to write content for a topic they know very little about.

This is a big deal, especially if you can do affiliate marketing relying on free SEO traffic.

2. Don't stay focused.

I know this all too well. It could be one of the biggest affiliate marketing mistakes you can make.

It boils down to this: Let's say you're starting a new niche website, and you assume your new niche website is about "dog training."

Now you are constantly writing content on your site, adding affiliate marketing products everywhere, yet… Get 0 affiliate sales.

What's happening?

Why isn't your amazing site getting traffic and sales? You've worked so hard to develop the site and create content.

And much more.

You have nothing in return.

So what will a newbie do to make money online and do affiliate marketing?

They will move into another niche, create another website, write another content for another topic, put all the affiliate marketing products you can find… and again, you are stuck with no results.

They repeat this cycle, buying multiple e-books and courses on " making money online, "but only spend a little time on one of these methods.

This was my for 2-3 years when I started, and once I realized the problem: THE PROBLEM IS ME.

I immediately stopped turning down any new projects I started and focused on just one of them until they made me money.

And trust me, after a while, I went around all the sites I launched and made them profitable, one by one.

So yes, if you start somewhere, keep going because staying focused on only one thing will help your affiliate marketing efforts.

3. Try to copy others 100%

Oh, it's pretty simple, but also one of the most annoying affiliate marketing mistakes I see newbies make every time.

They try to copy others… ALL THE TIME

From niche to website design, ad layouts, products they promote, and sometimes even all content, even without copyright.

This will not happen; you will only get rich after copying someone else's niche and content.

Also, if everyone who reads some blog suddenly had to copy the ideas and niche of one of the sites, and 1000 of you do... How will this end for all of us?

None of us will make incredible money from it, or the site will most likely outperform and outperform yours simply because they have been working on it longer than you.

Does it make sense?

You need to STUDY and understand how and why some affiliate marketers do what they do on their affiliate sites. But you only copy some things.

Eliminate the best tactic someone is doing for their affiliate marketing website and then apply the same tactic to your niche and website.

Here's how you do it.

You collect the best ideas and techniques from everyone and then combine them all to create a super affiliate site, but in your niche and in your way, without copying anyone else's content, images, links, etc.

4.   Chasing Insanely Competitive Keywords

Look for something other than the most competitive keywords on the internet. If you don't know what you're doing and aren't ready:

- Spend plenty of time writing and optimizing great content
- traffic payment

This is a further common affiliate marketing mistake; you're just getting started, maybe you don't even know the basics of affiliate marketing, but you're trying to rank an affiliate site for the keyword: " lose weight"?

Sorry, but that will never happen.

Too many big fish are swimming around this keyword, writing the content and then optimizing their websites for AGES.

You should look for long-tail keywords with lower search and competition and try to write content around those keywords if you desire free traffic from Google.

If not, that's fine. You can pay for traffic; that's how it works too.

5.   Promotion of junk products

You can have the best affiliate marketing with high-quality content and get lots of search engine traffic.

But, If you advertise junk products. Your earnings will also be junk.

It's that simple. Some products are real scams. "Take this magic pill, and you'll lose half your body weight in 2 days." Okay, that's an exaggeration, I agree, but you know what I'm talking about, these products are there.

Not only scam products are garbage.

You can also have legitimate products that are rubbish simply because their landing page sucks or they use outdated designs, payment software, etc. On affiliate marketplaces like Clickbank, you'll find thousands of products for promotion; knowing how to find a good product to promote will be difficult.

You always want to try and analyze a product before you start promoting it:

- View product name
- Look at the product picture

- website check
- Who are the creators and owners of the product? Are they reliable?
- Are there any legit reviews of this online affiliate product or service on sites like TrustPilot?
- Is the site loading fast?
- Does the product have a high return amount?
- Are there a large number of partners promoting it?

I also check who is, the date the company was founded if a company is behind the product, etc.

You don't take a product willy-nilly and fill your site with banners and links that promote it, do your first research and try to find the best possible products and then services to promote. All the time

6. Dream of getting rich quickly

Okay, this hurts a little. But I have to do it, and I have to say it.

You don't get rich overnight.

Only after a week or a month, sometimes even after a year, especially if you are starting. Of course, there are exceptions to the rule, but in most cases, this does not happen.

This is one of those affiliate marketing mistakes newbies make without realizing it; they are only fed e-books and courses that promote a rich lifestyle; they only see fast cars, big yachts, and villas; they buy these products they think are happening to them, and too, and FAST.

But it only sometimes works.

Most of these supercars, boats, and villas are for rent. You know that, right? Most people in these videos are paid actors who act as experts and gurus. I hope you knew; if not, now you know.

There is a lot to be done in this area.

Sometimes I have 12 working hours daily, even pushing it up to 16 if what I'm trying to do calls for it.

Of course, this rarely happens, but the point is still relevant. Don't think that if you make money online, you will suddenly do it quickly without doing all the work.

You need time for Google to proceed to index and then rank your site, you need time to learn how to collect the best niches and products, and you also need much time to figure out how to write good content as well as how to market your site.

You can't force everything to happen in an instant.

7. Put all your eggs in the basket.

Don't just promote one affiliate marketing product from an affiliate network.

Join several affiliate networks and try several other products.

The same goes for everything else that has to do with the internet and affiliate marketing; another example is never relying on a single source of traffic (paid or free).

You should have backups for every situation. Oh yes, make sure you also back up your site regularly.

8. Rely on Free Traffic

Free traffic from Google or Bing is great. I understand that. But sometimes, especially at first, you won't be able to rank for specific keywords and niches.

Google updates its ranking algorithm almost daily, with hundreds or thousands of criteria to rank a website.

It's wild to put all your affiliate marketing activities in the hands of Google.

With a quick update, millions of websites will lose their ranking and end up at the bottom of the internet.

And it happens more often than you might think. Even legitimate websites get hit sometimes, not just black hatters.

It's also very good to get paid traffic to a new website because Google will consider that (they see users coming to your site and think it is good, so they rank you higher). You'll also earn faster.

9. Think you're an expert

They say that somebody becomes an expert in their field after doing it for over 10,000 hours. How close are you to that number?

You may need to learn how to rank for a keyword on Google and that you have traffic and sales to become an expert immediately.

Sounds harsh, but you need some time to understand and learn every affiliate and online marketing aspect.

The best online marketers are constantly learning, improving, and adapting.

Like doctors, their education continues even after they leave the university.

Internet marketing is the same. You should always learn and adapt with every Google update, every new rule that comes into effect from your favorite ad network or affiliate platform, etc. Always strive to improve and expand your business on affiliate marketing by researching the industry and testing things out whenever you get the chance.

Otherwise, if you think you're the best, you won't improve or learn new things, and you won't neglect the important things you need to do to succeed, so you end up failing.

Never stop learning.

10. Ignoring SEO

I'm a big believer in paid traffic. But you must pay attention to SEO. That's just stupid.

Of course, as I said earlier, don't rely solely on organic traffic, but not worrying about SEO at all is not a good way to do things, even if you are paying for traffic.

Ensure all your websites and blog posts have at least basic SEO before sending paid traffic.

11. Not Knowing What You're Promoting

This is similar to the junk products I did above. The difference is that even if you don't promote a junk product, you still might not get affiliate sales.

But why?

The majority of the time, the affiliate product doesn't match the site's content. This is another one of those affiliate marketing mistakes that I always see.

I've seen automated blogs (yes, it's still a thing for some reason) copying content from general lifestyle and health blogs, but their affiliate banners were for GoDaddy and then how to build a website. Like what?

Sometimes this can work, and you might get some sales, but that's different. Usually, you want affiliate products, banners, and links closely related to your content.

So for the example above, it would make much more sense to promote lifestyle and also health products instead of GoDaddy.

12. Ignoring Site Speed

The speed of your site may seem insignificant to you, but this is another big affiliate marketing mistake newbies make. The time it takes for your users to load your site is extremely important.

It can cost you a headline, an AdSense click, a sale, and also your Google rankings.

Yes, Google has said many times that it cares about the speed of your site and the speed at which it loads your traffic.

People typically leave websites that load more than 3 seconds (especially on mobile devices).

Then go to a site like GTmetrix and Pingdom and test your site's speed, and if it's in red, try to improve it as soon as possible, following the suggestions you see on the results screen.

13. Posting low-quality content

I'll make it simple and straight to the point.

- Create great content
- NEVER copy/ don't embed articles from other websites
- Use social media when appropriate in all your content (images and videos)
- Format your content so it looks good on the screen, don't make long paragraphs without breaks in the middle
- Count the words. Make sure every article you post is at least 500 words, although these days, the number is as high as 800, so try to write more.
- Create guides and lists if you're stuck and don't know what to write about
- Invite users together. I have your feedback on your content, so I know where to improve
- If you have writer's or blogger's block, spy on the competition and see what they're talking about, but keep their articles distinct; create your own around the same idea.

There is a lot to talk about, but overall these are the important ones, so if you want to rank on Google and have an engaged audience on your site, follow these content tips.

14. Prioritize Sales Over Help

While it may sound silly, trust me, it's true. I know you want to make money immediately by doing the best you can in your affiliate marketing journey.

But sometimes. You may need to catch up on what is most important here.

Provide value and help your audience.

All these people come to you because they have a specific need, whether it's a review of a product they're not sure about or to cure a terrible disease; you want to make sure your content helps them in the first place and then makes you money.

A happy audience means you will always have returning visitors to your site; they will also tell their family and friends about you, so even more traffic. They can leave your site with amazing reviews on Google, which is also great.

All this translates into more earnings for you. It's really simple if they don't find value in your articles or videos, they will go to some other site or video to get the advice and help they need, so you lose out. Affiliate commissions when it happens.

Also, don't forget that Google has a new YMYL (Your Money or Your Life Sites) site policy, so they will rank your site lower in the search results if you are not able to provide any real value and will instead try to get the money right away. Scaring visitors.

15. Don't invest in your business.

Feel free to spend money on tools to keep your affiliate marketing business running smoothly and efficiently.

Yes, it's hard at first...

Even paying for a domain name and a hosting server can prevent someone from starting and doing affiliate marketing.

When you're new, it's not a big affiliate marketing mistake, but when you're making money and trying to raise it, sometimes you have to pay to make things easier.

1. If you don't know how to code, proceed buying the theme and plugins you need
2. If you don't like to write, entrust it to freelancers
3. If you don't like waiting for free traffic, pay for paid traffic
4. the list goes on and on.

The biggest NO-NO you can do is to use deprecated plugins and themes at launch. Just don't do it. If you can't afford them, look for free alternatives.

Do not use canceled software from shady websites or try to use it to run a legitimate business. Almost all canceled items contain malicious code that someone can use to attack your site and gain access to everything just by running the entire partnership business.

"Frightened money doesn't make money." At least, that's what some rappers say in their songs; you must agree.

16. Wait to FOLLOW everything.

Affiliate marketing is mostly a numbers game; I've said it before and will always say it. If paying for traffic, you must properly track your campaigns with an affiliate tracker like RedTrack or FunnelFlux.

If you're into SEO, you need to track your rankings and the competition to see how your site is ranking and how you can improve it to get even more traffic.

Collecting more data than you can is one of the biggest affiliate marketing mistakes I can think of.

I know I've said before that these errors are all the same, but if I had to choose one that is the biggest of all, it would be the one.

Track everything you can.

How do you think Facebook makes all its money? From you, you are their data; they track everything you do and everything you like, not only on their website but all over the web.

They then sell this data to affiliate marketers, who use it to find the exact audience I want with high accuracy for the products and services I promote.

You need to track your paid traffic campaigns to know which keywords or publisher IDs to block, which landing page converts the best, or which GEO brings you the most money.

Not tracking your SEO ranking and competition with tools like Semrush will not provide you with the edge you need to increase organic traffic.

You need to understand your site's audience and which posts perform better than others regarding shares, time spent on the site, etc., to help you better sell products and services that accurately serve your traffic.

17. Lack of initial capital

Working with affiliate programs is a business, so it requires start-up investments. They will be required to pay for contextual advertising and advertising on social networks. In addition, you need to understand: that almost all affiliate programs have time limits and a minimum withdrawal amount. Therefore, investments are the first step to high earnings.

18. The theme of the advertisement does not match the theme of the site

Teasers offering to lose weight or get rid of parasites look strange on the website of the electronic library. This means that the number of transitions and conversions will be almost zero. When placing ads, consider the interests of the target audience.

19. Poor audience knowledge

With a huge number of visits to the site, you may only make a few purchases. You may need to analyze the target audience and the places where it lives on the network. The traffic generated from them will be much cheaper, and the opportunity to meet a large client will be higher.

20. Wrong partner choice

Its age and reviews on thematic forums will tell about the program's reliability. Pay attention to a clear interface and convenient advertising formats, sizes, and payment procedures. Before finding a suitable affiliate program, you must go through several options.

The other extreme is attempting to work in all affiliate programs simultaneously. It will be challenging to control and manage the effectiveness of advertising.

21. Inappropriate ad text

The advertisement pressures the client and praises the product - but you are not a seller but an intermediary! Your task is to attract and redirect a buyer to the seller's website. This means that ads should not sell but offer a solution to a specific problem.

For example, the ad "Promotion and support of sites, great experience, guarantees" is trying to sell the services of a web studio. You also need to identify the problem of the client: "The site crashed in the search? Lost sales? Call - we will help! Important: The ad must contain a clear call to action.

22. exaggeration of quality

Any adequate person understands that "Learn English in 3 days" is an exaggeration on the verge of a foul. Do not offer the impossible not to lose customers' trust.

23. Too many ads on the site

Everyone at least once visited a site where there were too many ads. Everything is bright and flashing - it needs to be clarified where to look and where to click. Even worse, when you open the site, annoying music or video with sound automatically starts playing. You can provide musical accompaniment, but the site should be "silent" unless the visitor himself presses the sound button.

24. Lack of systematic control of statistics

Any indicator change requires your reaction, whether for the better or the worse. The more experience you have and the desire to earn, the more time you will need to analyze statistics.

Conclusion

When managed well with the best partners, affiliate marketing is one of the most effective and profitable models for gaining new revenue, new customers, high-value leads, and incremental sales.

Like all marketing strategies, affiliate marketing requires time, money, and, most of all, online marketing and advertising knowledge.

In all the niches described, you can make a profit. The main thing is to find the one with which it will be easy and comfortable for you to work.

At the same time, remember that some verticals are more profitable but will require more costs. You must find the best traffic source and advertising strategy to get conversions.

Getting started with affiliate marketing is easy. You won't find an easier online venture than this. While it takes knowledge, practice, and effort to produce noticeable results, affiliate marketing can lead to financial success if done right.

There are multiple approaches to affiliate marketing, but the most effective one is to create a website dedicated to the practice and fill it with useful information for your target audience.

If you want to turn affiliate into a profitable business, this strategy will help you to reach your goals. If you do consistently provide high-quality content on your website, people will begin to consider you an authority in your field.

Making an affiliate marketing website and updating it frequently with relevant content will help you look more convincing and attract visitors actively looking for what you have to offer.

SEO & Online Marketing - Conclusion

To sum it up, in our ever-changing world, with many Google changes per year, illegal SEO practices are no longer in vogue.

Thus, we should focus on useful content and better user experience.

This will always stay in style!

I hope you find these SEO basics helpful and help you change how you think about online marketing!

Here are 16 affiliate marketing mistakes I highly recommend you try to avoid as much as possible. Each one can hurt your earning potential, so why take the risk?

Don't look for shortcuts; it's rarely worth it. Like everything in life, to have a successful affiliate marketing business, you'll have to give it your all, always try to learn from your mistakes, and improve without losing focus.

Book 2: Driving Traffic
Introduction

As hundreds of thousands of web admins confirm yearly, affiliate marketing can make a fortune. Cleverly selected affiliate programs go with a bang and bring affiliates a stable income. However, as in any business, there are some nuances. Where to drive traffic to affiliate programs - we figure it out together.

How CPA Marketing Works

As you already understand, an advertiser and a webmaster are in affiliate marketing. The advertiser draws up an affiliate program (offer), where he indicates all the conditions for promoting his services and goods: payout, payment model, percentage of conversions, and prohibited types of traffic. The webmaster connects the offer and receives an affiliate link with a personal ID code, by which the advertiser can track the number of conversions, that is, completed target actions.

Where can I find an advertiser with an offer? You can search on your own by contacting each company individually. Where else?

Now we come to the third member of affiliate marketing - the affiliate network or CPA network. What kind of networks are these?

The affiliate network brings together advertisers and web admins, allowing one to find site owners with a target audience and the other to find relevant and profitable affiliate programs for their online projects. Some affiliate networks focus on a specific niche, such as gambling, dating, crypto, etc. There are also those in which affiliate programs are simultaneously presented in dozens of niches, such as ours.

Let's see how it works:

The sporting goods brand has placed its offer in the affiliate network. A webmaster with a site with reviews of sports goods and who is registered in this CPA network connects an offer, places an affiliate link on his site, and starts attracting traffic.

The webmaster receives a fixed percentage from each sale made by the user who came from him. More sales equals higher earnings. Once a month, the webmaster withdraws the earned funds to an electronic wallet or by bank transfer.

The webmaster can work in this mode, combining his activities with his day job or without being tied to a specific place. Therefore, affiliate marketing is associated precisely with freedom in the distribution of working time.

Where to get traffic for offers?

This question is the most important for a web admin. Traffic can be paid and free. The main free source is your resources: websites, blogs, and social media accounts. In addition, there is an e-mail newsletter that has served affiliates faithfully for decades, thematic forums, the Quora website, sites with reviews and reviews, and social journalism platforms.

Paid traffic is varied. Here are distinguished:

5. Search traffic: Google Adwords, Yandex Direct. It is also called contextual advertising. Here you can target by keywords and current user requests. It is one of the most powerful advertising tools and is very effective. But experience matters here. Setting up contextual advertising for a beginner takes work.
6. Social networks: Facebook, Instagram, TikTok, Pinterest. Here you can run targeted advertising by geography, age, and interests. Ads will be shown to those who meet the criteria set.
7. Mobile traffic: Push, Pop, Display, Pop-unders. Here we target operating systems, operators, and phone brands.

Free traffic sources

Your website is a proven source of traffic for most web admins. You must design the website, order a programmer, or use website builders. Many (but not all) affiliate programs require a website. However, more is needed to create and launch a website - it must be promoted by creating high-quality regular content. Effective website promotion is facilitated by the presence of promoted accounts in social networks, ensuring a constant traffic flow. Therefore, the difficulty in working with the site is directly its promotion and promotion, which takes time.

Social media accounts

Social media has made affiliate marketing even more lucrative. A promoted account on Instagram, Youtube, Telegram, or TikTok can be an excellent platform for promoting affiliate offers and redirecting traffic to your website. Now many people promote several accounts on different social networks and redirect users' flow from one site to another.

Affiliate links can be used directly in social networks and on the site. Still, bloggers often resort to unique promotional codes that give users a discount and allow advertisers to track which blogger a person came from. Bloggers on Instagram, Youtube, and TikTok often use promotional codes.

It also takes time to promote social media accounts. Given the high competition now on almost all sites, as well as the growing demands of the audience for authors' content, be prepared that you will have to invest much effort into promoting accounts.

You can promote affiliate offers on social networks even without a promoted personal account or public. You can still leave spam comments with affiliate links under other people's posts or send messages with promotional mailings in a personal message.

E-mail newsletter

One of the dinosaur affiliate marketing tools, but by no means obsolete. Millions of people buy, sign up and download because they are interested in the information in the email, so don't discount this method. It also takes time to create quality email content and, of course, to collect addresses. However, the latter can be bought on some services.

Forums

As you know, a little spam never hurts. We're joking. New users' spam messages on the forums are almost immediately banned. Therefore, so your messages do not suffer such a fate, you must first benefit the forum members by answering questions and giving useful advice. And only after waiting can you try sending messages with affiliate links, of course, disguising it as advice or personal experience.

Quora

This is where you can get a question for any question and a useful resource for building a personal brand, especially if you have expert knowledge in some area and your site has information that people might be interested in. To build credibility, you must answer detailed questions, express your opinion, and give useful advice.

Social journalism platforms

You can post your articles on free platforms such as Medium or Cossa. Interesting and useful content and, of course, expertise in the field are important. Then users will go to your site or blog, subscribe to you, and eventually follow affiliate links. It is necessary to write interesting articles with valuable information. Articles with general and widespread information will not attract users.

Paid traffic sources

These are sites, resources, and social networks where you can place ads for a certain amount. And here we come close to the topic of traffic arbitrage.

Traffic arbitration

This is the purchase of traffic on third-party sites and social networks and redirecting it to another resource, with earnings on the price difference.

How does it work?

The arbitrator starts promoting the advertiser's products. To do this, he sets up advertising in one of the sources of paid traffic, pays for impressions, and as a result, the advertiser's goods are bought, and the affiliate earns income. He earns on the difference between income and expenses. For example, he spent $300 on Google Adwords and received a payment of $600 from the advertiser - the profit here was $300. An arbitrator can be the same webmaster who, in addition to his resources, also uses paid sources. The task is not just to get traffic to the advertiser's website but to earn.

Traffic arbitrage is quick user acquisition, but this method requires working capital and a clear understanding of the entire structure of traffic purchase.

What is better: free or paid traffic sources?

There is no definite answer to this question. Both free and paid sources do attract users and generate traffic, confirmed by the experience of millions of web admins. What source to choose?

We recommend free sources for beginners because they are safe for your funds and useful for further development. Your website or blog on social networks will always come in handy, and the skills to promote it will be invaluable when working with CPA marketing. Select relevant affiliate programs if you already have a website or blog on social networks with an active audience. If confident, try paid sources, calculating investments and possible profits. Experienced web admins test different approaches and working links because, in affiliate marketing, everything is tested only in practice.

Chapter 1: Leveraging Social Media for Affiliate Marketing

Affiliate marketing is one of the most interesting ways to get ahead in internet marketing. You can consider it in two directions (which we will do in this chapter): collaboration to attract free traffic and work with partners in the CPA system.

But the basis of affiliate marketing in social networks is in cooperation with thematic accounts, groups, or channels. In this chapter, we will analyze the 5 most popular types of collaboration between bloggers or brand pages.

Mutual PR

Mutual recommendations with similar accounts remain one of the most popular ways to promote yourself on social networks for free. You select an account similar in subject matter and coverage of the target audience of readers, contact its administrator and offer to publish recommendation posts about each other.

You can exchange anything: posts, reposts, and publications in stories - the main thing is that this exchange is effective for both parties.

It is worth paying attention to the fact that now there are more and more influencers - mini-bloggers. Almost every regular social media user thinks about starting to develop their account. And it doesn't matter if he will develop his brand or shares his thoughts or photos.

Therefore, you can use the mechanics of mutual PR even with your subscribers.

One of the subtypes of mutual PR is SFS. In this case, the blogger (or company) asks to place information about him on the subscribers' pages. After a certain time, he chooses among those who have posted some of the best publications and tells the rest of his subscribers about the accounts of their authors.

For authors, this is a great way to get a free mention, and for a blogger or company, it's a quick way to collect dozens or even hundreds of recommendations on the pages of subscribers and clients.

Collaborate on content

Another way to build partnerships is to produce useful content together.

The main ways of interaction in this format:

8. Client case.

In the b2b sphere, publications of customer cases are often used and work well.

Write an article about a company that uses your services or products. They, in turn, should share their experience of successful cooperation with you in this article: give an interview and share their expert opinion about your product.

9. Shared live broadcast.

Team up with potential partners and prepare joint expert content. For example, the founder of a women's club and a stylist can talk about personal image-making in a joint live broadcast, which will interest subscribers of both accounts. This will help increase engagement and get more reach and new page followers. Of course, provided that the content is really of high quality.

Often bloggers use the format of "collaborative content preparation." Some even unite and prepare joint products in addition to content - collections, checklists, or even full-fledged courses.

Holding joint competitions

Collaboration for contests is another frequent way of partnership with thematic accounts.

You can simultaneously hold a contest for two (or even more) accounts. To participate, for example, invite users to subscribe to the pages of all the contest organizers and put likes on the last 3 posts.

And to start working with an account much larger than yours, invite its administrator to run a contest and give him prizes from your company (this is called "competition sponsorship") in exchange for mentioning your page.

CPA partnership

Affiliate programs are alive and will live. Even if you have a limited advertising budget, or you, in principle, are not ready to spend large amounts on advertising, you can think about finding one or more partners who will cooperate with you on the CPA system and bring new customers.

Partners will offer to purchase your products from their customers; they will receive a predetermined percentage from sales. For them, this approach will complement the product line and increase the average check without additional financial investments.

As a rule, such a partnership is concluded between companies whose offers complement each other. For example, a web development studio can offer affiliate SEO services to its clients, receiving 20% off each sale.

Loyalty programs

They offer your customers a discount or a gift in other services and stores: this will help increase their loyalty and sales of partners. And Partners, in turn, will provide discounts and recommendations for your products or services to their customers, which will help you increase your income.

Loyalty programs are an ideal example of Win-Win cooperation. By participating in them, you and your partners can increase sales and the quality of your customer service.

As a rule, you can offer such cooperation to companies that are not your competitors but have a similar target audience. For example, a furniture manufacturer may offer customers discounts on ordering mattresses from partners and vice versa.

It isn't easy to find a person who does not have at least one account on social networks. Some use them to communicate with friends and like-minded people, the second uses them as albums for their photos, videos, and texts, and the third reads the latest news or entertainment content. But some make money through social networks - and affiliate marketing.

Today we will analyze what business models web admins use in social networks, what traffic is unwanted within this channel, and also take a look at each of the most popular networks separately.

Why social networks?

Many web admins start working in affiliate networks from social networks. The reasons are simple:

The social network is a ready-made platform for posting content: text, photos, illustrations, links, video, and audio. Some are tailored for certain formats (for example, Instagram is always images, and YouTube is always videos). The webmaster does not need to make a separate site for himself - he has personal pages, public, groups, and business accounts in his arsenal, and all this functionality is free of charge.

A social network is a ready-made audience that only needs to be targeted. Since in social networks, users voluntarily share information about themselves (gender, age, marital status, education, geography, work, interests), the web admin can create a portrait of the target in the most accurate way.

Social networks are ready-made mechanisms for advertising and promotion. At the same time, the mechanisms are easy to use and quite cheap - the webmaster decides how much he is willing to invest in advertising, and the entry barrier is very low here.

Business models in social networks

Despite the variety of possibilities of social networks, there are few working schemes in affiliate marketing. By workers, we mean those that bring tangible earnings comparable to the average monthly salary.

Groups/communities/publics about discounts. They usually specialize in a specific segment (clothes, shoes, children's products, online games, gadgets, and goods from China). Publishers check discounts and coupons from advertisers within the affiliate network and place the best offers in their groups daily.

Unusual/trend products. Here, the webmaster attracts attention with goods that are difficult to find in physical stores or with fashionable, hype things, the price of which is lower online. Usually, these are goods from Chinese stores, mainly from AliExpress. Such groups are designed to find the most interesting and profitable offers from various suppliers, and web admins spend much time choosing the most hit ones from the product catalogs.

Travel. Flights and tours should be placed in a separate business model since the web admin must always be alert. It is difficult to offer users cheap flights and tours: their prices change at lightning speed, so making a "burning offer" in a direction is a real talent. Particularly bright representatives make several dozen groups according to the cities of departure ("Cheap tickets from Khabarovsk," "Cheap tickets from Rostov," "Cheap tickets from Sochi," etc.) and develop each group separately.

Reviews/unboxings/comparisons. This cohort of web admins is closer to bloggers: they make video and photo reviews of products and services. Goods from China "enter" well in unpackings - such blogs help buyers choose honest suppliers whose expectations about the quality of goods correspond to reality. In the reviews, cosmetics and products for children are popular, mainly in women's direction; the target audience is girls and mothers of small children. According to the comparison model, they usually work with gadgets (smartphones, tablets, and other user equipment); here, the audience is more male. As soon as a webmaster reaches extensive coverage of live users and becomes an opinion leader, advertisers send them goods for review.

Arbitration. Everything is simple: web admins buy targeted advertising on social networks, place ads, and lead directly to the advertiser's website, from which they receive rewards for placed orders. The mechanism of work is close to contextual advertising - buy traffic cheaper and sell more expensive. The segments are very different - from consumer goods to financial and travel offers. The main disadvantages of this method are the inability to accumulate content (as soon as the advertising budget runs out, the ad disappears) and track statistics (the web admin can only access data from the personal account in the affiliate network and the results of reconciliation by the advertiser).

Prohibited traffic in social networks

There are few options for fraud on social networks, and most of them are easily tracked. Moreover, not all of the fraud they call it: for the most part, this is the kind of traffic advertisers do not want to receive from web admins. Typically, such traffic is users who are already customers of the advertiser. Here the situation is ambiguous: on the one hand, the advertiser has already invested a certain amount of money, time, and effort so that the user is familiar with the brand and has already made the first purchase from it (and as we know, attracting a client is much more expensive than retaining it).

On the other hand, if the user has yet to make repeated purchases (or makes them too rarely), the advertiser cannot convert him into a buyer, and the webmaster must step in here. Moreover, the webmaster needs help accessing the advertiser's statistics, which means he cannot know which buyer he brought, old or new. In this case, the finer the advertiser "sets up" his offer, the more profit he will receive: some set the bid for new customers higher than for old ones, and others prescribe brand names and formats that cannot be mentioned. There are general rules that most advertisers lean towards:

Creating groups and communities with the advertiser's brand in the name is forbidden. A particularly strict violation is when a web admin passes off his group as the brand's official community. The main risk here is the brand image. The advertiser needs to learn how the webmaster will represent him or how he will communicate with potential buyers. In a conflict situation, the brand itself will be responsible for them. Another reason such traffic is prohibited is the double investment of the advertiser, who has already spent on promotion and brand awareness growth, and must once again pay the web admin, who essentially earns on this brand.

Persecution of users - members of the brand's official communities. Here the situation is similar: if the webmaster starts to write to each member of the group purposefully, firstly, this will create negative associations with the brand (no one likes spam), and secondly, this is the advertiser's base, and deliberately aiming at it means to beat it off from the brand itself and resell it to him.

Targeted advertising is another channel that some advertisers don't like. By analogy with the context, there is competition for impressions, and the more participants in these auctions, the higher the rates will be. Overbidding is not in the advertiser's interests. Some prohibit the ability to engage in targeting, but this does not happen so often: due to the wide audience coverage of social networks, there is enough for everyone, and thanks to the creativity of web admins in creating advertising materials and targeting, their audiences may not even overlap.

Features of social networks

Not all social networks are equally useful. Built-in tools make them more or less convenient for monetization in affiliate networks.

Twitter. One of the least effective channels in terms of CPA work. The content format of 140-280 characters is already becoming obsolete: it is well suited for breaking news, and a simple hashtag system helps to get into the search. Still, there are better channels for working in an affiliate. The most promoted accounts of humorous or political topics are the least-selling topics.

Instagram. It is very good from the point of view of "showing the product with its face" - the format itself implies an image and short videos to which users are more than loyal - they comment on them with pleasure and react with likes. The problem is that there can be only one active affiliate link to external sites - in the profile description. Therefore, the main monetization mechanism here is the sale of advertising in promoted accounts. It is possible to arbitrate advertising posts recently appearing in the Feed and Stories (launched through the Facebook advertising account). There is also a new development, available only to a few companies in the experimental format: active links that can be placed directly on the image. If this topic takes off, we can expect Instagram to overtake other social networks in terms of CPA turnover in certain categories.

Odnoklassniki. Despite the biased attitude regarding the commercialization of leads on this social network, experience shows that an active solvent audience has gathered here, which is well converted into sales. In addition to content projects (blogs and groups), there is also targeted advertising from which you can drive traffic directly to the advertiser's website (launched via MyTarget).

Vkontakte. This social network is already quite saturated with groups of CPA webmasters, but you can still find your niche. The secret of success is the narrowing of targeting: it is worth making not just the "Best Discounts" group but "The Best Discounts on Children's Goods in Orenburg," for example. It remains to choose offers that deliver specific goods to a specific city and drive traffic to these offers. Yes, the coverage will be smaller, but targeting and converting such an audience into sales will be easier. Do not forget targeted advertising (in the feed, communities, and side block) - from here, you can drive traffic to your groups and the advertiser's website. It can be launched both directly on VKontakte and through MyTarget.

Facebook. It is better to work through Facebook in cases where you sell services in B2B (but this is no longer a CPA), enter a foreign market, or plan to arbitrage on traffic targeting. In various countries, consumer goods "enter" mainly through advertisements, while content projects do not work like other social networks. But you have to give credit to Facebook: if you understand the not-so-friendly interface of the advertising account, its targeting mechanisms can very accurately select the right audience.

Social networks include channels in Telegram and the microblogging format of the last couple of years. However, this has its specifics, and they should be considered separately in the context of affiliate networks.

The use of social networks in affiliate marketing

Affiliate marketing is part of online marketing focused on achieving results. Affiliate marketing is performance-based by which affiliates promote products in exchange for a fee for each action.

Social networks are considered one of the best strategies to promote affiliate products and monetize blogs and web pages. It is a fact that the use of social networks has increased in recent years, which has favored changes in habits and behaviors of use at a global level.

Consumers research social networks before purchasing and positively value the comments of other satisfied customers with the product. As a result, affiliate marketing has become very popular among businesses, and today many of them have a marketing budget to generate more sales through the content created by affiliates.

5 Steps to Promote Affiliate Products on Social Media

1) Choose the market niche and audience.

Identify the trends and needs of an audience group that shares the same topic of interest as yours. Choose a niche where you have the experience to offer your content's highest quality and credibility. Once the niche is found, you must find the target audience to be able to sell them the products related to the market. Segment by age, geography, interests, languages, buying habits, and behaviors to find your audience and identify the most relevant product.

2) Promotion of media and distribution channels

After identifying your target audience and the product you want to sell, you must choose the most appropriate social platform and means of promotion to reach your target audience. Here are the social platforms we recommend for promoting affiliate products:

- FACEBOOK

It is one of the most relevant platforms and the social network best known by consumers. Currently, Facebook allows you to sell products through the following methods:

The page or personal profile

It is the easiest method to start affiliate marketing but possibly the least effective. Your contacts, who are your audience, may not be interested in your products, so you should find the most relevant products. To do this, you will have to spend time learning about the interests and needs of your contacts.

Groups

In the same way that a blog is considered to offer content on a specific topic and thus add affiliate products, it can be done in the same way with a Facebook group.

Create a group according to the chosen market niche and offer related products. For example, you can create a group on "E-learning" (digital training) and offer information on this topic, including recommendations, trends, the latest news, interesting data, etc. The affiliate products you can add to the content must be related to the topic: training courses, e-books, resources, learning tools, etc. Likewise, encourage interaction and conversation with the audience to create your community of followers.

Fan page

Although it works similarly to groups, fan pages have less interaction and participation than groups. Fan pages are designed to keep a community updated on a specific niche. In this way, working with a fan page is a good method to share relevant information and thus be able to add affiliate products.

- INSTAGRAM

The most used social platform to research products before making a purchase. Likewise, the arrival of Instagram shoppable posts, on the one hand, has increased the trend of online shopping on this platform, and on the other hand, the trend of selling products has been enhanced. Selling on Instagram is easy since you can start selling affiliate products in simple steps.

- YOUTUBE

It is a fact that video generates more sales than other advertising formats, and more and more marketers are choosing this format to sell their products. Getting started in affiliate marketing on YouTube is relatively easy since you can start by sharing home videos on a specific niche. Consolidating a personal brand will be a little more complex because it takes time, technical skills, and expertise in a topic or niche. Start by sharing educational and informational content to capture user interest and consistently post content.

- PINTEREST

The social platform looks beyond online shopping and focuses on offering inspiration and a great user experience when researching products. Pinterest is like a blog with less text and more visuals that increase content visibility and conversion rates. Promoting affiliate products on Pinterest is very easy, and to do so, you only need to create an account, describe your business, and create boards by theme according to a specific niche.

- TIKTOK

The social network has more than one billion monthly active users worldwide. With the new live shopping feature, brands sponsored on TikTok can link with users in the community in real-time and share dynamic links to products and services while content is broadcast live.

3) Relevant, reliable, and quality content

Capture your audience's attention by offering solutions to their questions and trying to understand their needs and problems. Lead your community by describing product specifications with user-focused content. Conquer your audience with images and videos and offer them a satisfying shopping experience. Describe the product's positives and negatives to promote your business's credibility and increase sales.

4) Encourage the participation of your community.

Beyond creating content about the products, a key objective will be to get the interaction and participation of the followers to measure the degree of interest in the niche and the products. This way, you can offer your audience the most relevant products and increase sales. Here are 6 effective techniques to encourage participation in social networks:

- Respond to followers' comments as soon as possible
- Create a content calendar for important dates
- Proposes debates on current issues and asks questions
- Mention other users in posts
- Informal, close, and friendly communication style
- Use images and videos

5) Loyalty your community

Retaining the active participation of the community of followers is a challenge every affiliate pursues daily. Loyal customers provide brand value and those that generate the greatest benefits in the long term. A satisfied customer attracts a relevant audience, increasing your reach and visibility. Next, 5 strategies to retain your community of followers on social networks:

- Offer bonuses or discounts.
- Talk to your community face to face and connect with it emotionally and closely.
- Make sure that the content is always useful and adds value
- Offers efficient and exclusive customer service channels
- Share content generated by satisfied customers

Affiliate links and social networks

Amazon affiliate links can be distributed on social networks like Facebook, Twitter, or YouTube. These networks can also be used to increase traffic to your website, which means your audience will no longer rely solely on traffic from search engines.

Amazon affiliate links can be posted on social media. Even so, it is important that you follow Amazon's guidelines and always respect the conditions of use of each network because they can change. For example, the social network Pinterest strictly prohibited users from sharing affiliate links for long. But that rule changed, and.

What is allowed in the Amazon Associates Program?

It is allowed to distribute affiliate links as long as it is seen that the social network account from which it is made is operated by the affiliate who creates the links. Affiliates must update their account information in Affiliate Central to include the exact URL of the social network where the links will appear.

On Twitter, the account must be verified. This occurs when Twitter includes a blue check mark next to the username. For more information on how to verify your Twitter account,

What is not allowed in the Amazon Associates Program?

Sharing affiliate links on social media is not allowed if you are an Amazon affiliate but do not own the account on which the link is shared. It is also not allowed to use Facebook apps to distribute links.

Identify affiliate links on social media.

Affiliate links are considered advertising and must be marked as such. To do this, you can include a notice next to the link. This is also a form of transparency for other social network users.

Users should know that you will receive a commission if they buy through one of your affiliate links. Do not ask your visitors to make those purchases to support your website, as the Amazon Affiliate Program prohibits it.

Here's an example:

'The links included are affiliate links. I may receive a commission from that sale if you buy through them, but this will not affect your price.'

YouTube and Affiliate Marketing

On YouTube, affiliate marketing can also be used as a further source of income alongside sponsorships. This makes even more sense when it is a product video, whether an analysis of a specific product or a review based on one's experience. In these cases, affiliate links can be included in the video description that appears just below the video.

As with the articles on your site, it is important that you are rigorous and honest with your visitors or followers. Always keep in mind to add value and focus on making quality content. It is a good practice to gain an audience and ensure that no one questions your credibility.

- Tip: On YouTube, always include affiliate links at the beginning of the video description. This does increase the chances that visitors will click on it.

YouTube and your website

YouTube allows you to include banners with interactive elements in your videos that link to the URLs of your choice. These interactive banners appear at the top right of the screen when you play the videos.

You can adjust when and how often informational icons with links appear in your videos. You can also include descriptions and text with these links.

To create links to your website in the informational links, you must first verify the website and link it to the YouTube channel. These options appear in the advanced options of your YouTube account. You can create multiple YouTube channels on different websites with one Google account.

It may also make sense to embed videos uploaded to YouTube in related articles on your website. If the videos are viewed through your site, the time users spend on your pages will increase, which positively affects the positioning of your site in Google.

- Tip: YouTube also allows you to hide playback controls and other actions when you embed videos on your site. In this way, users cannot rewind or view other additional content that may distract them from the content of your website.

Other Ways to Use Social Media in Affiliate Marketing

Search engines are the only traffic source for many bloggers or website owners. But social networks can be a new and important source of visitors if you are active on them and use them well. Your site will have the advantage that its audience is independent of search engines. If your positioning in them fails, you will still be able to count on the traffic that comes from your social networks.

Platforms like Facebook are also ideal for creating a community through shares, comments, or 'Likes.' This does increase the organic reach of your posts to Facebook users, which may contain links to your website that people click on.

You should focus on more than just the number of 'Likes' your Facebook page receives. It is much more important to have followers and fans on this network who are genuinely interested in the topics you write about and are likely to continue to engage with your posts.

To achieve this, it is important that you create interesting and high-quality content. You have to understand your potential audience as well as possible. This will help you ensure your content is well received and respond appropriately to changes and trends.

Similarly, you should post regularly and in a consolidated style. You can also try different times to post on Facebook and compare the reach of each one (Facebook itself gives you that information). In this way, you will get an idea of what hours of the day are those in which your publications receive the most attention. ,

The Best Affiliate Marketing Strategy for Electronics

The operation of affiliate marketing is relatively simple. The affiliate signs up for an affiliate program, selects the electronic products they want to promote, and gets their unique affiliate link. You then place those links in your content through reviews, recommendations, or ads. When somebody clicks on your link and then buys, the affiliate earns a commission.

Benefits of using affiliate marketing to promote electronic products

There are multiple benefits to using affiliate marketing to promote electronic products. First, it is a low-risk business model since you do not need to create your products or make significant investments. You also don't have to deal with shipping, customer service, or inventory storage. You focus on promoting the products and earning commissions on the sales.

Another benefit is flexibility. You can choose which products to sponsor based on your interests and knowledge. For example, if you are passionate about technology, you can focus on promoting cutting-edge electronics. In addition, you can work from anywhere and at any time, as long as you have internet access.

Also, affiliate marketing allows you to generate passive income. Once you've created and promoted your content, you can continue to earn commissions on future sales, even while you sleep or take a break.

How to Find the Best Affiliate Programs in the Electronics Industry

To succeed in affiliate marketing for electronics, finding the best affiliate programs in the industry is crucial. Different affiliate platforms and networks allow you to connect with companies that offer affiliate programs. Amazon Associates, ClickBank, and ShareASale are some of the most popular affiliate programs in the electronic arena.

When choosing an affiliate program, it's important to consider the reputation of the program, the variety, the quality of electronic products available, and the commission rates offered. Research and compare different programs before deciding which one is best for you.

Steps to create an effective affiliate marketing strategy for electronics

Creating an effective affiliate marketing strategy requires careful planning and execution. Below the main steps to creating a successful strategy:

1. Define your target audience: Before promoting electronic products, you must understand your target audience. Clarify the demographics and interests of your target audience to tailor your marketing strategy and select the right products.
2. Research products and programs: Research the electronic products in affiliate programs and choose relevant, high-quality ones. Ensure you know the products' benefits and features to promote them effectively.
3. Create relevant content: Quality content is key to engaging your audience and promoting electronic products. Create detailed reviews, tutorials, comparisons, and other useful and informative content for your readers. Include your affiliate links strategically within the content.
4. Social media promotion: Utilize the power of social media to promote your electronic products as an affiliate. Create profiles and business pages on platforms relevant to your audience and share valuable content that includes your affiliate links.

5.   Analyze and Adjust: Track your affiliate marketing efforts and analyze the results. Use analysis tools to understand which strategies and products generate the most sales and adjust your strategy accordingly.

The importance of choosing quality electronic products to promote as an affiliate

When promoting electronic products as an affiliate, it is essential to choose only quality products. Promoting inferior or low-quality products can negatively affect your credibility and trust with your audience. Make sure you do your research and learn about the products before you decide to promote them. Consider the brand's reputation, customer reviews, and the overall quality of the product.

By choosing quality electronics, you'll be able to provide your audience with trustworthy and valuable recommendations. This will increase the chances that your visitors will purchase through your affiliate links.

Tips to increase your earnings as an electronics affiliate

If you want to increase your earnings as an electronics affiliate, consider the following tips:

- Build an Engaged Audience: As you build your audience, focus on quality rather than quantity. Seek to attract people interested in the electronics niche and create relevant and valuable content for them.
- Use SEO strategies: Optimize your content for search engines using relevant keywords. This will help you improve your visibility in search results and attract more qualified traffic.
- Offer exclusive bonuses and promotions: Work with sellers to offer your followers exclusive bonuses or promotions. This will incentivize your visitors to purchase through your affiliate links.
- Constantly update yourself: Stay abreast of electronic product trends and news. Keeping your knowledge up to date will allow you to create quality content and promote relevant and popular products.
- Build relationships with vendors and other affiliates: Building strong relationships with vendors and other affiliates can open up new opportunities and allow you to gain valuable industry insight and advice.

Useful tools and resources to optimize your affiliate marketing strategy in the electronic field

There are several useful tools and resources that you can use to optimize your online affiliate marketing strategy. These include:

- Affiliate Management Platforms: Use AffTrack or Post Affiliate Pro to manage and track your affiliate links efficiently.
- Analysis tools: Use tools like Google Analytics or SEMrush to study the performance of your website and understand which strategies are working best.
- Link Generators: Use link generators like ThirstyAffiliates or Pretty Links to shorten and personalize your affiliate links, making them much more attractive and easier to remember.
- Educational Resources: Spend time reading blogs and books and taking courses related to affiliate marketing. This will help you to make your knowledge and skills better in this area.
- Affiliate Communities: Join online affiliate communities, such as forums or Facebook groups, to share knowledge, ask questions, and learn from other successful affiliates.

How to take advantage of social networks to promote electronic products as an affiliate

Social media can be a strong and effective tool for promoting electronic products as an affiliate. Consider the following tips to get the most out of social media:

- Choose the right platforms: Not all social networks are equally effective for promoting products. Research the most popular platforms among your target audience and focus on them.
- Create compelling content: Create compelling and visually pleasing content highlighting the benefits of the electronic products you promote. Use high-quality images, how-to videos, and customer testimonials to grab your followers' attention.

- Engage with your audience: It's not just about posting content. Interact with your followers, respond to their questions and comments, and build strong relationships. This will build trust and increase their chances of purchasing through your affiliate links.
- Use relevant hashtags: Use specific hashtags in your posts to increase the visibility and reach of your content. Research the most popular and used hashtags within your niche and then use them strategically in your posts.
- Promote valuable content: Do not limit yourself to promoting products directly. Create valuable content related to the use and benefits of the electronic goods you are promoting. This will position your profile or page as an authority in the field and increase your credibility with your followers.

Common mistakes to avoid when implementing an affiliate marketing strategy in the electronic sector

When implementing an affiliate marketing strategy in the online industry, it's important to avoid common mistakes that can hinder your success. Some of these errors include:

- Promote low-quality products: As mentioned above, promoting low-quality products can negatively affect your credibility and trust with your audience. Be sure to do your research and choose quality electronics before promoting them.
- Do not disclose your affiliation: Being transparent and honest with your audience about your affiliation and earning commissions is important. Don't hide the fact that you are promoting products as an affiliate. You must disclose your affiliation and affiliate links in your content.
- Not monitoring your results: It is essential to monitor and analyze the results of your affiliate marketing strategy. You need to monitor the performance of your links and the impact of your strategies to improve and optimize your efforts to obtain better results.
- Focus only on the sale: Although the ultimate goal is to generate sales and profits, do not focus only on the sale. Instead, focus on providing value and solutions to your audience. Create quality content and focus on building strong relationships with your audience.
- Do not diversify your sources of income: Do not limit yourself to a single affiliate program or niche of electronic products. Diversifying your sources of income gives you greater security and flexibility. Look for opportunities in different affiliate programs and consider expanding into other related niches.

Chapter 2: Email Marketing Basics for Affiliates

One of the most traditional ways marketers have gotten word of mouth is through affiliate marketing. This is considered a surefire way to increase reach and exposure for your brand. The best way to do this is through.

Why email marketing? Email is the widest marketing channel and a great affiliate marketing medium. While selling products or services other than your own company in your email campaigns may seem strange, there is nothing wrong with including advertising in your newsletters if you send emails to achieve your marketing goals.

Becoming an affiliate is quite simple; While each program has unique approval standards, participation is usually free, and no prerequisites are needed. Search engines are a great way to identify acceptable brands to promote: "[Brand] + Affiliate Marketing Program."

Some companies run internal affiliate programs, although this industry is highly specialized. As a result, most organizations favor partners who have already developed successful programs for their clients and firms with years of affiliate marketing experience.

Email marketing is one of the best alternatives for affiliates who want to maximize their income.

Email is and will continue to be a strong marketing channel valued by professionals, managers, and purchasing influencers.

However, having so many platforms and communication networks, some affiliates wonder: what is the best way to capture leads and encourage their engagement until the final conversion?

Although the ideal is to carry out a holistic strategy, combining social networks and different content formats, such as podcasts, blogs, and videos, in this topic, my mission is to show you the advantages of email marketing for affiliate campaigns.

I will also bring you the most precise tactics to apply the method and tips so that you start structuring your emails on the right foot. Accompany me!

Why should affiliates have an email marketing strategy?

Mailing campaigns represent a powerful process to improve the cost-benefit ratio of your initiatives as an affiliate.

Today, empirical evidence makes it clear that email marketing is the digital channel that generates the highest ROI. Generally, every dollar invested returns between $38 and $42 in profit.

Email becomes interesting for its scalability and recurrence in the context of affiliate marketing strategies. Over time, you can increase your email list with high-converting forms and landing pages.

At the same time, you send them messages of different types to understand their preferences and segment them more and more, automating your email campaigns to obtain more openings, clicks, and future sales.

It is not so easy to measure the ROI of affiliate marketing because the income depends on several factors, such as:

- the level of specialized knowledge you have acquired,
- the commercial and promotional tactics that you apply to share your links;
- and the model of commissions that you receive is different.

But there is a fundamental difference between email marketing and other media concerning the volume of expenses it requires.

While ad campaigns, for example, depend on a more aggressive initial investment, the mailing structure is cheaper and more organic.

With a multifunctional email marketing platform like GetResponse, you can send up to 2,500 emails monthly and create forms to attract new recipients without paying anything.

To make your mailings more sophisticated over time, you can sign up for a paid plan for more advanced list segmentation and campaign automation features. It is a worthwhile investment because you concentrate all your activity on a single platform.

After putting together your entire operation in it, you have to explore the creativity to write the texts of each email, which will change according to the objective you assign to it.

The process is also speeded up by the ease of using newsletter templates and other emails, which you can customize to suit each campaign.

Finally, there are many opportunities for experimentation in email marketing, which allow you to optimize the results.

In GetResponse, you can, for example, A/B test various mail subjects and messages to see which generates the most interactions.

Email marketing or social networks: in which channel should we invest more?

Many affiliates put almost all of their efforts into ads and social media posts but could use a balance with email marketing.

The key question you should ask yourself is: what would I do if a social network went down or went bankrupt?

You could continue generating sales only if you were the actual manager of your contact base rather than a big tech like Twitter, Google, or Meta.

Such a scenario makes us reflect on the decision to go fully into social networks and consider email marketing as the foundation of our strategy.

And what to do if one-day GetResponse or another Email Marketing platform ceases? You don't lose control of your contacts because you can export them to offline files from those tools.

In any case, this does not mean that you cannot or that it is not convenient for you to use the networks because they are channels with a wide audience and are capable of generating new contacts for your email marketing lists with well-targeted ads.

Email campaigns have evolved with the power of algorithms. I invite you to read our guide to the applications of artificial intelligence in email marketing to visualize this phenomenon.

4 interesting types of email marketing for affiliates

Mailing is a fairly flexible communication model. Therefore, you can structure your mailings in different formats, which can be useful if you act as an affiliate.

The idea is to integrate them to expand your possibilities and cover all the conversion funnel stages since some emails will be more informative. Others will be more directed toward a purchase objective.

Let's take a quick look at some types of campaigns you can explore.

1. Invitations, calendars, and promotions

Using emails to send news, launches, or events is a great way to segment your contacts and understand their interests. Thus, you will build a more mature and active audience base, which will generate sales in the long term.

Work as an affiliate of a marketplace like Amazon, for example. You can share links to new products regularly, providing information about their impact on the market and competitive advantages.

Thus, your contacts will always be aware of the news that you share to make a purchase when they feel ready.

You can share specific links to receive direct commissions by building your segmented lead lists.

The interaction rate will depend on the relationship between the contacts' preferences and the offers you share.

2. Newsletter

The newsletter is one of the main email marketing formats. It works as a selection of news and useful content for contacts, helping to form a true community around the brand that sends it.

Affiliates often create newsletters to further their engagement with recipients, especially when they provide them with specialized knowledge.

Consequently, it is a tactic that goes beyond direct sales. By offering emails with relevant insights and advice, you can keep your readers engaged and encourage them to follow your posts.

In addition, it is an excellent channel to educate your contacts and conquer them for your ability. By sharing messages with different levels of depth and topics, you will have much information about the characteristics and needs of those who read you.

Another advantage is the ease of the conversion process to a newsletter. With a simple, you can capture the email address of your users and grow your list instantly.

At GetResponse, you will find ideal newsletter templates for your strategy; they are free and work automatically on mobile devices or computers.

3. Lead nurturing

Especially for affiliates, this strategy always stands out for the good results it generates. With the automation of email sequences, you create a flow of messages with high conversion potential.

As its very name suggests, lead nurturing emails are about increasing the level of knowledge and maturity of the contract, thus preparing them to buy at the right time.

In short, you create content, such as blog articles, ebooks, podcasts, and videos, to show how the solution you sell helps eliminate a specific problem.

For example, if you offer an online course, you can automate a series of lead-nurturing emails, each containing snippets of the points you present in your classes.

GetResponse has autoresponders to schedule automatic responses on certain dates based on user actions on your website. For example, when they sign up to receive your newsletter or register for one of your webinars.

You can also create lead nurturing flows with customizable templates automatically activated to educate and warm up contacts.

We have the following specific workflows for affiliate campaigns:

- Online course promotion;
- affiliate online course;
- webinar promotion;
- cross-selling for affiliates;
- affiliate welcome message;
- assignment of engagement tags;
- attribution of activity points for contacts.

4. Seasonal Email

These emails are tied to specific dates important to your strategy or the market in general. Today, many content creators consider viral trends and topics to provide relevant insights.

Taking advantage of these windows of opportunity, in which the minds of your contacts are already prepared to receive information on the subject, you can approach them with your instructions, which will be the most precise for the occasion.

It's also a great tactic for online store affiliates because there are many business dates to explore, like Christmas, Black Friday, or Easter.

4 keys to building your email marketing campaign as an affiliate

The process is simple; there are clear steps and good practices that you can follow to improve your.

However, it should be noted that the results and liquid commissions depend on the closeness you can establish with your contacts, the credibility they see in your communication, and the quality of the segmentation you attribute to your recipient lists.

To overcome such challenges, choosing the right email marketing platform is critical. Let's look at each stage in more detail so you can put your plan into action.

1. Think about every aspect of your campaign.

One of the first steps is the definition of your persona, that is, the ideal contact profile you want to address with your messages.

Put yourself in their shoes to understand their needs and what concepts you have to teach them so they want to buy what you offer, be it a product, service, or material.

You must complete all stages of the conversion funnel because your contacts are at different times in the purchase process, and for each one, there is a more appropriate type of email.

Diversify your strategy, creating informative campaigns with newsletters, others to share more advanced materials and transmit your knowledge, others to promote your launches, and, finally, commercial messages to make your sales.

Integrate them, conditioning the sending of one to the results of another. For example, if one of your newsletter topics generated more opens and clicks than usual, consider doing an event or ebook with a similar proposition to expand performance in the long run.

2. Use GetResponse

GetResponse is the leading email marketing solution on the market and today stands out for its affiliate-specific resources that maximize engagement and sales results.

With a generous free plan and cheap contracting options, our platform stands out for having various solutions to structure your campaigns, such as:

- tool to create landing pages ;
- pop-up windows to attract new subscribers;
- artificial intelligence website builder (with affiliate website templates);
- platform to create and present webinars ;
- automated conversion funnels, which I just mentioned;
- AI email generator ;
- and many more.

Indeed, it provides recurring commissions of 33% per month or one-time payments of $100; we will explain it fully later. Still pending!

3. Create a lead capture plan.

Lead generation can be a complex task. Here, you can also create different entry doors for your contacts, taking advantage of the power of content marketing to arouse their interest.

An accurate tactic is to, or rich materials that you can offer the user at no cost in exchange for their data on landing pages or forms. Some examples are ebooks, webinars, and spreadsheets.

Then, you wait to consolidate a base or make announcements to push your content to interested profiles.

Try different types of forms to capture information from the users of your website.

Use more than just landing pages with several data fields. Sometimes it is best to start with a form that only asks for the user's email address, adding them as subscribers to your newsletter list and converting them into leads at another time.

Another essential point is compliance with data protection regulations, guaranteeing that all contacts are permitted to receive your messages, preventing your email from being considered spam, and protecting your recipients from malicious emails.

4. Take the first shot and correct what is necessary.

Email marketing is a strategy you can constantly refine to maximize click-through, open, and conversion rates.

After the first delivery, look for relevant insights by analyzing the map of user interactions in your message, perform A/B tests to discover the best version of your content, experiment with shooting at different times and days of the week, etc.

All these changes depend on permanent monitoring. Therefore, manage your campaigns from a growth hacking perspective, identifying small factors that you can implement in the following ones to obtain better results.

Suppose you are interested in finding reference data for your strategy. In that case, I recommend reading our email marketing benchmark, which provides information on the average performance of emails in different countries and market segments.

What email marketing KPIs should you analyze as an affiliate?

KPIs (Key Performance Indicators) are valuable sources of information for affiliates because they indicate optimization points for future campaigns.

Undoubtedly, such analysis must be part of your email process. But many metrics are available, and some are less important than others. So let's see the ones you must follow to evaluate your performance.

1.   Open rates

This indicator refers to the percentage of recipients who clicked on the emails you sent to open them.

Today, an email with more than 20% opening is considered efficient, while a regular email usually has between 10% and 20% opening.

The email subject line is crucial in determining your numbers on this metric and the accompanying preview text.

2.   Click-through rate per email open.

Here we have an excellent resource to measure the engagement in your emails, which varies greatly depending on the objective of the email and its entire composition (content, design, and call to action).

For example, in a newsletter or promotional email, you want the click-through rate higher than in a transactional email because this is generally only sent to inform the user about a completed action.

The number of links you use also greatly influences this indicator. If you include your personalized affiliate link at various points in the message, with texts like "click here" or "buy my products now," you can annoy the reader and hurt your click-through rate.

3.   Cancellation rate

The unsubscribe rate indicates the number of recipients who no longer want to receive your emails.

It is a metric that is quite susceptible to the strategic changes you make, such as a drastic increase in the number of emails or a reduction in the quality of the content.

For example, if you made template changes without an A/B test to justify them. If contacts aren't very fond of your new version, the rate of requests to cancel shipments can grow significantly.

4.   Spam Complaint Rate

Email providers frequently ignore spam and complicate your relationship with the contact base. When you get to a very high level of spam, your communication can be invasive.

If this problem happens to you, it is convenient to try some factors to solve it, such as avoiding the excessive use of images or guaranteeing the security of the links you share to avoid the frustration of the contacts.

These metrics are available on GetResponse email marketing dashboards, which update in real-time and provide a clear view of your performance on each one.

Learn about the GetResponse affiliate email marketing program

With our two program options, you earn money while using the most powerful email marketing tools on the market and capturing more leads.

First, you receive continuous commissions of 33% during all the months that your lead continues with the active plan in GetResponse.

The second program is simpler: you earn a fixed commission of $100 for each client that contracts our platform from your personalized link.

Here are some of the reasons to join our programs:

- two commission formats that you can explore;
- informative guides with clear sales instructions for affiliates;
- reports in real-time;
- cookies active for 120 days after the click;
- access to key email marketing and promotional tools;
- Exclusive discounts for GetResponse paid plans.

I invite you to the program's official page to learn more and take your first steps. Let it surprise you! Give the first step; sign the invitation by clicking the button below!

Tips to promote affiliate marketing products to your email list

Affiliate marketing is a way to make income online. It is a marketing strategy that requires promoting other companies products and receiving a commission for each sale made through your affiliate link. Your email list is an effective way to promote affiliate marketing products. This topic will present tips and strategies to help you effectively promote affiliate marketing products to your email list.

If you're an affiliate marketer, chances are you're looking for ways to sponsor your products and services to your email list. In this topic, we will show you how to do it effectively.

1. Understand your audience

You must know your audience well before promoting any product to your email list. What kind of people subscribe to your list? What are their interests and needs? By understanding your audience, you can select affiliate products that are useful and relevant to them.

2. Select quality products

Do not promote any affiliate product that comes your way. Instead, select quality products that you think your audience will find useful. Read other users' reviews and opinions and ensure the product has a good reputation.

3. Create a compelling email.

You must create a compelling email to promote your affiliate products to your email list. The email should be short, but it should include all the important details, such as the features and benefits of the product. In addition, you must include a clear and compelling call to action to get recipients to click on the affiliate link.

4. Use an interesting subject.

The email subject line is the first thing your recipients will see, so ensure it's engaging and relevant. Use relevant keywords and ensure the subject line is interesting enough for people to open the email.

5. Offer an incentive

Offering an incentive to your recipients can increase the click-through rate on your affiliate link. You can offer an exclusive discount, a gift, or a special offer. Ensure the incentive is relevant to the product you're promoting and compelling enough to make people want to click on the link.

6. Follow up

Once you've sent the email, tracking and measuring the results is important. Use email tracking tools to find out how many people opened the email, how many clicked on the link, and how many made a purchase. Use this information to improve your future email campaigns.

You can increase your chances of success by understanding your audience, selecting quality products, creating compelling emails, using compelling subject lines, offering incentives, and following up.

How to promote affiliate products?

If you are a product affiliate, you have wondered how to increase sales and promote your products effectively. Here are some tips to help you promote your affiliate products effectively.

1. Know your followers

Before you start promoting your affiliate products, it is important that you know your audience. Who are your followers? What are their interests and needs? By knowing your audience, you will be able to select the affiliate products that are most relevant to them and, therefore, more likely to be purchased.

2. Use quality content

The content you share on your social networks and website must be interesting and high-quality. If you share low-quality content, your followers will unlikely be interested in your affiliate products. Use eye-catching images and create compelling content that grabs your followers' attention.

3. Share testimonials from happy customers

Testimonials from happy customers are a great way to promote your affiliate products. Share real testimonials from customers who have used and are satisfied with the product. Testimonials can be shared on social networks, websites, or YouTube videos.

4. Offer discounts and promotions.

Offering discounts and promotions is a fantastic way to encourage your followers to buy your affiliate products. Offer exclusive discounts to your followers and promote these offers on your social networks and website.

5. Use SEO techniques

Use SEO techniques in your content to make your affiliate products more visible in Google search results. Use relevant keywords in your posts and your affiliate product descriptions.

6. Participate in forums and discussion groups.

Participate in online forums related to your affiliate products. Provide valuable information and share your knowledge with other members of the group. If you offer useful information, group members will likely visit your website and buy your affiliate products.

7. Communicate effectively with your followers.

Communicate effectively with your followers through your social networks and website. Respond quickly to your followers' questions and comments, making them feel valued. Maintaining a good relationship with your followers makes them more likely to buy your affiliate products.

Following these tips can effectively promote your affiliate products and increase your sales. Promoting your affiliate products requires time and effort, but the results can be very satisfying.

How to do email marketing?

According to a study by the consulting firm McKinsey, email is up to 40 times more effective in acquiring new customers than social networks such as Facebook or Twitter.

To do email marketing effectively, it's important to follow a few key steps:

1. Create a contact database

The first thing you need to do in email marketing is a list of contacts interested in your company or product. You can capture new contacts through website registration forms, social network promotions, or events.

Ensure you get explicit consent from your contacts to email them and segment your list according to their interests and preferences.

2. Design attractive emails

The design and content of your emails are key to capturing your contacts' attention and getting them to open and read your messages. Use a clean, attractive design, include images, and use clear and direct language.

Also, your emails must be personalized and relevant to each contact. Use the information you have about them to send them messages that are interesting and useful to them.

3. Define clear objectives

Before sending any email, clearly define your message's purpose. Do you want to encourage a purchase, promote a new product or service, or keep your contacts informed about your company's news?

Define a clear goal for each message, and make sure your email content and call-to-action align with that goal.

4. Measure and analyze your results.

One of the advantages of email marketing is that it allows you to monitor and analyze your results precisely. Use analysis tools to measure the rate of opening, clicks, and conversions of your messages.

Use this information to adjust your strategy and then improve your results in the future.

5. Comply with data protection regulations.

Finally, it is important that you comply with data protection regulations, such as the GDPR in Europe or the data privacy law in the United States. Ensure you get explicit consent from your contacts to send them emails and respect their right to unsubscribe anytime.

How to promote a product as a Hotmart affiliate?

Hotmart is a digital marketing platform that allows digital entrepreneurs to sell and promote their products online. As a Hotmart affiliate, your job is to sponsor other people's products and receive a commission for each sale made thanks to your promotion. But how to promote a product as a Hotmart affiliate effectively? In this topic we will explain it to you.

1. Know the product well.

Before promoting any product, it is important that you know it well. Read all the information you can about the product, use the product yourself to see it firsthand, and make sure you fully understand the needs of the audience the product is intended for.

2. Create valuable content

One of the most effective ways to promote a product as a Hotmart affiliate is by creating valuable content that does attract your target audience. You can create articles, videos, infographics, podcasts, among others. Make sure the content you create is useful, informative, and related to the product you're promoting.

3. Use social networks

Social media is a great channel to promote products as a Hotmart affiliate. Use social media profiles to share product-related content and engage with your target audience. Make sure you use the right keywords so that search engines easily find the content you share.

4. Offer bonuses or discounts.

Offering bonuses or discounts to your followers can be a great way to promote a product as a Hotmart affiliate. For example, you can offer a free ebook related to the product you are promoting or an exclusive discount for your followers. These bonuses or discounts can encourage your followers to purchase the product through your link.

5. Use email marketing

Email marketing is a way tool to sponsor products as a Hotmart affiliate. Build an email list with your followers and send regular emails with product-related content. Be sure to include your affiliate link in the email so your followers can purchase the product through your link.

How to succeed in affiliate marketing?

Affiliate marketing is a strategy where a company pays a commission for each sale made through an affiliate link. It is an effective way to earn money online and can be profitable if done correctly. Here are some keys to success in affiliate marketing.

1. Choose the right products.

It is important to choose products that are in line with your lifestyle and your niche. You must be sure that the products you promote are of high quality and that your followers will be interested in them. If you promote products that aren't relevant to your audience, you won't generate many sales.

2. Create quality content

Quality content is key to engaging your followers and getting them to click on your affiliate links. You must create useful and relevant content that is attractive to your audience. If your content is quality content, your followers will be more willing to trust you and buy the products you promote.

3. Use multiple marketing platforms.

Affiliate marketing is not limited to blogs and social networks. There are several methods to promote affiliate products, such as paid ads, email marketing, and influencer marketing. Use multiple platforms to reach a larger audience and increase your chances of success.

4. Be transparent

It is important to be transparent with your audience about the fact that you are sponsoring affiliate products. You must disclose that you are receiving a commission for the sales made through your affiliate links. Being transparent will help build trust with your followers and increase your chances of success.

5. Measure your results

It is important to measure your results to know what is working and what is not. Use tracking tools to measure your sales and conversions. If certain products are not generating many sales, you can adjust your marketing strategy to skyrocket your results.

Choose the right products, create quality content, use multiple marketing platforms, be transparent, and measure your results to increase your chances of success.

Chapter 3: Content Marketing

Marketing is a broad concept representing many activities designed to advertise products, services, or the companies themselves. Content marketing is an element of marketing campaigns, which is the opposite of classic advertising. It focuses on long-term customer relationships, helping to gain their trust and instill loyalty.

Content marketing is an online advertising strategy used to attract a consistent group of customers. Therefore, it is not a one-sided advertising message praising and recommending this product or service. This kind of enterprise leads to building long-term and intensive relationships with a selected group of clients.

How Content Marketing Works

Content marketing activities include:

- creation and publication of interesting content: articles, videos, webinars, multimedia presentations, diagrams, graphics, infographics, and so on;
- attracting the attention of a select group of customers;
- increasing commitment and customer loyalty.

While content marketing can also be done offline, such as by delivering ads, flyers, and so on, online content marketing offers more opportunities. As you can see from the above, the content presented to customers can also take a different form. Most importantly, it should be substantive, contain useful information, and encourage user participation.

Internet customers try to find interesting goods, services, and reliable information there. They are looking for proven tips, recommendations, and opinions. According to various studies, this trend is becoming increasingly important, and today it is normal for seven out of ten Internet users.

Therefore, more than one beautiful website is needed; consumers seek reliable information in blogs, forums, or social networks. The decision about which product they choose depends on the opinions and comments they find and how the information is presented.

But content marketing is about providing customers with the information they want online. These may include manuals, tutorials, and so on. Meeting expectations, if the content looks professional and relevant will encourage customers to use the offered products or services.

Viral content

At the same time, content marketing is also about discussions and viral content. It is worth creating interesting, even controversial, reality-based content encouraging users to discuss.

If it is an interesting topic, they will personally and unknowingly contribute to advertising by distributing articles, videos, graphics, or other materials.

So in content marketing, you can get the effect of viral marketing. However, choose the right content channels for the target group in addition to quality content, such as social media channels, mailing lists, blogs, and so on.

Content marketing and SEO

Content marketing is about providing content to recipients that they are interested in and key SEO actions.

Remember that Google's search engine algorithms primarily value quality content. They have a high ranking factor, which results in a better search engine visibility of the website and a higher position. Content marketing articles usually contain links to a website, and as we know, link building is critical to SEO. Activities that combine SEO and content marketing are time-consuming, so third parties are needed, such as:

1. Copywriters create quality written content: sponsored articles, blog posts, copy for the company website, and product and service descriptions. Content should be optimized, focused, and written according to SEO principles.
2. Graphic designers create graphic materials: graphs, infographics, and diagrams.
3. Also, interactive content such as video creation, live chats, quizzes, virtual explorations, and so on is gaining more and more importance.

Building your content strategy

What content do you think your audience will want about the product or service?

The content you create will be one of the most important factors, which in most cases, will prove to be the gap between success and failure. Unfortunately, most people usually focus on creating promotional content that only resonates with their audience. You need to create a funnel to guide your prospects every step of the way and ultimately convert them.

- Top of the content funnel

The first thing to look at is the top-of-the-funnel content. This content is at the top of your sales funnel, so it is not intended to sell a product or service. Instead, your primary purpose for content at the top of the funnel is to educate and inform your readers about something important in the niche.

Creating such content aims to target people at the "awareness" stage. It's your chance to make people "learn" about your digital presence or platform. If your ToF content is good, people will return to your blog repeatedly and read what you have to write.

- Middle-of-funnel content

This brings us to the next step: the middle of the content funnel. You slowly introduce your readers to your main products and services at this stage. However, instead of boring them with deep details and specific points, your main goal is to let them know what value the product or service you promote can be useful to them.

This can be done by creating case studies, comparative articles, or specs. When creating MoF content, you must add a CTA to get a subscription and eventually build an email list. This will give you a better understanding of the people willing to receive offers or promotional content from you.

- bottom of funnel content

And finally, the bottom of the content funnel. This type of content is designed to convince your audience to buy a product. You must do your best and convince them of the product's value. By now, your audience will have earned at least some trust in your brand and need one last "push" to make a purchase.

Ideally, all bottom content of the funnel should contain a call to action (CTA) button or a compelling offer designed to get people to convert. This is your chance to close the deal, and you can only do so when you know your audience's pain points. Always focus on their needs and offer them a solution. You will notice an important increase in sales.

6 Affiliate Marketing Content Writing Tips

Affiliate marketing is a good income source for bloggers. However, to make money from affiliate marketing, you must know how to easily create interesting content that includes your affiliate links. This can be a real test. You don't want your readers to think you've sold out or are more interested in promoting products than educating them. Of course, the best way to make your affiliate marketing efforts work is to drive traffic through interesting and engaging content. After all, the more interested your readers are, the more likely your affiliate links will grab attention. To help get you on the right track, we've provided six content-writing tips for successful affiliate marketing.

1. Focus on your readers.

The reader should always remain in the spotlight when you write any content. This remains true when you also focus on affiliate marketing. When choosing topics to write about, consider what your readers want, what interests them, and what will help them solve their problems.

When you write about affiliate products, keep it user-centric. What about the product will benefit your reader? How can they use it to make their lives easier?

2. Find ways to include products in your stories without selling too much

The best affiliate marketing content needs to look organic. You shouldn't feel like you're selling a product. Instead, you should look like a trusted source, even a friend who recommends a product.

To do this, keep your recommendations always in the form of stories. For example, if you tried a kitchen product to cook dinner for your family, write about your family life over the past few days and think about your homemade food. You can then discuss your experience with the affiliate product, even if it doesn't feel forced.

This allows you to focus on an interesting product and inspire confidence. Also, when you discuss products in real-life situations, it builds trust. Showing people you like something is much more interesting than just telling them. Write in detail and use lots of visuals to create an interesting story about your affiliate products. Use tools like, Trust My Paper and Grammarly to help.

3. Focus on products you know your customers will love.

This is another area where your clients should be your priority. Yes, it's helpful if you love your products, but you should focus on products and services that fit your customers' wants and needs.

Don't post products you don't like. At the same time, remember that your tastes may not match your audience's. In these cases, your audience wins. These are the ones who are more likely to buy the products you promote.

They should be in your mind when you choose the products to look out for. Look for healthy foods. When describing them, keep in mind customers' needs and tastes.

4. Priority of honesty and reliability

You have many followers because your readers trust you. You can keep that trust as a marketing partner. You must commit to being honest about it. Highlight the foods you've tried and love. Yes, it's okay to promote products you don't like. We'll take a look at this below. However, you must have first-hand experience with any product you support. There are so many products available on the market. Choose the ones that are either related to you or your audience.

Why is it important? You have earned the trust of your readers. They will believe in the truth of your recommendations. That trust will quickly erode if they conclude that you only promote products to make a quick buck. It's not something you can get rid of easily, if at all.

When you recommend a product, please provide details. Tell them what you liked about this product. Share a real-life example of how this product makes your life easier or more enjoyable.

5. Give your honest opinion.

No one will believe you if you claim that every product is a home run and that you love it. With this approach, your posts will seem like commercial offers. Also, when you have something you want to commend the roof for, your audience won't be thrilled about it. You should never criticize an affiliate product. You can give a constructive point of view on the positive side. For example, you can focus on the positive things you notice. You can also write about the product from the point of view of one of your readers who might like the product. Imagine that you have tried out some exercise bands. You don't care about them and prefer to work out in the gym. You can still describe the training groups positively and recommend them to your readers who want to train at home. Ultimately, you will come across a product you cannot approve of. This is fine. There are many other products. Affiliate marketing is a long game. Never sacrifice your credibility or the needs of your audience in a market for a product that you just can't approach.

6. Diplomatic handling of recalls

Chances are your readers won't hesitate to tell you what they think of your products. When the feedback is positive, it's great. You can thank the reader and ask them a few follow-up questions. The real problem comes when the reviews are public and negative. This must happen, and you must be ready to respond sensitively and productively without letting things develop. You can use these.

A step-by-step guide to creating high-converting content in affiliate marketing

In affiliate marketing, content is critical in driving conversions and increasing your revenue. If you want to be successful in this field, it is crucial that you create high-converting content that talks to your audience and motivates them to make purchases through your affiliate links.

For this reason, we will provide you with the key strategies and tips to create high-converting content in affiliate marketing and stand out in the competitive online market. So let's get started once and for all!

Step 1: Understand your audience to create high-converting content

The first step to creating high-converting affiliate marketing content is understanding your target audience. Thoroughly research and analyze your target audience, and identify their needs, desires, and problems. What kind of products or services are they interested in? What are your most frequently asked questions and concerns? The better you understand your audience, the more effectively your content will address their needs.

Step 2: Conduct Thorough Keyword Research

Keywords are essential to optimize your content and achieve greater visibility in search engines. Do extensive keyword research related to your niche and find the ones that are relevant and have good search volume. Use tools like GKP to discover the most relevant keywords for your content.

Step 3: Create catchy and catchy titles

Titles are the gateway to your content. They must be attractive, eye-catching, and generate curiosity in your audience. Use keywords in your titles and add a touch of creativity to stand out from the competition. Some examples of effective headlines could be: "Top 10 products to solve X problem" or "Discover how X product can transform your life."

Step 4: Develop relevant and useful content throughout the year

The content you create must be relevant and useful to your audience. Provide valuable information, practical advice, and solutions to the problems your followers are facing. Avoid excessive product promotion and focus on offering truly beneficial content to your readers. Trust is key in affiliate marketing; creating quality content is one way to build that trust.

Step 5: Use storytelling for high-converting content

Storytelling is a good technique that you can use to connect with your audience emotionally. Instead of presenting scant information about a product or service, use personal and success stories to illustrate how that product has improved people's lives. Storytelling builds empathy and creates a stronger bond with your audience, growing their chances of purchasing through your affiliate links.

Step 6: Add compelling visual elements

Compelling visual content can significantly improve the effectiveness of your affiliate marketing posts. Accompany your content with high-quality images, infographics, charts, and relevant videos. These visual elements make your content more visually appealing and help convey information more effectively and capture your audience's attention.

Step 7: Optimize for SEO

Optimizing your content for SEO is important to make sure it stands out in search engines. Use keywords in the title, headings, paragraphs, and internal links. Also, make sure your content is easy to read and well-structured with headings (h2) and subheadings (h3). Also, consider your website's loading speed and user experience, as these factors also affect your search engine rankings.

Step 8: Incorporate persuasive calls to action (CTAs)

Calls to action (CTA) are key elements to generate conversions in affiliate marketing. Include persuasive CTAs in your content to motivate your audience to act, such as clicking an affiliate link, signing up for an email list, or purchasing. Use clear and direct sentences that indicate what action you want your readers to take.

Step 9: Provide testimonials and reviews

Testimonials and reviews are a good way to support the effectiveness of the products or services you are promoting. It includes testimonials from satisfied customers, reviews from experts in the field, and examples of success stories. This social proof will help build confidence with your audience and grow their likelihood of purchasing through your affiliate links.

Step 10: Monitor and analyze the results

Once you've created high-converting content, monitoring and analyzing the results is important. Use tools to monitor the performance of your posts and grasp what type of content resonates best with your audience. From this information, you can adjust and improve your content strategy in the future.

Other recommendations: Stay up-to-date with the latest trends and news

The world of affiliate marketing is dynamic and constantly evolving. Stay updated with trends, news, and changes in the industry. Follow blogs, participate in online groups and communities, and attend relevant conferences and events. Staying updated will allow you to create fresh and good content that engages your audience and keeps you ahead of the competition.

Lastly, be consistent and persevere.

Last but not least, consistency and perseverance are key in affiliate marketing. Don't expect instant results; keep going even if you don't see immediate conversions. Continue to create quality content regularly, adjusting and improving your strategy. With time and effort, you'll be able to build a solid base of loyal followers and increase your affiliate marketing conversions.

Chapter 4: Affiliate Marketing Without Subscribers

Affiliate Marketing Scale – Is it worth the fuss?

Keep reading to learn why affiliate marketing is such a successful earning strategy!

Multiple bloggers and online business owners find that affiliate marketing is the most effective way to monetize their efforts.

In truth,

- Affiliate programs are critical to the success of 81% of brands.
- To date, $12 billion has been made through affiliate marketing.
- 15-30% of all purchases are made through affiliate networks, a huge advantage for advertisers and marketers.
- Affiliate marketing is so successful that companies allocate 15% of their marketing budget.
- Affiliate marketing is utilized by almost 84% of content providers to monetize visitors to their sites.
- 40% of marketers consider affiliate marketing a required competency.
- Unlike most online scams, these examples show that affiliate marketing is a great way to make money online.

A tidbit of an affiliate marketing program

The affiliate marketing program is quickly gaining popularity as more and more people get into the market. Anyone with Internet access and a minimal online presence can benefit from this business approach.

As a result of digitalization, people's daily lives have completely changed. Everyone needs money to survive, and more and more people are turning to the internet to do just that. Affiliate marketing is the best method of making money online due to its high success rate and low difficulty level.

Simply by advertising and selling others' products, a few affiliate marketers can completely change their lives. This is why many people are considering getting into affiliate marketing. Affiliate marketers often brag about their earnings and accomplishments on blogs and video channels. However, many of them still need to speak up about their technique to achieve success.

This topic details practical strategies for starting a zero-subscriber affiliate marketing venture.

How to do affiliate marketing without subscribers: initial steps

Learning the basics of affiliate marketing is the first step to success in the field without an established fan base. You will then need to select a niche, launch a website or blog, browse the web for relevant keywords, identify suitable affiliate programs, create keyword-optimized content, and then submit it to search engines.

- Choose your market.
- Sign up for affiliate programs and apply.
- Register as a partner.

- Choose from many brands, individuals, or companies you want to promote.
- Choose the right affiliate program for your target market.
- Adopting effective methods to advertise your affiliate links.

How to promote affiliate links without subscribers? Tips to Know

The beauty of affiliate marketing is that the method of getting started with or without subscribers is the same. The only significant difference lies in the channels and methods to promote partnerships.

Affiliate marketing is a major online business where affiliates sell other companies products or services and earn commissions on each sale. This topic will discuss affiliate marketing without subscribers and how to use it to your advantage.

- Paid traffic

Every free strategy for attracting visitors will be time-consuming and labor-intensive. Work on a partner site can take from several months to several years.

Running a campaign with purchased traffic is the fastest and easiest way to earn affiliate commissions. This is a great alternative to a website to advertise affiliate products but it comes with monetary risks.

There was the potential for quick financial gain and quick financial losses. To maximize your ROI and minimize losses, you must be well-versed in managing sponsored ad campaigns on your preferred platform.

The best way to run a sponsored traffic campaign is to sponsor high-paying affiliate links and direct people to the affiliate web page or sales funnel before sending leads to the purchase offer.

Consequently, sales will increase, and losses will be reduced.

- Making a website or creating a blog

The crucial thing to this strategy is to create content that ranks on search engines.

It takes a lot of time and effort, but the results from targeted visitors from search engines are worth it.

You can earn as much money as you want from a blog or website you create and host on your web address.

There may come a time when you decide to sell it. When you do affiliate marketing by gathering followers on social platforms, you are not the true owner of that firm.

Websites can attract natural visitors in two ways. Both of these topics will be discussed below.

- Getting an automated affiliate marketing website

Since this choice simplifies content development, attracting visitors is less hassle.

Automated affiliate marketing sites are usually specialized WordPress websites legally importing videos from YouTube channels.

With this program, you can launch your first fully automated affiliate website in an hour if you already have a domain name and hosting.

- Website for affiliate marketing

This is usually a slower and more complex option. If that's your goal, you must keep releasing new search-engine-optimized content to attract readers.

However, it is a much more efficient strategy for attracting targeted visitors.

By offering helpful content in the form of guides, you can increase the number of people visiting your affiliate links.

When performed correctly, the results can surpass those of a robotic affiliate platform.

Even if composing music isn't your forte, you can still use this strategy to achieve huge success with minimal effort.

- Send an email to your heart to sell a product.

Email marketing is another easy way to spread your partnerships if you still need to get a significant social media following.

Email marketing efforts that involve building a list of subscribers and delivering emails to that list are an easy and effective way to acquire new customers.

Embedding the email signup form on the partner's homepage described above is a fantastic way to start collecting email addresses.

- Influence Influencers Through Your Affiliate Links

Since you don't have plans to become an influencer with a large following, you can promote affiliate links with the help of those who have already made that decision. Find people with a significant audience in your target market and offer them partnerships.

You can either agree to pay them a flat fee based on the number of sales associated with them promoting your affiliate links to their audience.

- YouTube channel

You can reach the largest audience with YouTube affiliate links even if you are starting. Affiliate marketing through YouTube videos can be done with

- product reviews
- instructional videos

You must place affiliate links in the video description. Also, ask people to subscribe to your channel, watch your videos, and leave comments. In the end, this will lead to an increase in your channel's audience.

- Amazon Associates Program

It is a common way for new blogging parents like me to make money, even if we don't have a large readership.

The question, "Can I become an Amazon affiliate even though I don't have a web page?" maybe it crossed your mind at some point. The correct answer is obviously "no." The reasons are as follows.

Amazon is aware of consumer aversion to overt selling. This is why Amazon's affiliate policies prohibit you from promoting your link without providing useful context.

- Own website

Building your dedicated website will allow you to reach those who have yet to become familiar with your affiliate links.

Instead of updating your website with new information, as with a blog, you can direct visitors to your most popular pages. Once you determine which posts are the most popular, you can then join the legion of affiliate marketers who swear by them.

- Social media marketing

Read on if you enjoy using platforms but need help building an audience because you can use social media to advertise your affiliate links even if you don't have any followers.

How? Affiliate marketing in the form of working with social media influencers is like using someone else's email list to promote your links to their audience. Find an influencer whose readership matches yours to get the best return on investment.

- landing page

If you want to promote affiliate links in such a concise and focused way, landing pages are the way to go. Our favorite aspect is that you don't even need a website or blog to do this.

Your landing page can be a simple one-page to a free one (like a chapter, list, print, podcast, blog post, or free lesson) that solves your reader's problem and promotes your affiliate product.

Chapter 5: Paid Advertising

Affiliate programs allow web admins and bloggers on social networks to earn money by promoting affiliate services and products without mandatory investments. This type of marketing has already made thousands of website and blog owners millionaires. Let's talk about how to promote affiliate programs effectively.

Ways to promote partnerships

Affiliate programs can be promoted in different ways. With the development of social networks, there are more and more ways.

So, where can you place an affiliate link?

- on the site: on your own or someone else's;
- in their accounts on social networks - Instagram, Youtube, Tik Tok, Telegram,
- on blogging platforms, such as Yandex Zen;
- on thematic forums;
- in the email newsletter;
- in paid advertising.

Among the listed methods, only placement directly on your site requires your site. Other methods allow you to promote offers without your website.

Promotion of affiliate programs on the site

Some affiliate programs make it a requirement to have a website, but not all of them. If you already have a website and a live audience, it is enough to register in the affiliate network and select offers for your audience. Affiliates that are relevant to your topic work best. For example, if your site is dedicated to reviewing modern gadgets, then advertising children's products will not bring profit.

You place an affiliate link in the text of your articles or mask it with banners. You are rewarded when the user clicks the link and completes the target action.

In the same way, you can place links on third-party sites - for example, if you are a guest author of a post on another blog.

Promotion in social networks

Social media advertising is a powerful affiliate marketing tool. You can promote affiliate services and products on your pages and others.

Instagram

You will need to create your account and gain live followers. There are few places on Instagram where you can place an active clickable link, so personalized promo codes that replace links are very popular here.

Youtube

You need to create a channel and gain views and subscribers. Affiliate links can be placed in the video's description; you can also use promotional codes similar to Instagram.

In contact with

This social network has several ways to make money on affiliate programs. You can create a personal brand from your account and promote affiliate products, or create a public with interesting topics for the audience and post advertising content there.

Telegram

In Telegram, partner products are promoted through the function of mini-blog channels. You can create your channel, buy a ready-made one with a live audience, or buy advertising from popular channels. Links are posted as posts.

Tik Tok

TikTok has a problem with placing active links, as well as on Instagram, so personal promotional codes with discounts for users are used more. You can also redirect traffic from Tiktok to Youtube, where it is very convenient to place affiliate links.

Promotion on blogging platforms

These are services where anyone can create their blogs or publish articles. The most famous such service in Runet is Yandex Zen. Here, the authors create their channels dedicated to some topics: travel, cinema, health, lifehacks, stars, news, and others. As part of such a channel, bloggers write articles that collect views, comments, and subscriptions to the channel.

Advertising is placed here by analogy with your website - links to partner services and products are placed in the text of the articles.

Promotion of thematic forums

Affiliate links can be placed in forum posts on relevant topics. Since there are too many ads on the forums, moderators often delete such messages. To avoid this, you must first increase your reputation: answer questions from forum members, provide useful information, and share experiences. Only after that your messages with affiliate links will not look overtly promotional.

Promotion via Email

The popularity of email marketing continues today. Although the algorithms of mail services are constantly being improved, and many promotional emails go to spam, this can be avoided with the right mailing settings. A link to partner products is placed in the text of the letter. You should carefully consider the text and visual design when compiling such letters.

Promotion in paid advertising

Paid advertising is contextual, targeted, and teaser advertising. That is, paid traffic sources. Contextual advertising is paid advertising through Yandex and Google. Targeted - promotion through Facebook, Instagram, VKontakte, Odnoklassniki. Here, ads are targeted to a specific type of user by age, interests, geo, user behavior, etc.

It is also possible to place affiliate links in such ads, but you need to consider the ratio of advertising costs to rewards. Otherwise, it is easy to lose money. To place an affiliate link in Instagram advertising through the Facebook advertising account, you need to know about traffic arbitrage because this method has nuances.

Best Pay-Per-Click Affiliate Programs

Affiliate marketing continues to evolve in 2023 as an opportunity for brands and retailers to introduce their products to a receptive audience. Pay-per-click affiliate programs can provide a fast and steady income stream for affiliates, but choosing the right affiliate program or PPC network is essential to success.

Affiliates and PPC (Pay Per Click)

Affiliate marketing continues to gain momentum as a source of income for content creators and the brands they sponsor. The COVID lockdown likely helped as more people shopped online and interacted with websites that matched their hobbies, ambitions, and interests. Wishes, but this trend has continued strongly after the pandemic.

Brands seek to work with influencers and content providers (bloggers, YouTubers, pintersters, Twitter, etc.) whose audience is constantly growing. As an affiliate, you will want to sign up for a marketing program that delivers fast results in your area of interest. Many have income-generating offers, including pay-per-click, which can give quick results.

Pay Per Click is just one type of affiliate marketing earning model. You most likely know that the other popular earning models are CPA, CPS, CPL, CPI, and Revenue-Share.

Context advertising is still a big business with lucrative opportunities; Remember that Google makes a huge amount of money from AdSense website ads. It simply means there are fewer PPC affiliate offers than other performance marketing models for affiliate marketing and PPC work.

Advantages and disadvantages of pay-per-click for affiliates

The affiliate marketing ecosystem has different elements, KPIs, and opportunities with various benefits. This allows publishers to choose the best options for the type of content they provide and the audience they want to create.

Here are some of the key benefits and benefits of PPC for partners:

- Instant - Pay-per-click occurs when a viewer clicks on an ad, ready and removed without further interaction.
- No Conversion Required - Unlike most other earning models where an affiliate depends on a referral conversion to earn, with pay-per-click, you earn as soon as the viewer goes to the seller.
- Simplicity – With fewer elements to manage and optimize than other affiliate offerings, PPC advertising is easier and faster to implement and maintain.
- Some crucial disadvantages of PPC for affiliates:
- Low payouts - The quantity paid per click is usually very low, with some niches earning only a few cents per click. Some niches command, but the values are much lower than CPA or CPS.
- Traffic volume – To get a good income from PPC campaigns, you need a high volume of traffic that leads to clicks. This can be a huge hurdle for new publishers if they don't have much traffic.
- Arbitrage Yield – This refers to affiliates who use paid traffic sources to create traffic and then try to monetize the traffic with PPC. Without management and optimization, traffic can quickly reduce profits.

Why Focus on Pay Per Click Affiliate Programs?

Pay-per-click affiliate marketing is similar to signing up for Google AdSense, one of the biggest pay-per-click players. Still, more focus is on linking content and ads through an affiliate program.

PPC affiliate advertising requires minimum engagement (sometimes called independent affiliate marketing), so you can easily move from trend to trend to find the best content and marketing tactics that work for you.

Some key reasons why you should consider paying per click:

- It's easy to create content around the keywords that the ad belongs to.
- A constant stream of new ads, videos, or other content
- Fast income independent of conversions
- Can quickly create affiliate content across multiple markets
- No need to invest heavily in one topic
- Generally easier to track and manage than other affiliate methods.

How to Find the Best Pay-Per-Click (PPC) Affiliate Program

When considering different pay-per-click affiliate programs, you must evaluate two important things: their application requirements and payout terms. For example, most programs require you to exceed a minimum monthly traffic threshold and may have traffic source requirements.

It is also important that you go through the payout terms. For example, if you're new and want to join a program that requires you to get 50,000 views per month or more, you might want to reconsider. After all, it is very difficult for new website owners to get 50,000 page views in a month.

Likewise, if you are starting, you should also pay attention to the minimum payment threshold. If you sign up for a program with a minimum payout of $500 or even $100, watching the money peel up in your affiliate account can be frustrating.

Ultimately, it may take several months to notice any of these funds appearing in your bank account.

Then you also need to check other things like UI and formatting tools. Some programs are more for beginners, while others are more for advanced users. The most important factor you must consider is how much you can earn by joining the program.

Several key metrics indicate your earning potential: revenue share, revenue per thousand impressions, and incoming traffic. Essentially, it comes down to the performance of your website. The more traffic you get on your site, the more you earn.

Comparison of payment structures

One of the key things you should consider before joining any affiliate program is how you will get paid. As a beginner, you should consider joining. First, you must ensure that the information posted on their website is accurate and current.

Sometimes, advertisers may charge a fee for transferring money to your bank account. So this might be something you need to consider. There are several key points to consider here.

- Minimum threshold:

You must earn this minimum amount to be eligible for a payout. Some pay-per-click affiliate programs have a $10 minimum threshold, while others can go as high as $500. So you won't get paid if you don't reach the threshold within one of your billing cycles. You will have to wait for the next billing cycle, and hope you reach the threshold to receive your funds.

- Payment time:

Another important factor to consider is the billing cycle. These days you must wait until you receive payment from the program. Some affiliate programs pay per click. Others may have a longer payment period, such as a month.

- Payment method:

This is also critical. Few affiliate programs pay via PayPal or popular payment methods such as wire transfers. Others also provide additional features, such as Payoneer or Skrill. You should check and choose the best one.

- CPC:

When searching and promoting with a pay-per-click affiliate program, your biggest question is how much you will earn per click. This is not an easy question. The cost-per-click value will vary depending on the niche, product, or service, geographic location of the traffic (clicks from some countries cost more than others), and many other factors. While it's great to know you'll get $0.10 per click, it doesn't matter because CTR (Click Through Rate) determines how much you put in your pocket. CTR can be affected by minute factors such as the quality of the banners you display, and it can even vary for every banner size and placement on your site.

How to Promote PPC Affiliate Programs on Social Media

The Affiliate Network can help you find the right pay-per-click offers from various niches, including entertainment, gambling, finance, health and wellness, education, and many more.

Today, you don't have to focus primarily on traditional marketing. Instead, one of the best ways to promote affiliate products and services is through social media. A thoughtful, well-planned strategy is great for affiliate marketers who want to earn decent commissions.

- Search and promotion in niche groups

Social networks like Facebook make joining relevant groups focused on specific topics and niches easy. As a partner, this should be your primary focus. You can search for groups that are closely related to the niche you work in. But once you find such groups, it's important that you take a measured approach to promoting your affiliate offerings.

Many affiliate marketers use these groups to effectively drive traffic to their pay-per-click offerings. However, they tend to be subtle about how they sell. First of all, you need to create value for participants. Instead of shamelessly posting links as comments on every post, you must provide interesting content to make the viewer click on your banners or links.

- Include product images

The human brain is wired to respond better when we look at photos and videos. You're doing it wrong if you're weaving in text content. You must emphasize graphics as much as possible to be a successful affiliate marketer.

Many people who have succeeded with pay-per-click affiliate programs use product images effectively in their content. People are generally more likely to buy a product if they see it in a photo or video. Social media platforms like Facebook and Instagram also use algorithms that greatly increase the reach of posts containing photos and videos.

Instagram is a photo-sharing app, so you must add photos and videos to your content. Apart from this, you also need to develop interesting promotional text or captions for it.

Providing accurate information and details is essential for your users to make an informed decision. If you can match the description of a product or service with the appropriate features, you can greatly increase your success.

- Use link shortening

Usually, people are wary of following a longer link. This is also common among successful marketers; they only post links after first hiding them. You should shorten your URLs because it greatly increases the chances that other users will share them online.

When using social media to promote, you must create shared content that others will share. Shortened URLs usually have a higher CTR. You can use many shorteners, and Bit.ly is one of the most popular options.

Social Media Can Help You Grow Your Email List

Experienced affiliate marketers are always looking for multiple ways to make money. One of the best ways to leverage your social media subscriptions is to grow your email list. After all, you can send affiliate promotions to your audience through another channel, email and maximize your income.

You should never rely on one affiliate channel to generate traffic. So, if you're only focused on social media, you must do it right. Instead, you need to work on building your social networks and growing your email list simultaneously.

Luckily, all major platforms, such as LinkedIn, Facebook, and more, now allow you to capture emails. You can get their email by offering your audience interesting content as lead magnets. You can offer many things as a lead magnet in exchange for contact information, such as a newsletter subscription, ebook, style guide, templates, and more.

While you might be wondering what the value of email collecting addresses is when you're a PPC partner interested in getting as many clicks as possible, you're right. Of course, there are many cases where you just want to click and move on; however, if it's possible to create an email list, that list is valuable, and you can use it to promote products that pay good commissions. You can get more out of the same traffic over and over again.

An active online presence can work wonders.

As an affiliate marketer, it can be easy to get lost and focus more on other channels while ignoring social media. It is a bad idea. You must maintain an active online presence to maximize your income through social media channels.

Get an eye-catching cover and profile picture (you can use Canva to create custom templates) and then use them on Facebook and Twitter. You should also never ignore Instagram for more traffic. Create posts and schedule them regularly so you can engage your audience.

Almost all major social media platforms, such as Facebook and Instagram, provide you with a dedicated dashboard to track your campaigns' success. If you're advertising on social media, this will give you a better understanding of engagement and reach.

Eventually, You can optimize and tailor your content to boost your CTR. Keep in mind that social media affiliate marketing requires a huge investment. However, running paid ads or searches can increase the chances of your posts going viral.

Facebook has a variety of filters that you can use to target your audience and target them carefully. Even Twitter gives you the ability to promote tweets!

Top 10 Pay-Per-Click (PPC) Affiliate Programs

Whatever type of content your site is about, affiliate marketing programs have spent years creating categories of related brands and ads to match the theme. They also have a wide range of payment options and thresholds. You'll want to consider your options for each affiliate program before deciding whom to work with.

With that in mind, you can monetize your content with these top pay-per-click affiliate programs. Please note that most of them use a variety of ways to generate income and pay, but PPC continues to be an important part of many affiliate programs.

- Google Adsense Pay-Per-Click Program

We can also start with the elephant in the room, the giant Google AdSense, which has dominated the online advertising market ever since the search engine became the web platform for billions of users. While not exactly an affiliate program, our list wouldn't be complete without Google.

First, although AdSense is free to register and use, click-through revenue has plummeted recently. This is because Google AdSense is increasingly focused on making ads and brands work with it (the business side of Google Ads) and less so on sites that show their ads at the other end of the funnel.

If you're starting with affiliate pay-per-click, you can use the Google AdSense calculator to estimate your revenue across regions and subject areas. But for regular content creators, Google's increasingly complex algorithms and systems seem increasingly complex.

Instead of affiliate and relationship managers, for most sites, Google AdSense uses a combination of contextual targeting, placement, personalization, and network targeting to reach the right audience, but this can lead to very generalized and disparate results on your site.

PPC and AdSense partners receive 68% of the cost of advertising, depending on the content area, how much the brand pays for placement, and other factors, including impressions that require high-performing sites to generate substantial revenue.

The Google AdSense Dashboard is easy to use, displaying recent earnings, various properties of your site, and a performance comparison with the previous month. The minimum payout is $100, and if you have a YouTube channel, you can also see the effectiveness of video ads.

There is nothing wrong with using AdSense and other affiliate programs, but be careful not to overload your content with ads and scare your audience.

Pros of Google Adsense:

- The service is free for content creators
- Easy to use with minimal web skills
- Google takes over all advertising management
- Unwanted ad-blocking options

Cons of Google Adsense:

- Less flexible than a full-service affiliate program.
- Outcomes for small content creators worsened.
- You may be banned from using AdSense, so read the rules carefully.

- Algo-Affiliates Pay-Per-Click Program

While Google AdSense may be the main starting point for many on their affiliate journey, transitioning to a proper affiliate program can be quite straightforward. Take Algo-Affiliates, for example. We deliver performance-based ads tailored to your content with thousands of targeted offers and funnels. They cover popular topics, finance, home improvement, health and beauty, business, technology, etc.

With powerful automation and a strong customer focus, we deliver some of the highest PPC rates from a dynamic and fast-growing player in the affiliate space. We also provide 24/7 expert support to help partners needing advice (try it with Google)!

Our smart dashboard shows your active offers, your offer's current performance, and reports (also available on the iOS and Android app). The featured offers tab shows the latest offers from our partners and makes it easy to add them as links or codes to your site. It's easy to manage the creation of your editorial calendar or strategy based on our proposals, and you can see the results appear to adapt or change them as needed.

Our partner company combines technology and expertise to deliver the best ads to your audience, generating the most clicks.

Pros of using Algo-Affiliates:

- High commissions and conversion rates
- Excellent range of offers
- Easy-to-use control panel

Cons of using Algo Affiliates:

- Need to expand payment options

- SkimLinks PPC Partner Program

Aside from the unfriendly registration process (did you guys work on the UI/UX a bit?), SkimLinks offers a slightly different way of presenting ads. As an affiliate, all you have to do is add code to your website above the BODY section, and when you're approved, you'll see ads they recommend based on your content.

SkimLinks is very similar to Google AdSense in this respect, but this time the split of payments is 75/25 to partner for PPC clicks, and these ads come from other affiliate programs, so they are effectively middlemen, saving you from working with another partner. Goods.

If you are starting, it will save you many registrations and learning about different systems, but you are at the mercy of their algorithm. On the other hand, there are no site size or traffic requirements, but it takes up to three months to pay, which can be a problem for those looking for a quick income.

Advantages of using Skimlinks:

- A largely automated system that makes things easier for publishers.
- There is no need to check and add links as they are updated automatically constantly.

Cons of using skylines:

- 90-day payment terms are not exactly fast

- Outbrain PPC Partner Program

Taking a different approach to pay-per-click affiliate marketing, Outbrain has high entry requirements (about 3 million visitors per month) but offers access to some big brands. The functionality differs from traditional PPC in that Outbrain acts like a native ad network.

Outbrain positions itself as a referral network offering programmatic affiliate advertising. All those sponsored stories at the end of news articles are just one example of what he can do. So your business (and you'll need at least $300 a month or more to generate significant income to participate) can buy ad space from other affiliated publishers on the network.

Outbrain recently introduced Keystone technology to help improve revenue opportunities, but if that flies over the heads of typical small publishers, it might be something to miss out on. However, those with the ambition, budget, and interest in ad tech will find it worth exploring.

Pros of using Outbrain:

- A unique approach to affiliate marketing
- Integrate with Google Analytics for easy reporting
- Focus on quality content

Cons of using Outbrain:

- Partners stuck using their formats and display options
- Less earning potential than some other programs
- Media.net PPC Partner Program

Media.net claims to have over half a million ads on its list that affiliates can use. Through contextual and programmatic advertising and machine learning for program optimization, Media.net uses a custom display-to-search (D2S) ad format to match search queries to serve pay-per-click ads.

The company claims to have hundreds of blue-chip clients on its list, with a focus on media brands on its front page. It is working with search engines Yahoo and Bing to move away from Google's hegemony and give it some competitive edge.

Publishers can run up to three ads per page, along with Google AdSense ads, so Media.Net (which should be a useful domain in its own right) works well for those who want to wow their audience with targeted ads. Ads and works in mobile, display, native and other formats.

Media.Net was part of a nearly $1 billion buyout deal in 2016, and many of its stats are from 2018, so there may be some concern that this service is no longer the best but with decent payment terms and thresholds. May have a lot to offer.

Pros of using Media.net:

- Focus on Bing! and Yahoo for alternatives to Google traffic
- Lots of ads on the page

- Focus on quality content

Cons of using Media.net:

- Lots of published content

- Bidvertiser PPC Affiliate Program

There are several players in the PPC market, and Bidvertiser chooses the path of bidding for your content. This is fine if you have an authoritative site, an authoritative voice in your niche, or just heavy traffic, but this should be avoided for everyone else.

Even so, you can sign up for Bidvertiser fairly easily, but if your ad placement bids aren't coming in, don't get your hopes up. Their game is about transparency and quality, which is valuable for the big players. Still, if there is no traction, all the targeted segmentation, targeting, and optimization worldwide will not help.

For those who do find affiliate value in Bidvertiser, there is a wide range of ad types to place alongside your content, and the service is approaching 500 million ads per day, so they must be doing something right.

Note that there is a bonus of up to $50 for publisher referrals when these pages start making money, which is one way to engage a wider network.

Pros of using Bidvertiser:

- Bids can add value to strong content and features
- Many types of promotional content to achieve high results

Cons of using Bidvertiser:

- There could be a battle for less-stellar content or new niches

- Infolinks PPC Affiliate Program

Infolinks is another player that works similarly to Skimlinks. By advancing its technology with real-time traffic analysis, Infolinks delivers the most relevant ads from brands, including Kellogg's, Microsoft, Mastercard, and more.

Increasing performance, Infolinks partnered with IPC Pricing (Impressions Per Connection), a proprietary technology company, in 2021 to reward advertisers with real-time bonus impressions based on ad performance. This can go a long way for large sites, ensuring that Infolinks publishers get more creative ads and higher click-through rates.

Benefits of using Infolinks:

- Highly automated and instant ad delivery
- Strong list of brands and ad types

Cons of using Infolinks:

- 45-day payment frequency

- GuruMedia PPC affiliate program

GuruMedia focuses on Nutra, health, e-commerce, and other popular affiliate niches, which is perfect for content creators in these areas. GuruMedia promises a personal touch that is always welcome in the land of gigantic all-digital operations.

Using Hitpath technology and a set of partner apps for security, payments, and performance tracking, you can see how small partners can thrive and focus on deals, not back-office technology. This allows GuruMedia to work with the network and affiliates' highest-quality partners, sales, and leads.

Pros of using GuruMedia:

- A strong partner for those working in the health/beauty/Nutra industry
- Shows most of its offers upfront, so don't subscribe just to be disappointed
- Weekly payouts for quick earnings

Cons of GuruMedia:

- It would be better if they expanded their portfolio of niches

- Ezoic PPC Affiliate Program

Ezoic is Google's award-winning publisher platform that aims to deliver higher RPM for PPC operators. But look at the Ezoic website; there's a lot to love about all areas of the publisher.

Essentially, their goal is to boost your revenue by improving content performance by leveraging smart technology for exceptional content. This means automatically selecting and placing ads to show the best ads to your audience. Ezoic claims their publishers are seeing 50-250% revenue growth.

Ezoic has 6 different tiers depending on the publisher's traffic volume. The base tier, called Access Now, is for sites with fewer than 10,000 monthly visitors. Levels 4-10 and VIP are for sites with more than 10,000 visitors. As traffic increases, you will move up the levels. Each tier offers more income, additional features, and access to more advertisers.

Ezoic Pros:

- Automated Income Technology
- Provides user experience information to improve the content

Cons of Ezoic:

- You won't get much if you're at the Access Now level

- Mediavine PPC Partner Program

If you thought Ezoic had tough entry requirements, brace yourself for Mediavine, which wants to work with the cream of the publishing crop. You'll need over 50,000 monthly visitors to start playing with their ComScore Top 20 business.

For Mediavine users, they provide a complete ad management solution, doing all the back-end work to provide content creators with a fast and flexible ad partner. This allows you to continue working on your content while the best ads appear, which should be generating strong clicks.

In 2021, Mediavine launched PubNation "to fill this gap and provide these site owners with the same industry-leading ad revenue opportunities currently enjoyed by content creators under the umbrella of Mediavine Ad Management." You need over 1 million visitors a month to use this, again - it's geared towards the high-end but provides its users with business-class tools.

Pros of MediaWine:

- Powerful, intelligent technology for the best advertising experience

Cons of MediaWine:

- Enterprise-class technology suitable for large venues

PPC Marketing (pay per click): what is it, and how much does it cost?

The auction process

The operation of PPC is based on an auction process in which advertisers compete to show their ads in search results or on other websites and digital platforms. Here are the main steps:

The advertiser creates an ad campaign and sets a daily budget and maximum bid per click.

When someone searches on a search engine or visits a website associated with an ad network, an auction occurs between advertisers who compete to display their ads.

The auction is based on several factors: ad relevance, landing page quality, maximum bid per click, and daily budget.

The auction winner displays their ad in search results or on the associated website, and the advertiser pays a fee each time someone clicks on the ad.

The cost of ads

The cost of the ads depends on the competition and the maximum bid per click set by the advertiser. The cost per click may be higher if many advertisers compete for a keyword or ad space. On the other hand, if there are few competing advertisers, the cost per click may be lower.

Ad Rank

Several factors, including ad quality and maximum bid per click, determine Ad Rank. Google Ads, for example, uses a scoring system called a "Quality Score" to determine ad relevance and landing page quality.

Bid Strategies

Bid strategies include setting a maximum bid per click that is competitive and allows your ad to be displayed in an appropriate position. Advertisers can also use smart bidding strategies using artificial intelligence and machine learning to optimize bids and improve campaign performance.

The importance of keywords in PPC

Keywords are terms or phrases users enter into search engines or ad networks to find information or products. In the context of PPC, keywords are crucial because they allow advertisers to show their ads to users actively searching for what they offer.

Here are some important things about keywords in PPC:

What are keywords?

Keywords are terms that users enter into search engines or ad networks to find information or products. Advertisers use these keywords to show their ads to users actively searching for what they offer.

How to choose the right keywords?

To choose the right keywords, it is necessary to consider the target audience and the objective of the advertising campaign. Advertisers must research relevant and popular keywords for their business and ensure they align with users' search terms.

How to use keywords effectively?

It's important to use keywords effectively in your ads and campaign settings. Advertisers must include keywords in their ads and landing page to make them relevant and attractive to users. Additionally, advertisers should use keyword analysis tools to monitor keyword performance and adjust strategy effectively.

In short, keywords are critical to PPC success as they allow advertisers to show their ads to users actively searching for what they offer. By choosing the right keywords and using them effectively, advertisers can improve the performance of their ad campaigns and maximize their return on investment.

Effective Ad Design

Effective ad design is crucial to the success of a PPC advertising campaign. Here are some important aspects of effective ad design:

How to write compelling ads:

Ads must be attractive and relevant to users. To do this, it is necessary to use clear, concise, and persuasive titles and descriptions highlighting the benefits of the offered product or service. In addition, clear and compelling calls to action should be included to encourage users to click on the ad.

Use of images and videos in ads:

Using images and videos can significantly improve an ad's appeal and effectiveness. Advertisers must use images and videos that are relevant, high-quality, and engaging to users. It is important to ensure that images and videos do not affect page load or distract from the main offer.

Design and effective ad formats:

The design and formats of the ads are crucial to attract the users' attention and increase the click-through rate. Ads must be visually appealing and meet the ad platform's format requirements. Also, ensuring your ads are consistent with your brand and landing page is important.

In short, effective ad design is critical to the success of a PPC campaign. Advertisers must write attractive ads, use high-quality images and videos, and use layouts and formats appropriate to the ad platform. By designing effective ads, advertisers can significantly improve the performance of their ad campaigns and maximize their return on investment.

Landing Page Optimization:

Landing page optimization is crucial to maximizing the conversion rate in a PPC campaign. Here are some tips for creating an effective landing page and increasing the conversion rate:

- Design and relevant content: The landing page must have a clear design consistent with the ad's offer. The content must be relevant, attractive, and compelling to users.
- Clear and attractive title: The title must be clear, attractive, and related to the ad's offer.
- Call to action: The landing page should include a clear and compelling call to action that encourages users to take a specific action, such as making a purchase, filling out a form, or signing up for an email list.
- Responsive design: The landing page should have a responsive design that adapts to different devices and screen sizes.
- Load speed: The landing page should load quickly to prevent users from leaving it before it loads.
- Contact form: If users are required to fill out a form, it should be short and easy to complete.
- A/B Testing: A/B testing your landing page is recommended to determine which design elements and content drive the highest conversion rate.

In summary, landing page optimization is essential to maximize the conversion rate in a PPC campaign. Advertisers should consider relevant design and content when creating an effective landing page, a clear and eye-catching headline, a call to action, responsive design, loading speed, a contact form, and A/B testing. By implementing these best practices, advertisers can significantly increase conversion rates and maximize the performance of their PPC campaign. We will further cover this topic in the next book in detail.

Tracking and analysis of PPC campaigns

Campaign Tracking Tools

PPC campaign tracking and analysis are essential to the long-term success of PPC advertising. Some common campaign tracking tools include Google Analytics and PPC-specific tools like Google AdWords and Microsoft Bing Ads.

How to Track ROI

Tracking ROI is important to determine the effectiveness of PPC campaigns. ROI can be calculated by dividing the revenue generated by the campaign by the total cost of the campaign.

How to adjust and optimize PPC campaigns

Optimizing PPC campaigns is accomplished through A/B testing, which involves testing different campaign elements, such as ads and keywords, and determining which works best. Additionally, it is important to regularly monitor and adjust campaigns to ensure they are in line with marketing objectives and generate positive ROI.

Common PPC mistakes and how to avoid them

Several common mistakes can limit the effectiveness of PPC campaigns. Here are some of the most common mistakes and how to avoid them:

Bid too high or too low

One of the biggest advantages of PPC advertising is that you can set your bids and budgets. Your ad may only appear in relevant searches if your bid is high. On the other hand, if you bid too high, you could pay more than necessary. The solution is to find the right balance for your goals and budget.

inappropriate keywords

Choosing the right keywords is key to successful PPC advertising. It is important to avoid keywords that are too general or irrelevant to the product or service you offer. Also, keywords with high competition can be more expensive, negatively affecting your ROI.

Unattractive ad design

Ads that aren't attractive or attention-grabbing may not generate enough interest for someone to click on them. It's important to ensure your ads are clear, concise, and engaging with your target audience.

Ineffective landing pages

A poorly designed or unclear landing page can cause users to quickly leave the page without converting. It's important to ensure the landing page is relevant to the ad and provides the user with all the information they need to make a purchase or conversion decision.

What benefits does PPC offer for companies?

PPC offers several benefits for businesses, including:

Increase in traffic and conversions

PPC can help businesses increase traffic to their website and drive more conversions as ads target users searching for specific products or services.

Advertising budget control

With PPC, businesses can set a daily budget for their campaigns and adjust their bid per click based on their needs. This allows them to have more control over their advertising spend and maximize their return on investment.

Highly targeted ads

PPC allows companies to show ads to specific audiences based on their location, language, interests, and other demographic criteria. This allows them to target more relevant leads and increase the chances of conversion.

Overall, PPC is a powerful tool for businesses to promote their brand and reach their target audience effectively and efficiently.

How much does PPC cost?

Factors Influencing PPC Costs

The cost of PPC can vary depending on several factors, such as the industry, type of advertising, keyword competition, and geographic location. Some markets may be more competitive and require higher bids for your ads to appear in a good position.

Average cost per click (CPC)

The average cost per click (CPC) is an important indicator of the cost of PPC. Refers to the cost an advertiser pays each time someone clicks on their ad. CPC also varies by industry, type of advertising, and geographic location.

How to Calculate a PPC Budget

To calculate a PPC budget, it's important to consider your expected CPC and the number of clicks you expect to receive. Multiplying the expected CPC by the number of estimated clicks will give an idea of the total cost of the campaign. You should also consider the campaign's duration and any additional costs, such as the cost of ad design and landing page optimization.

Trends and changes in the PPC

New ad formats

In addition to the familiar PPC ad types like search, display, video, and social, there are some emerging trends in the PPC world worth highlighting.

One is the rise of shopping ads appearing in product search results on sites like Google Shopping. These ads allow retailers to promote their products with images and detailed descriptions, which can attract online shoppers.

PPC Automation

Another trend in PPC is automation, which uses machine learning tools to optimize advertising campaigns in real-time. The largest advertising platforms, such as Google Ads and Facebook Ads, have developed automation solutions to save time and improve campaign performance.

New PPC advertising channels

Finally, there is a growing trend towards advertising on new channels, such as Amazon, LinkedIn Ads, and podcast advertising. As more businesses look for new places to reach their audiences, more PPC advertising options on different platforms are expected to emerge.

Frequent questions

Is PPC Right for Every Business?

PPC (Pay Per Click) can be a very effective tool for many businesses, but it's only sometimes right for some. It depends on several factors, such as your advertising budget, business type, and marketing goals. Businesses looking for quick results and increased online visibility may find PPC an effective strategy. However, it is important to note that PPC can be very competitive and expensive in certain industries. Furthermore, it requires ongoing investment to sustain results and may only be sustainable in the short term for some businesses.

How long does it take to see results in a PPC campaign?

The time it takes to see results in a PPC campaign can vary, but you can generally see immediate results in traffic and clicks. However, you must constantly test and tune your campaign for optimal performance and

ROI, which can take weeks or even months. Therefore, it is important to note that the long-term success of a PPC campaign requires a carefully planned and executed strategy.

How can I optimize a successful PPC campaign?

To optimize a successful PPC campaign, the following steps can be followed:

- Perform an in-depth analysis of keywords and competition.
- Create attractive and relevant ads for the chosen keywords.
- Direct ads to an effective and relevant landing page.
- Constantly follow and analyze the results of the campaign.

Make adjustments and improvements in the campaign according to the results obtained.

Use remarketing techniques to increase conversions and return on investment.

The key to optimizing a successful PPC campaign is constantly staying informed, analyzing the data, and adjusting based on the results.

What is a conversion rate, and how can it be increased?

Conversion rate is the percentage of website visitors who take a desired action, such as purchasing or completing a contact form. To increase the conversion rate in a PPC campaign, it is important to optimize the landing page, ensuring it is relevant and persuasive to the user. It's also helpful to target keywords properly and adjust bids strategically. In addition, the design and content of the ad can influence the click-through rate and, ultimately, the conversion rate. A/B testing and data analysis can also be useful in identifying opportunities for campaign improvement.

What is the difference between search advertising and display advertising in PPC?

Search advertising refers to ads that appear in the search results of engines such as Google or Bing and are based on specific keywords that users search for. On the other hand, display advertising refers to ads that appear on websites, mobile apps, and ad networks, targeting users based on their online behavior and demographics. Search advertising is more effective at driving direct conversions, and display advertising is more effective at building brand awareness and audience reach.

What is pay-per-click marketing?

Pay-per-click (PPC) marketing is a form of online advertising in which advertisers pay for each click a user makes on their ad. This form of advertising is commonly used on search engines and content websites, where advertisers select keywords relevant to their products or services and create ads displayed to users searching for information related to those keywords. PPC allows advertisers to target specific users and only pay when users click on their ads, making it an effective form of online advertising.

Cost per click: How does it work?

Cost per click (CPC) is the amount an advertiser pays each time someone clicks on their ad in a pay-per-click (PPC) marketing campaign. CPC is determined through a keyword auction in which advertisers compete to show their ads in search results relevant to their chosen keywords. Ads are ranked based on several factors, including max CPC, ad quality and relevance, and landing page. The actual CPC paid is determined in the auction and may be less than or equal to the maximum CPC set by the advertiser.

Chapter 6: Make money with affiliate marketing:

The best products

Various products from different areas are suitable for affiliate marketing. So there is no such thing as the best affiliate marketing product. Rather, it is important that the website has a product reference or that the product and content fit together. Therefore, for example, these types of websites are particularly good if you want to make money with affiliate marketing:

- theme portals
- niche sites
- blog
- online magazines
- Test and comparison portals
- Social media networks
- Video platforms like YouTube
- voucher portals

It is also advisable to rely on niche products. These may have a smaller audience, but you can also rank better for keywords.

Start your affiliate marketing business now!

The affiliate business is characterized by flexibility and a low weekly time commitment. Of course, in the beginning, you must invest time and effort to fill your website or social media account with basic information about your topic. Affiliate business is the right model for you if you are looking for a business model that runs perfectly on the side and requires little technical know-how and little attentionIt is even "The simplest business model in the world" for us!

Frequently Asked Questions About Pay Per Click (PPC)

1. What is pay-per-click affiliate marketing?

These programs that offer pay-per-click campaigns provide publishers with ads that the publisher then places on their site. Every time a visitor clicks on an ad, the affiliate earns a commission, hence the name pay per click.

2. How do pay-per-click programs work?

Brands sign up for affiliate programs and provide a list of ads, keywords, or campaigns for their products. The partner can then select advertisements (or they are selected automatically) that best match the content. The affiliate program platform tracks clicks, payments, and performance to help optimize revenue generation.

3. What are the benefits of pay-per-click?

The main advantage of pay-per-click affiliate marketing is that you earn once a visitor clicks on an ad. You don't have to rely on the seller to close the sale, i.e., convert your traffic. You also don't have to worry about how well the seller retains the customer, which can make a big difference if you're earning a commission based on revenue share, for example.

4. How do advertisers benefit from pay-per-click?

In short, they are getting a new stream of potential customers to their front door. This is a bit more difficult for the advertiser because only a tiny percentage of clicks will result in a sale. Thus, the advertiser should get a positive ROI with effective campaign management.

5. Are pay-per-click affiliate programs legal?

Yes, just like any other advertising or marketing business. The question arises because some advertisements (as in any market) may push boundaries with questionable claims or not comply with regulatory or legal requirements in all countries.

Chapter 7: Affiliate marketing through videos and podcasts!

Videos in affiliate marketing

I like reading texts, especially when they convey facts and solid information because you can quickly look up certain things. This isn't easy in videos, but you can better convey or arouse emotions. In addition, it is often easier to present and show products in videos.

For this reason, affiliates should increasingly rely on videos in the future. More and more people prefer to watch videos than read an article, and you should consider this on your affiliate website. Otherwise, you will no longer pick up part of the target group. And if you don't feel addressed or can't find the content you want, you won't buy a product either.

Video types for affiliate websites

Different types of videos are possible on affiliate websites. The following video types are used most frequently:

- review videos

First, there would be a video in which a product is presented. This is the classic case. The product is presented in detail, data and facts are discussed, and a judgment or recommendation is made.

- experience videos

Experience videos are much more personal. The focus here is not on the product but on a specific experience or story that you have had. This creates stronger viewer loyalty. But of course, the experiences revolve more or less strongly around a product, so this is usually also discussed.

- tips videos

Tips videos are very popular in which best practices, tips, or background information are given. These are more problem-related than product-related, but they convey know-how and increase our reputation as experts. This helps later when you make product recommendations in another video or text.

- Haul videos

Haul videos are very common on YouTube. It simply shows what you have bought with a purchase, without any real evaluation of the products.

- news videos

Another approach is news videos. In these, you go into the latest news in a subject area and describe your opinion on certain product announcements, for example.

- vlog

The classic vlog is most comparable to a video diary. These videos are the least "professional" ones, but they're usually not perceived as advertising and come across as very personal.

Which of these video types makes the most sense for you depends on whether you own the product.

Videos with product

You can create very good review videos if you bought the product or were provided a copy. You don't have to meet any official test criteria, but you shouldn't indicate that in the video. Instead, a personal review of a product you use yourself is a very good way to present it in a video.

Haul videos are also possible if you have the product (or products). Whether you bought or received the products from the manufacturer is unimportant. However, for reasons of transparency, you should always be honest about where you got the product from. It quickly becomes surreptitious advertising if you pretend you bought a product yourself, even though it is a review copy.

And, of course, experience videos usually only make sense if you describe your experiences with a product you should have used.

Videos without a product

However, there is also the possibility of making experience videos if you do not own a certain product yourself. Then you don't describe your experiences with a product, but, for example, a problem you have or something that happened to you.

Tips Videos are a typical example of videos without products. Background tips and information can be conveyed well in such videos without mentioning a product.

News videos are another way to regularly create videos without having the products in your hands. If, for example, you talk about a newly announced smartphone in a video, give information about it, and describe your opinion, then that also attracts many visitors.

The vlog is something you can do with or without a product. Many use this format in social networks such as Facebook or Instagram to build a personal level, and the focus is rarely on the product. Nevertheless, you build up so much, and that, in turn, ensures many sales for later product recommendations.

Supplement articles with videos

Anyone with a larger affiliate website should consider adding a video to older articles. This is not so difficult with many articles since the content is already available, and you "recycle" it in the video.

For example, if you describe a certain experience in an article, you can do the same in the video. If you list certain tips in an article, you can also go through these tips in the video.

And they don't have to be long videos, on the contrary. Many viewers want information quickly and to the point. A few minutes are usually sufficient. This is also good because the videos can be created, uploaded, and integrated relatively quickly.

How do I use video marketing for affiliate marketing?

Video marketing is a good way to reach a wide audience while increasing sales. It is one of the most powerful affiliate marketing strategies due to its capability to reach a wide audience while increasing the number of sales.

Video marketing is an effective way to get more customers and generate sales. Video marketing grants you to reach your audience uniquely, engaging them with various visual and audio elements.

To use video marketing for affiliate marketing, there are a few steps you should follow. First, you should choose a target audience and create a video specifically tailored for that audience. The video must convey the message clearly and concisely so the target audience can easily understand it. It's also important that the video helps create an interest in your product or service.

After creating the video, it must be promoted to reach a wide audience. A good way to achieve this is by using social media like Facebook, Twitter, YouTube, and Instagram. You can also post the video on various websites and blogs to promote it to a larger audience.

Once the video is created and published, you must ensure it comes with relevant affiliate links. These links should lead your website to increase interest and conversion rates.

It's also important to update your videos regularly to ensure they're still relevant and up to date. This is important to ensure that the target audience is always up to date when things change.

Video marketing can be a very effective strategy to attract customers and generate sales. However, it is important that you follow all of the above steps to get the best success. Following the above steps, video marketing can greatly improve your affiliate marketing business.

Affiliate marketing for YouTubers

Being a partner means always staying in the know. It may be challenging to catch all the trends at once, but this is the only way to find the most profitable ways that will work for your affiliate business. Instagram is a promising trend that you should try out, Facebook is one of your gems, and now it's time to try something new!

Mass distribution of Youtube is not a secret. Every month, every living person watches 6 billion hours of video on YouTube, about 1 hour per month. It is the second-largest search engine in the world, with over 1 billion users, and the number continues to grow. So you still need to see if YouTube affiliate marketing exists? This topic examines who does it, where to start, whether it works, and more. Let's find out.

Who does it?

Many, many YouTubers, if not most of them.

Where to begin?

YouTube affiliate marketing is creating videos and placing affiliate links in the videos themselves (using annotations) or in the video descriptions. It's very simple. Just like you can write a blog post, "The Best Cat Homes," with an affiliate link, you can create a video showing an overview of several cat homes and include the affiliate link in the description. The goal is simple and clear: redirect traffic to an affiliate page, or of course, you can also direct users to an email signup form if you have a thinner funnel that promotes affiliate products. If you're serious about YouTube content creation, one of your videos likely has at least one affiliate offer.

Costs?

YouTube is so popular that it makes no sense to. Profitability, as always, depends on several factors. Content, as always, is one of the keys, but everything is in your hands.

What types of videos can you make to generate affiliate income?

There is always room for fantasy. However, several standard formats have proved successful. Although most are not ideal for affiliate marketing, several formats provide an opportunity to promote products and services.

1.   Video with product reviews

Individual product reviews or comparison videos are a good way to make videos that can promote products.

It has been advised that 62% of consumers watch review videos before making a purchase, and 52% of customers are more open to buy a product in a YouTube product review video.

This is a great opportunity to create content to help retailers achieve maximum sales while earning good commissions through affiliate income.

2.   How to make / DIY video

This type of video showing people how to organize your child's birthday party and inflate 250 balloons alone, or how to fix a roof, is a great example of a video that can be informative and recommend products simultaneously.

3.   "Best of" videos

This type of video shows the best product, from our point of view, at the moment.

It's easy to imagine similar summary videos across different niches, such as the best headphones, golf drivers, skateboards, running shoes, etc.

How to monetize your videos with affiliate programs

If you're a video content creator, you've probably wondered how you can make money from your videos. One way to do this is through affiliate programs. This topic will explain what affiliate programs are and how you can use them to monetize your videos.

Affiliate programs are a good way to monetize your videos, as they allow you to promote products relevant to your audience and earn money from them.

How do video affiliate programs work?

To use affiliate programs in your videos, you must follow the following steps:

1.   Find an affiliate program: To get started, find an affiliate program that suits your niche and audience. Some companies offer affiliate programs directly on their website, while others use affiliate networks like Amazon Associates, ShareASale, or Commission Junction.

2. Sign up for the affiliate program: Once you've found an affiliate program that interests you, you must sign up. This usually involves providing basic information about yourself and your website or YouTube channel.
3. Get your affiliate link: After signing up, you will get a unique link used to promote the advertiser's products or services.
4. Promote the product or service: You must use your affiliate link to promote the product or service. You can do it in the description of your videos or a sponsored video.
5. Earn commissions: If somebody clicks on your affiliate link and buys, you will get back a commission for that sale.

How to find affiliate programs for videos?

Finding video affiliate programs can be long and tedious, but there are a few ways to make it easier. Here are some ideas:

1. Search Google: You can search Google for affiliate programs specific to your niche or industry.
2. Use affiliate networks: As mentioned, affiliate networks such as Amazon Associates, ShareASale, or Commission Junction group affiliate programs from different companies.
3. Contact companies directly: If there is a specific company whose products or services you would like to promote, you can contact them directly to ask if they have an affiliate program.

What products or services can I promote in my videos?

You can promote any product or service relevant to your audience and related to your niche or industry. Some ideas could be:

1. Tools or Software: If you create videos about technology or digital marketing, you can promote useful tools or software to your audience, like Filmora video editing software.
2. Physical products: If you create lifestyle or beauty videos, you can promote physical products like makeup, clothing, or accessories.
3. Services: If you create videos about business or finance, you can promote services like financial advice or accounting services.

Remember that choosing products or services relevant to your audience and related to your niche or industry is important.

How can I make my videos effective for affiliate program promotion?

There are a few strategies you can use to make your videos more effective for affiliate program promotion:

1. Do a review or demo of the product or service: An effective way to promote a product or service is to do a review or demo of it in your video. In this way, your audience will be able to see how it works and what benefits it has.
2. Include your affiliate link inside the description: Make sure to include it in the video description so that your viewers can click on it if they are interested in the product or service.
3. Create a sponsored video: If you have an established relationship with a business, you can create a sponsored video to promote their product or service more explicitly.

What affiliate programs are the best for videos?

There are many affiliate programs that you can use to monetize your videos, but some of the best are:

1. Amazon Associates: Amazon Associates is among the most popular affiliate programs. It offers commissions for the sale of physical and digital products on Amazon.
2. ShareASale: ShareASale is an affiliate network that combines affiliate programs from different companies. It has a wide variety of affiliate programs in different niches.
3. Commission Junction: Commission Junction is another affiliate network that combines affiliate programs from different companies. It has a wide variety of affiliate programs in different niches.

How to do affiliate marketing with a podcast?

While most content creators make their podcasts out of passion and love of the craft, they must turn their passion into a profitable income method. Podcasts are particularly good for this, and affiliate marketing is one of the best methods.

It is a business model in which you can obtain commissions for the sales of products of a certain brand to your audience, generating a source of income that depends to a large extent on how you present the product to your listeners.

In the next few paragraphs, we will teach you everything you need to know about affiliate marketing and how to apply it to your podcast to start generating income through it like a pro.

Benefits of affiliate marketing for your podcast

One of the business models that offer the most benefits for both the advertiser and the content creator is affiliate marketing because it can be mixed coherently and fluidly with other marketing strategies, increasing the possibility of obtaining optimal results.

As for the benefits it will bring to your podcast, affiliate marketing is one of the best ways to get the most out of your program through monetization while improving your advertising resources by promoting the advertiser's products or services.

Among the most notable benefits that affiliate marketing can provide to your podcast are the following:

- Profitability: Through affiliate marketing, you can turn your podcast into a legitimate source of income that will depend on the number of users who purchase your product.
- Payment facilities: unlike other online monetization models, affiliate marketing does not pay for clicks or impressions; its earnings are based on the commission model.
- Influence: the quality of the products offered and the type of advertising that is applied can lead to increased views for the podcast, attracting listeners interested in learning more about the products.
- Valuable connections: affiliate marketing will allow you to use your podcast as a powerful social tool to attract new customers and increase the impact of your message and that of the advertiser.

Learn how to do affiliate marketing with your podcast.

There are several factors that you must take into account before starting to do affiliate marketing with your podcast to achieve it successfully. For starters, you must ensure you're serious about producing your content, giving your listeners the best possible audio experience so they more seamlessly receive the product's message. In addition, it must be promoted naturally and fluidly since the message's naturalness determines the sale's success.

- Define your niche

Be sure to specify your podcast's topic as much as possible. Staying within a topic can help you gather a more focused audience and improve your search engine rankings. You can access pages like Amazon Affiliates, Awin, or Hotmart to find profitable affiliate niches.

Find affiliate programs

The types of affiliate programs that you can select vary depending on their sales volume and the size of their commissions, classified as follows:

- High Commission, Low Volume Affiliate Programs
- Low Commission, High Volume Affiliate Programs
- High Commission, High Volume Affiliate Programs

The third affiliate program is completely saturated by professionals with high budgets who resort to spamming, so it is incredibly difficult to excel in this field. The first two are the most profitable options.

To select an affiliate program, consider factors such as your experience level and niche. For example, the low commission, high volume program is ideal if your target audience is end consumers. In contrast, the high commission, low volume program is better suited for a more professional or business audience.

- Create quality content

An affiliate podcast can only be successful by creating high-quality content that naturally incorporates affiliate links and promotions to enhance audience reception. The passion for the subject and the charisma of the podcaster are important factors since it is not only about reviewing the best-selling products of your advertiser but about creating content that engages the listener and convinces them to buy the products or services you offer.

- Drive traffic to your affiliate podcast.

This step is about spreading the content of your podcast as much as possible, which you can do through your social networks and alternative means of dissemination.

This can be done through various methods:

- Paid traffic: This is about using payment methods to increase traffic to your podcast through methods such as PPC ads. One of the advantages of this medium is that once you start paying, you will start receiving visits.
- SE0: is a web page optimization strategy to increase its positioning in search engines so that your podcast can appear organically among the first search results through the use of words target key.
- Contact list: They are one of the best ways to stay in touch with your podcast listeners so that you can notify them about the publication of each new episode, as well as send them affiliate promotions, of course, with the consent of your subscribers.

- Promote your affiliate links.

Affiliate links are the most common way a Podcaster, or content creator, can generate income through affiliate marketing. It is a link that takes the user directly to a product promoted by the advertising brand and that is linked to the podcaster's affiliate account, so if the visitor decides to purchase this product, the podcaster will receive a part of the profit.

It is necessary to take into account that quality content does not guarantee that the listener will enter the affiliate link, so it is necessary to resort to different methods to get clicks on them:

- Link mention: During your podcast narrative, you should look for opportune moments to mention the affiliate link. This can be located both in the podcast description and in one of your social networks, but you must ensure the listener knows it is there.
- Context: The moment and context in which you mention your affiliate links must be well-defined to keep your podcast's narrative and feel in the right place for your listeners.
- Reminders: Depending on the length of your podcast, it may be a good idea to remind your listeners about your affiliate links or other social networks. However, this resource must be treated with care not to overwhelm your audience with constant mentions of affiliate links.

Chapter 8: The 7-Steps Checklist of the Successful Affiliate Marketer

We have reached the heart of the matter, but the points previously covered are still just as relevant.

We have given our opinion on what goes into a fool proof affiliate marketing strategy.

We have decided to share these tips with you so that you can discover what you need to make money with affiliate marketing. Here we go!

1. Select the most appropriate platform.

Currently, there are many options for affiliate marketing using platforms.

Although the variety of options represents a benefit, it can also seem tedious for those deciding the best alternative to implement marketing strategies.

The best thing you can do is find out the platforms' reputation, compare commissions and volume of communities, and recognize the value of contributions available.

2. Identify the most commercially relevant niches.

You must have great objectivity and think about achieving sustainable benefits. If you choose a niche with little demand, your earnings will not be as attractive.

However, if you choose a niche with an impressive demand but an equally high level of competitiveness, you may be able to earn income, but your strategy will have to be much stronger.

It's all about balance, a key point for professional affiliate marketing.

Currently, many tools help identify best-selling products online on various platforms.

If you choose a relevant niche, you will get these benefits:

- It will be much easier to get visits to your website because the products are of public interest.
- Given the sector's demand, you can perceive sales in less time, but your strategies are relevant for this.
- Many of these products have already gained popularity because of the interest they have captured; it is a resource to be exploited.

3. Have a functional and error-free website.

The first impression counts a lot. This is something well-known by those who have been working with affiliate marketing for a long time. However, you can focus less than 100% on web design.

People often focus on displaying various banners; they provide designs that make up a dynamic (and sometimes loaded) website.

But, they need to pay attention to the small details, giving way to serious errors at the functionality level.

IMPORTANT that you focus on the following aspects for the production of your website:

- Work on Responsive that your website is adapted to use on various devices.
- Avoid errors like overlapping elements, broken links, etc.
- Work on creating information that connects with the user.
- Don't leave site loading speed in the background.

4. Prioritize transmitting confidence

The audience detects and does not appreciate empty, excessively technical content with little credible information in a good way.

Instead of promoting products guaranteeing that they are 100% perfect, you should focus on identifying their strengths to differentiate them from the competition.

How can you do it? With vision, putting yourself in the consumer's place and providing true information.

Those who have used the digital products, services, or physical items it promotes know more about the good and the not-so-good. So they manage to issue more objective reviews (this pleases the audience).

5. Create dynamic content

If you are here, surely you have asked yourself more than once how to do affiliate marketing on my website.

Many strategies focus on creating professional, complete, and detailed texts.

However, a clear difference exists between creating content to promote a complete affiliate product and creating a long, bland copy.

The difference lies in the dynamism. But how to generate it? Divide your content into several hierarchical diversity subheadings. Incorporate attractive images allusive to the content, leave textual quotes, statistical percentages, videos, and more.

It is also convenient to break down the information into paragraphs to make it easier for the reader to digest. In general terms, you must ensure that your audience connects with the quick text and appreciates what they need to satisfy their doubts about the product.

6. Stories drive sales

Many people value obtaining information on the products of their interest by knowing the experience of other people. This arouses emotions and makes readers feel identified.

Storytelling is a great strategy to connect with your audience from start to finish and helps create a good impression about the product being promoted.

Once you learn how to do Storytelling professionally and appreciate its benefits, you won't want to stop applying it to the growth of your website.

7. Keep an eye on SEO.

Google values the creation of extensive content, rich in information and elements and with enough internal links to cause more clicks among visitors.

It is important that you create a balance between the creation of an informative, friendly, and honest text, with the application of SEO strategies in copy generation.

Likewise, you must identify problems or errors on your website that affect web positioning. One of the most common is the excess weight of images that negatively impact the website's loading. You must avoid it!

Learning how to do effective SEO in affiliate marketing will help you capture web traffic professionally.

THE 7-STEPS CHECKLIST OF THE SUCCESSFUL AFFILIATE MARKETER

1

SELECT THE MOST APPROPRIATE PLATFORM
- Find out the platforms' reputation.
- Compare commissions
- Recognize the value of contributions available

2

IDENTIFY THE MOST COMMERCIALLY RELEVANT NICHES
- You must have great objectivity and think about achieving sustainable benefits

3

HAVE A FUNCTIONAL AND ERROR-FREE WEBSITE
- Work on a responsive website that is adapted to use on various devices.

4

PRIORITIZE TRANSMITTING CONFIDENCE
- You should focus on identifying the strengths of the products.

5

CREATE DYNAMIC CONTENT
- Divide your content into several hierarchical diversity subheadings.
- Incorporate attractive images allusive to the content

6

STORIES DRIVE SALES
- This arouses emotions and makes readers feel identified

7

KEEP AN EYE ON SEO
- Google values the creation of extensive content

Conclusion

Working in affiliate marketing means being flexible in choosing promotion methods and keeping your finger on the pulse. Focus on your target audience and the specifics of specific offers.

In terms of payback, affiliate marketing has long moved from a hobby to a source of income. This is your own business, requiring constant development and training. To reach the payback point, various tools are provided. You can act as a promotion intermediary without your website, blog, or official page.

Don't stop at the first hurdles; keep testing marketing scenarios, analyzing audience behavior, studying power user success stories, and you'll be able to capitalize on making money from someone else's product line.

In conclusion, promoting affiliate marketing products through your email list is a great strategy to increase your income and provide value to your audience. By following the steps mentioned above, you can create email campaigns that are compelling and engaging to your subscribers, leading to a higher conversion rate and better results. Remember to be transparent with your audience and choose only high-quality products that fit your niche. With time and practice, you can become proficient at promoting affiliate marketing products through your email list and achieve success in your online business.

The most successful affiliate marketers write about products they like. They provide honest and helpful product information. Most importantly, they focus on readers' needs, even at the risk of earning a few extra bucks. In doing so, they have established themselves as a reliable marketer whose priority is informing and entertaining customers.

Pick a specific market, explore affiliate programs that target that area, and then market your business with a standalone affiliate marketing website or blog.

But just like any other skill, your affiliate marketing skills will improve with practice. Although always remember that as an affiliate, you must put in a lot of time and effort to increase your sales.

However, once it's up and running and you focus on increasing your blog readership, it can make you money even if you need to maintain or update it actively.

When you become an affiliate marketer, you can talk about what you do, so choose a product or service to promote that you are passionate about. Your audience can see if you like something, which is a positive aspect of the situation.

People appreciate it when they understand that a person is genuine. Because of this, sincerity is the most effective strategy for building trust when working in affiliate marketing without followers.

If you are considering getting in the field of affiliate marketing, this is a fantastic step in the right direction. You are pleasant. In the 2020s, the affiliate marketing strategy will be the most successful.

If you want to be an effective affiliate marketer in your profession, you need to follow the steps above. If you are successful, you can quit your 9-to-5 job and be free to do what you want with your time and money.

This concludes the information we can provide you regarding how to do affiliate marketing without subscribers. We sincerely hope this was informative. It's time to get busy and take charge of your life.

Affiliate marketing can be made without social media, but using them can increase reach and revenue. By posting a link to promote your blog or website on your social media accounts, as most people do, you will help spread the word.

Promoting affiliate programs can bring solid profits. All methods above operate both independently and in conjunction with each other. Most web admins and bloggers use several methods simultaneously, testing different traffic sources and selecting working links. Affiliate marketing is all about flexibility, so don't be afraid to try different techniques.

Youtube channel is a great affiliate marketing platform, whether you are an experienced YouTuber or have yet to download videos. Everyone has to start somewhere; why not give Youtube a chance? By the way, if you are not planning on having a website, this is one way to build your Affiliate Business without websites.

Are you ready to start affiliate marketing on Instagram?

Always remember that the first step is always the most difficult. What separates you from being an employee to being a boss?

Another great way to start scaling your affiliate business is to post the same content on TikTok that you post on Instagram.

Affiliate programs can be an effective way to monetize your videos and make money from your content. To use them, you need to find an affiliate program that fits your niche, promote relevant products or services to your audience, and use effective video strategies.

Remember that affiliate programs are not the only way to monetize your videos, but they can be useful if used properly.

In conclusion, PPC is an effective form of online advertising that grants businesses to reach their target audience through highly targeted ads. The right choice of keywords, attractive ad design, and landing page optimization are critical to the success of a PPC campaign. In addition, monitoring and analyzing the results allow you to adjust and optimize the campaigns to obtain the maximum ROI. While PPC costs can vary based on several factors, control of your advertising budget and the ability to adjust bids based on results make PPC an attractive option for businesses. It's important to stay on top of PPC trends and changes to get the most out of this ever-evolving advertising strategy.

Book 3: Advanced Techniques for Higher Profits

Introduction

For professionals, SEO is the best tool to get more visibility, infinite visits, and sales at a low cost. This is due to consumer behavior. In a high percentage, when they need something, they will search (unless we have already made them loyal, and they go directly to us). If we appear in the first results, you will find us, enter our e-commerce, and increase sales.

Another quality of advanced SEO is worth noting: it is infinite. Because although it requires maintenance, a large part of these visits will continue to arrive even if we do not work on it for a while. And, even though it costs money, the investment is much lower than advertising online.

Chapter 1: Advanced SEO Techniques for Affiliate Marketers

SEO is a topic that concerns companies worldwide. Regarding page views, Google is the market leader: more than 85 percent of all search queries started worldwide run via the search engine.

According to a study by the German Institute for Marketing, around 30 percent of all clicks in a search query fall on the first result. Only one in ten takes a look at the third result.

One thing is clear for companies: If their websites end up on the back pages, they have little chance of converting interested users into customers. Anyone who is not yet concerned with search engine optimization risks valuable clicks and thus loses customers due to poor result positions in the rankings.

But how do you get to the top positions in the search engine results? To achieve number one, websites must cover certain ranking factors that the search engines evaluate, monitor, and optimize.

Google is constantly evolving, changing its algorithms and how it ranks websites. Google updates its algorithm about 500-600 times a year. That means there is at least one update every single day.

SEO tactics are trying to devise measures to do the algorithm justice. Many mistakes happen: Website operators rely on tactics such as link farms (e.g., through inorganic backlinks) or keyword stuffing, which used to work but are now consistently penalized by Google.

SEO tactics must be regularly reviewed and compared to new guidelines, as keeping track of changes is nearly impossible. That's why we've compiled the most important, most effective SEO tactics and methods for 2023.

Understand the search intent of your target audience

Search intent (user intent, search intent) describes the purpose of an online search. It's the reason someone does a particular search. After all, everyone who searches online hopes to get relevant results. Is the person looking for an answer to a question? Does she want to visit a specific website? Is she looking online because she wants to buy something?

Over the years, Google has worked hard to improve its algorithm to determine user search intent. Google lists the pages at the top that best match the search term used. Therefore, you should ensure that your post or page corresponds to the user intention of your target group with the appropriate content.

There are four types of search intent:

- informational
- navigational
- transactional
- Commercially

Information intent

Many searches on the Internet are conducted by people looking for informative content. This can be information about the weather, raising children, search engine optimization, etc. People with an information intent have a specific question or want to learn more about a specific topic.

Google's understanding of intent goes beyond just displaying results that provide information about a specific term. For example, search engines like Google know that people who type in "hollandaise sauce" are most likely looking for recipes, not the sauce's culinary history.

Most people who type "Pluto" are looking for the planet, not Mickey Mouse's dog. Google knows that for some search terms, like "how to build a paper airplane," it's handy to include videos and images.

navigation intent

People with this intention want to visit a specific website. For example, if you search for the keyword "Twitter" online, you usually go to the Twitter website. So you want to ensure your website can be found when someone searches for your business name online.

Transactional Intent

Users buy things online and search the web to find the best deal. People search with transactional intent when they aim to buy something right now. That means they already know exactly what they want to buy. Your goal is to get to this product page immediately.

Commercial Intent

Some people intend to buy goods or services in the (near) future and use the Internet for their research. Which laptop is the best? Which SEO Tactics Are Most Helpful? These individuals also have a transactional intent, but they need a little more time and persuasion. These search intents are referred to as commercial search intents.

Recognizing the right search intention is the most important step in keyword analysis and an essential part of an SEO strategy. Search engines are constantly changing: While in the past, the results were determined based on a single keyword and backlinks, today, the focus is on the user.

Website operators and those responsible for marketing must structure the appropriate content differently, depending on the search intention. The SEO strategy also determines the right choice of content.

So it's a good idea to optimize product pages for commercially oriented search terms. For example, if you sell animal supplements, you can optimize a product page (category) as a landing page for the search term "buy supplements."

Check the Core Web Vitals of your website.

Some time ago, Google announced "Web Vitals." They represent metrics to measurably assess and evaluate websites based on the page experiences provided (e.g., speed, user experience).

The page experience ("page experience") is a new, decisive factor for an optimal ranking. These include website speed, load time, interactivity, and visual stability.

To measure the essential aspects of the user experience, Google selects three corresponding metrics - also known as the Core Web Vitals:

1. LCP, Largest Contentful Paint

This measures loading time, i.e., how long most content appears on the screen. This can be an image, but also a block of text. A good rating gives users the feeling that the website loads quickly. A slow website can lead to frustration. A good guideline is 2.5 seconds at maximum.

2. FID, First Input Delay

This does measure how long it takes for the website to respond to the first interactions. This can be, for example, tapping a button. A good rating gives the user the feeling that a website reacts quickly to inputs and is responsive. A good guideline for FID is less than 100 milliseconds.

3. CLS, Cumulative Layout Shift

This measures the visual stability of the website. In other words, is anything moving on the screen while it's loading - and how often does it happen? Nothing is more frustrating than attempting to click a button when a slow-loading ad appears at that point.

Pop-ups, ads, or slow-loading fonts, images, or videos usually cause this experience. The lower the CLS value, the better. A good benchmark is less than 0.1 seconds.

Of all SEO tactics, improving the core web vitals of websites has one of the most noticeable effects on search engine rankings. Targeted results require the support of experienced web developers, as is the case with the Löwenstark Digital Group. To get an overview, Google has updated many existing tools for measuring the most important Core Web Vitals.

They provide reports that provide details and insights into the most important metrics and methods:

- Google Search Console
- Page Speed Insights
- Lighthouse
- Web Vitals Extension

With the Page Experience Update rolled out last year, Google put website speed and user experience back into focus. For holistic SEO, one should work on the web vitals to offer visitors the best browsing experience.

Find featured snippet opportunities.

Featured snippets are short snippets that appear at the top of Google results to quickly answer a user's search query. Many SEO experts and marketers also refer to the featured snippet field as "position zero" because it appears above the first search engine result page (SERP).

The content which appears in a featured snippet is automatically extracted from websites in the Google index. Typically, featured snippets appear as definitions, tables, guides, and lists. Sometimes a suitable video is displayed.

Featured snippets are important for your SEO tactics in two ways: On the one hand, they offer the opportunity to get more clicks in the organic search results. According to a study by Ahrefs, the average click-through rate for a featured snippet is 8.6 percent.

This is lower than for the first organic hit but generates more traffic than the lower rankings.

On the other hand, featured snippets increase the number of "click-free searches" where none of the search results are clicked.

That's because the featured snippet often provides the answer the user wants. However, this is only the case for very simple searches. Often, Google only displays a snippet of the text, list, or table, requiring searchers to click on the page itself to see all the information.

In this respect, this search result feature is an optimal opportunity in search engine optimization to generate more organic visibility and, thus, organic traffic and success.

What featured snippets are there?

Text

Text snippets are the most common form of featured snippets. The user does receive a direct, short answer to his question in text form. Google commonly uses definition boxes to answer "w" questions. Google definitions are short and sweet: The average definition of a featured snippet is between 40 and 60 words.

Video

In addition to the text snippets, Google shows video results for certain queries. However, video snippets have little relevance in Germany regarding website traffic potential.

The reason for this is simple: most of all, video snippets are generated by. Results outside of Google's video platform are almost impossible to find. Without an active YouTube channel of your own, video snippets have little meaning.

Lists and Tables

List snippets can often be found for search queries, the answer to which ideally consists of listing several individual points or criteria. Search intentions are, for example, instructions, tutorials, checklists, or lists.

In addition, featured snippets can also appear in table form. These are occasionally displayed when the search query is answered with a set of data. Suitable search intentions for these cases are, for example, information in the form of comparisons, distributions, or figures.

How can I optimize snippets for features?

To increase the chance of your content being included in a featured snippet, you should:

- Identify matching keywords and search queries
- Prioritize: Only try to optimize the pages where you can help users with better content than the competition
- Check the user's search intention and compare it with the answers
- Use easy-to-digest, easy-to-understand language
- Keep your answers short and sweet
- Use high-quality, trustworthy content that best fulfills the search intent and answers correctly and concisely.

Optimize your voice search.

Voice search optimization is one of the most important SEO tactics and trends in online marketing again this year. According to the consulting company, PwC, 59 percent of 18 to 24-year-olds use voice search daily, which is still growing (source: PwC). As its popularity grows, voice search becomes more relevant to businesses. Thanks to the now widespread smart sound boxes such as Google Nest and Amazon Echo, voice search has arrived in the mass market.

With voice search, users can search with their voice instead of typing. This works via an automatic speech recognition system that converts speech signals into text.

Search engines like Google then use the text like a normal search query and match the search query with the correct results. As voice searches become more commonplace, incorporating voice search into SEO strategy is necessary.

User intent

To optimize a website for voice search, the user's search intent must first be clear (informational, navigational, transactional, and commercial). In addition to the written content, the photos and graphics on the website should also be optimized to understand how much content is ranked.

Local searches nearby

Many voice searches are related to a specific location. Searches performed on mobile devices, in particular, tend to be more local and often used by voice. Useful information on local listings (e.g., FAQs, opening hours, or details on available items) help users to get better information about local businesses.

keyword research

Long-tail keywords make sense, especially for voice queries, as they are usually longer than text queries. So it's perfectly fine to use terms that seem voluminous - as long as they seem natural in the content. For example, instead of "pizza dough best recipe," use "What's the best recipe for pizza dough?"

Since a large part of the voice search queries can be traced back to questions, you should also look specifically for question sentences when building the keyword list for your website.

Content for Voice Search

Answering Questions

It pays to research what your target audience is interested in. Answers to these questions can be given in written form on the website.

Use schema markup

Structured data helps Google identify information more easily, and the site will appear for relevant searches.

Specifying your location

Voice-driven searches often contain explanations such as "near me" or "in my area." For example, if your business is based in Cologne, you should add keywords with the city name to your website. This gives the business a better chance of being listed in the results.

Advanced SEO strategies to improve the visibility and sales of Affiliate Marketers

Online positioning has two parts, what we can do on the page and what is done from outside of it. Let's focus first on those actions we can carry out from the e-commerce to improve its SEO.

On-page optimization depends on you since you are the one who controls everything on it. Its objective is to make things easier for Google and index the pages as quickly as possible, classifying them according to your interests. Of course, always remember the importance of the user experience.

Advanced content optimization for SEO

As you already know, content is the basis of positioning. If we talk about advanced SEO techniques, we must remember their optimization. It is necessary to improve the characteristics and other elements of content so that the web page where it is found is better visible than similar ones in search engines.

Optimizing content is essential for any website. With it, it is easier to appear in the search results related to the topic. And how to get it? These are the keys:

- Content quality.
- Identify indexing errors with Google Search Console.
- Choose the keywords well. You can use Google Trends or the Google Ads keyword planning tool.
- Combine different elements in that content, such as texts, images, videos… And structure it appropriately.
- Use link building.
- Make a periodic analysis of the performance of the contents. Thus, you will know which ones are not offering what is expected, and you will be able to improve them.

SEO-optimized URL structure

In addition to the contents of the pages, Google and the other search engines use their URLs to determine if the result matches the user's needs. For that address to be "liked," it must:

- It's easy to read.
- It does not use strange characters.
- It is related to the content of the page.
- Lets you know what that content is about.
- It only uses lowercase characters.
- Does not contain stop words.

If your store is based on a CMS, like WordPress or PrestaShop, you will have no problem making those websites friendly. Plenty of plugins and modules will help you achieve that goal.

But, to optimize the URL structure for search engines, you need to know the parts into which it is divided and take care of each of them:

- The protocol is the first part of a URL. HTTPS is the current preference, showing that the site is secure.
- The domain name must be short and easy to remember.
- A subdomain is a subset of a bigger domain. It appears in the direction between the protocol and the domain name, from which it is separated by a period. It is usually "www," although you can use any word to make a unique web address without changing the domain name. Thus, you can organize your e-commerce.
- The file path corresponds to the exact location of the content search on the web.

To understand it, let's take as an example "https://www.mydomain.com/featured-content," where "https" is the protocol, "www" the subdomain, "mydomain.com" the name, and "featured-content" the destination page.

Using rich snippets to improve visibility in search results

Rich fragments or snippets show additional information thanks to structured data extracted from web pages. Among other data, this information can be displayed as places, user ratings, or profiles of people. The most common rich snippets are:

- The opinions of the users (reviews).
- Upcoming events, including information regarding the event.
- Products, including price, availability, or user reviews. We also can insert a thumbnail image of the article.
- The contact details of a person. This is a feature that LinkedIn is working on.

- The preparation time, level, or general rating of the recipes.
- When looking for a group or a song, the link to listen to it.
- The videos include data such as the insertion date or the authors. We can also get a thumbnail of the video to appear.
- If breadcrumbs are included, we will greatly improve the indexing of the online store in its structure.

Advanced off-page optimization techniques

As we said, in addition to what we can do within the page to improve its positioning, advanced SEO includes what is done outside of it. Using off-page SEO techniques, we will be able to attract visitors to our e-commerce and increase the site's relevance.

Building high-quality, relevant links

Links have always been a fundamental pillar in search engine optimization. Those responsible for Google, for example, have explained several times that if there are quality websites with links to our content, we will increase our page rank. So, do we have to get other sites to link to us? It is somewhat more complicated because of the nuance of "quality." These must be relevant and have related content.

How can I get those links? These are some formulas to achieve it:

- Write a post for another website.
- Create an e-commerce blog on a different domain.
- Ask a relevant website to link to you.
- Analyze where your competition links and look for similar pages to get them to backlink you.
- Generate attractive content that others want to use. Let them do it as long as they link to your store.
- Increase your contacts, participate in forums and blogs, and create content on social networks.

Use of social media to increase brand visibility and reputation

Social networks are also a fundamental tool to improve the positioning of your online store. But is it worth opening a profile and waiting? No, you must have an activity following the following guidelines:

- Take care of the content.
- Post when your audience is online.
- Include the links to your profiles in a visible place in your e-commerce. They should also be easily found if you send a newsletter or blog.
- Includes a call to action (CTA). When you write new content, include a "Follow us on social networks" and links to the web when posting on your profiles.
- If you include questions in your posts, you will increase the responses and engagement.
- Grow your community with contests and giveaways.
- Promote the posts that work best.
- Get into the conversation using the most popular hashtags of the moment.

Advanced analysis and monitoring techniques

One of the great advantages of online sales compared to traditional models is the amount of data we have from the entire process. This analysis has improved in recent years thanks to the many tools that filter information for us, and we can keep only what we consider essential for our business.

Use of advanced data analysis tools

Professionals in the sector and those who are having more success in their online stores point out these models and tools as essential to improving business through data:

- Marketing mix model (MMM). It is a technique based on big data to measure the effectiveness of disseminating content through a specific channel. For example, it tells you if a landing page has performed well.
- Scope, Cost, and Quality (RCQ). Reach, cost, and quality is the way to use structured data. It offers us key information, such as engagement quality, the number of customers we reach, and the cost of each conversion.
- Predictive models allow us to find business opportunities. Also, they facilitate knowing the market share or identifying segments. We will use this data to make decisions quickly and correctly.
- Attribution model. It allows algorithms and rules to manage the resources that will help us convert and sell.
- Time series analysis is a mathematical prediction model that allows you to anticipate trends, seize opportunities of all kinds, and adjust strategies.

Monitoring and control of online reputation

How does online reputation management benefit from monitoring? The new technological tools allow us to know everything about our clients, what they say, think, or demand. As we have already pointed out, this is decisive for improving brand reputation and making strategic decisions. And it is that we can:

- Observe user reactions.
- Satisfy the needs of the public.
- Meet the influencers of the sector and the brand ambassadors.
- Stay alert and anticipate any situation of online reputation crisis that we may suffer.

Trends in SEO and the future of web positioning

Although, as we have already pointed out, SEO positioning consists of improving the user experience and appearing in the first search results, it is necessary to know the trends that will be the protagonists in the coming months.

Effect of SEO on voice marketing and image search

Voice recognition services, increasingly used, have affected the way of doing SEO. Since Siri appeared, the figures have only increased, due to the arrival, in addition, to of others, such as **Google Assistant or Alexa.**

Therefore, if users have changed their way of making queries, we must adapt and position ourselves for voice searches. Now, users have stopped entering phrases made up of keywords into the Google search engine. They have conversations with their devices that turn into searches.

And how to be the first of those results? Working our SEO with more natural keywords that can be used within the conversation.

Emerging trends in SEO and how to take advantage of them

SEO professionals point out that, in the coming months, it will be important to focus on :

- Clip markup and seek markup to improve the positioning of videos.
- Increased traffic through image searches.
- Queries based on complex questions.
- Core web vitals.
- Being in position 1 is no longer the most important thing.
- Passage indexing.
- Use new traffic sources like Google News and Google Discover.
- Google EAT sets the new rules of SEO.
- It is important to think about search intent to get leads and sales.
- Positioning in Amazon, local SEO, and the Google company profile.
- Know the role of artificial intelligence in SEO.

10 SEO Tips for Better Affiliate Websites

Affiliate websites are a good source of income. However, only if you find a lucrative niche on the one hand and pass the others with good search engine optimization (SEO) on the other. In this article, we've rounded up ten SEO tips for your affiliate websites.

Hard to believe, but even today, new niches still want to be filled. For example, many business models that used to take place offline are currently migrating to the Internet. A good chance to make money with affiliate marketing. In the age of content marketing, however, this means that the user demands added value for the product offer. He would like to obtain comprehensive information before making a purchase. Conversely, more than online listing offers is needed - affiliate websites must become their brands to convince and retain users.

These ten tips make it easier to get started in the affiliate business:

1. Keyword Targeting: Informational vs. Commercial Keywords

Before you make any money, visitors need to find your website or blog. Users who come via organic search convert better.

The key to more users is the right keywords. Most bloggers only do keyword research after writing their articles, or their keywords have difficulty asserting themselves against the strong competition. If you want to make money with your affiliate website, you must approach it systematically.

There are two types of keywords:

- Informational keywords (e.g., "What is affiliate marketing?")
- Commercial keywords ("best web hosting")

Make sure you use the right combination of informational and commercial keywords. When someone clicks on the informational keywords, they're not ready to buy, as opposed to commercial intent for keywords like "best hosting."

2. People don't buy online from strangers.

The reason it's important that you also use informational keywords is that website visitors don't just buy from strangers. Your readers trust you when you write blog articles that answer important user questions. That doesn't mean you shouldn't use commercial keywords – it's all in the mix!

Use informative keywords to increase traffic. You can only make money as an affiliate marketer if you have much traffic on your site. That's why using the right informational keywords related to your affiliate products is important.

With the commercial keywords, you make money. The best keyword combinations in this context are "test" or "evaluation." However, never write a product review if you have not used the product before. Use it for some time and only rate it if satisfied.

Summarized again:

- Informative keywords will help you increase your traffic.
- Commercial keywords will help you increase your sales.

3. SEO tools for affiliate websites

Three SEO tools will help you do better SEO for your affiliate website.

SEMrush: SEMrush helps you spy on your competitors. Not only is it helpful for finding your competitor's top keywords, but it will also help you find the right affiliate products for each niche. It's an all-around SEO tool that every affiliate marketer should use.

Google Keyword Planner: Free tool marketers use to find good keywords. Proceed to sign in to your Google AdWords account, and you will find many keyword suggestions by typing in your favorite keywords.

Long Tail Pro: You should use more long-tail keywords to increase traffic. Finding long-tail keywords is easy with LongTailPro. It's a keyword research tool that helps you find the most profitable long-tail keywords for any industry.

4. Affiliate Website SEO: Dos & Don'ts

If you plan to make more money from affiliate marketing, you should know the dos and don'ts of affiliate marketing:

DOS:

Start Small and Get Better Over Time: Most beginners want to make big money immediately. That does not work. Get the skills you need to sell first. Generating a decent income from affiliate marketing takes at least a year.

Build an Email List: The list is the surefire way to build trust with your blog audience. If it trusts you, it will be easier to sell your products. But ensure to provide information in the newsletter and write as little as possible about products - most about the highlights.

Don'ts:

Don't choose a broad niche: Beginners in affiliate marketing usually promote several products on their blog. But you won't make more money the more products you promote. That's not how affiliate marketing works. You better pick a small niche and focus on being good there. You make more money by promoting fewer and more targeted products.

Only promote products you like: This is beginners' most common mistake. Never advertise a product you don't use. Because that won't buy your blog audience, and your affiliate marketing will only be successful in the short run.

5. Find a potent niche.

Before you decide on a domain, research what niche you want to serve in the future. If it is a tangible product, it is worth combining the product with the keyword "test." Ensure that the main keyword combination has at least a search volume of 10,000. What sounds like a lot is due to the long customer journey that a user goes through. There are many ways to jump off. Another tip: high-priced products are worth much more because you have to sell less.

6. Competition stimulates business

It is usually said that if the keyword has much competition, it will be harder to gain a foothold. It's interesting to change your point of view here: when Brigitte, Elle, and Co. report on a topic at the top of the list, it first shows that there is interest. As long as there aren't already some niche sites out there, it's all good. With good SEO, niche sites quickly overtake the big players because they usually only have a few articles on the subject up their sleeves. If there are niche sites on the topic, you should consider using other keywords or promoting other products.

7. You must use these WordPress plugins for affiliate marketing!
   • Yoast SEO
   • Amazon Simple Admin
   • Yoast Google Analytics
   • Advanced Custom Fields

WordPress offers a variety of plugins and is one of the most commonly used content management softwares due to its size. A popular affiliate theme is Affiliseo, with many features that make affiliating easy from the start.

8. Don't overdo it with on-page optimization!

Hard to believe, but you can tweak too much:

- Over-optimized titles: Provide a readable and, most importantly, motivating title. What's the use of keyword-packed heads if nobody wants to read them?
- Keyword Density: Lots has changed in the last few years. The motto is: less is more. Use a long-tail keyword that you vary creatively.
- Similar Pages: Make sure your affiliate website is unique. If it resembles other sites, Google will penalize you.
- Internal linking: Two to three internal links are helpful for readers. With more, it will not only be too much for them but also for Google. Therefore, you should rely on something other than automatic linking.

9. Make sure to do the off-page optimization!

You can also do some things better than others off-page:

- Backlinks: Although backlinking has lost its importance, it is still important. However, you should carefully set only a few backlinks quickly or just let them refer to your home page.
- Link texts: When it comes to anchor texts, ensure you don't just use the main keyword.
- Suspicious link sources: In addition, backlinks only come from high-quality sites. It is best only to use the directory pages that were common in the past.

10. Content and always content

Content, content, content – what applies to online marketing also applies to affiliate websites. Only those who offer high-quality content will convince their visitors.

Here are a few more tips to optimize your affiliate content:

- Use a static page as your homepage in WordPress. So you can customize them with the best items.
- Think of an attractive layout and clear formatting with paragraphs, headings, and subheadings.
- Use images, video, and audio.
- Articles should be around 800+ words long.

Chapter 2: Crafting an Affiliate Email Marketing Funnel

How to create an effective affiliate marketing funnel

Affiliate marketing generates billions of dollars by helping others. Having the opportunity to become an affiliate, you can monetize well.

The problem is that it's more than just driving traffic to a site or offering a sale.

An affiliate funnel must be mapped and followed to increase conversions and sales. You have to "sell" the consumer, requiring an affiliate marketing funnel that will push the potential lead to action.

What is an affiliate marketing funnel?

The affiliate marketing funnel is the path a consumer or person interested in a product or service takes from exposure to purchase. A typical marketing funnel goes through four main stages:

The introduction is the first step in the sales funnel that determines what happens when a prospect first enters the funnel. This could be a potential customer who clicks on a link from social media, an e-book, an article, or another link. This is how you funnel traffic and get people interested.

Interest is the next part of the funnel, including how you educate the prospect. These may be articles teaching the reader how to solve their problems. If a user has signed up for a series of emails, you can send multiple emails to build trust and interest before making a sale.

The decision is difficult because you have to "sell" a potential client. Here you have a potential buyer landing on a sales page, where the funnel includes testimonials, reviews, and further information that aims to get a potential buyer to buy your offer. There are many competitors, and they will also try to sell. They'll go elsewhere if you don't grab the customer's attention.

Action is the last step in the marketing funnel, including a lead action. An action can be a subscription to a newsletter, a product purchase, or an action you have included as a target in a campaign.

The affiliate funnel often narrows down and can go through three stages, depending on the type of offer you plan to promote. Sales funnels can be as easy as that if it's enough for your target audience to make a decision and make a purchase:

Subscription (opt-in) or sale page, where the affiliate funnel leads to the landing page. A person can purchase or subscribe to a newsletter if you're trying to get someone to register for your mailing list or offer something for free, like emailing a PDF or email guide.

The page after the subscription (Thank you page), on which you thank the person for his action. Even an affiliate company can do this.

If you are planning to start your affiliate funnel from the subscription page, try to promote offers on the Thank You page. This is a fantastic way to convert social traffic or potential buyers just trying to expand their knowledge and better understand their needs.

Why an affiliate marketing funnel?

You are probably wondering why an affiliate funnel is a good choice for you. If you make sales and have many conversions, your funnel can be perfectly optimized for your audience. But let's say you only convert 1% of your traffic.

A funnel that is optimized or modified to match the needs of your prospects better can increase CR by up to 2%.

You will make twice as many sales and get twice as much income from the same amount of traffic. Marketers have been using sales funnels for a long time because they work so well.

Many affiliates make the mistake of believing that their sales are good and that they are happy with the money they are making. But big companies, even Amazon, optimize their funnel because they know they can squeeze even more money out of consumers.

You want to increase sales, and your funnel can do it.

A proper funnel is one with a CR of 1-5%.

How to create an affiliate funnel?

If you need to learn how to create your funnel, you can follow the steps above to optimize it. Some many different products and technologies can also help in this process:

A/B testing to determine which is the landing page that converts the best.

Studying the target audience to determine various aspects of your funnel and where a potential customer may be in it.

Optimization of banners, posts, or traffic generation methods for different funnels or parts of the funnel.

Start by figuring out what your funnel will look like depending on how you generate traffic. Let's say your offer can solve a problem, so you can sit down and explore the potential client's pain points.

These moments can bring a potential client to your site, or you can create content or e-books to help educate and educate potential clients.

As an affiliate marketer, you should always optimize your site and funnel. When you add new offers, add them to the funnel. A funnel can be as complex or as simple as possible.

By learning the basics, you will become more successful.

Create an affiliate marketing funnel in 5 steps.

If you have already dealt with affiliate marketing or passive income, you will have heard of them: affiliate marketing funnels.

- But what exactly are these affiliate funnels?
- And why are they not only incredibly important for the success of your business but also relieve you of much work in the long run?
- What is an affiliate marketing funnel?

As the name suggests, an affiliate funnel is a "sales funnel" for affiliate marketing.

Imagine a way to take your website visitors by hand and guide them step-by-step to your affiliate product.

The funnel, i.e., "funnel," symbolizes the path of the visitors who make a purchase decision at the end of the path - i.e., click on your affiliate link, place an order, and contribute to the conversion rate.

The classic model of a sales funnel consists of 4 phases. The awareness stage, i.e., the awareness phase where a potential customer has a need; the interest stage, where that customer develops an interest in your product; the desire stage, i.e., the phase of purchase intention; and the action phase, where a purchase is completed.

This model can also be applied to affiliate marketing. You, as an affiliate partner, come into play, especially in phases 2-3, where it's really about convincing customers of the affiliate products and guiding them over to phase 4 so that you get your commission.

An important tool in affiliate marketing

The funnel is the largest at the beginning. It gets narrower and narrower towards the end as the focus on your goal, i.e., the conversion from website visitor to customer, increases.

Comparable to a camera that you sharpen with each step within the funnel.

These funnels are the perfect strategy to make sure you are directing your visitors to your product.

In practice, an affiliate funnel can be set up effectively with simple means and is now part of affiliate marketing like a hammer in a toolbox.

Note: The GetResponse Conversion Funnel feature allows you to tailor your marketing efforts to each stage of your affiliate marketing funnel with a visual funnel planner.

What does an affiliate marketing funnel look like?: Stages & how it works

You have probably already come across funnels on the internet:

Your search for a topic using your favorite search engine, maybe you want to find a solution to a problem (phase 1: awareness), and you end up with an interesting blog article that addresses exactly your question (phase 2: interest).

Then at the end of the article, you will find out that the author is offering a free eBook - suitable for your topic! (Stage 3: Purchase Intent). Ultimately, you download the ebook (phase 4: conversion/purchase).

But what does all this look like in affiliate marketing? Here is an example of what an affiliate marketing funnel might look like for niche sites:

Phase 1: The affiliate marketing funnel begins, and a need is developed

It all starts with a customer's need or problem. Be it finding the right dating app, wanting to take an online language course, or subscribing to Kochboxen.

The customer googles his needs and finds out that there are different suppliers for his preferred product. This is how he gets to a comparison, niche, or affiliate site.

Therefore, Your site should be easy to find to intercept and forward potential customers.

Phase 2: Develop interest on the niche side

Now it is up to you and your side to inform the customer as best as possible about the general topic, your affiliate partners, and their offer. Not only so that they develop buying interest but also so that they can make the best decision for themselves.

This is where your content comes in, especially top and middle-of-the-funnel content that gives your website visitors enough information.

Phase 3: Develop purchase intent & decide on an affiliate

Now it is really important to help the customer with his decision. That means you should show the advantages of your affiliate partners and leave no questions about their offer unanswered. This happens primarily through bottom-of-the-funnel content, e.g., articles or reviews.

Upon completing this phase, the customer has chosen an affiliate and then clicks on the affiliate link, where they are redirected to your affiliate's sales page or sign-up page.

Phase 4: The Sales Page

Now it's up to your partner to close the affiliate funnel. This includes a functioning sales or registration page.

Once customers sign up and verify their email address, they're taken to the bottom of the funnel.

This is where the affiliate funnel ends. However, that doesn't mean the buyer cycle is over - the Thank You page isn't just a way to say thank you for your interest:

In the best-case scenario, the customer is offered something – usually a reduced product related to the website's topic or the article.

Less is more

So you see, an affiliate marketing funnel can be simple.

On the contrary – less is more.

With your affiliate marketing strategies, focus on providing your website visitor with added value at every step.

It starts with the landing page or your blog article.

It is important that every visitor to your website feels valued at every stage of your affiliate funnel and knows exactly why they should click on the affiliate link at the end. So make sure to make your site spammy, but inform your customers in detail and honestly.

Be authentic

Suppose you authentically convey why you recommend this product from your affiliate partner to your website visitor. In that case, the chance of a conversion is much higher than if you place the offer.

Your customers gain trust in you and are more willing to visit your website again or read your newsletter.

Affiliate marketing is not only fun for you but also your customers.

Trip Wire Offer

The free offers at the beginning of an affiliate funnel are called "trip wire" offers. For example, if you lure people into your affiliate funnel with a free e-book or by subscribing to a newsletter.

The visitor of your affiliate website ends up in the "trip wire" of the path you have carefully planned for your target product at the end of the funnel.

Take your customers by the hand.

A perhaps more friendly idea is to take your website visitor by the hand – you are the "guide" and want to help your potential customer find the best way to your product.

How to build an affiliate funnel (step by step)

Creating an affiliate funnel takes just a few simple steps and will improve communication and engagement with your potential customers.

5 steps to a successful affiliate marketing funnel:

1. Generate traffic:

You can attract people to your site with paid ads, SEO blog posts, or social media. Know your audience, then create tailored content that brings them to your site.

2. Convert the traffic: Think about how to drive the collected traffic to an opt-in. This can be with a free offer, a discount, a download, or via webinar. Make your offer interesting enough that they develop an interest in buying it.
3. Leverage buying interest & direct customers to the sales page: Give your customers everything they need to make a purchase decision. Inform them about the offer, integrate social proof, and compare competing offers.
4. Create the sales page: Direct them to an attractive sales page. This again contains all the information about the offer, such as a registration form, an order form, and a CTA that completes the conversion. From there, customers can place the order.
5. Create the thank you page: This is perhaps the most underestimated page of your funnel - on this landing page, you thank your visitor for their interest and trust and, at the same time, draw their attention to an additional offer that you can also advertise with an affiliate link or forward the visitor to your sales funnel.

Complete Guide to Email Marketing for Affiliates: learn the best practices to create, manage and optimize your campaigns

Email marketing is one of the best alternatives for affiliates who want to maximize their income.

Email does continue to be an effective marketing channel valued by professionals, managers, and purchasing influencers.

However, having so many platforms and communication networks, some affiliates wonder: what is the best way to capture leads and encourage their engagement until the final conversion?

Although the ideal is to carry out a holistic strategy, combining social networks and different content formats, such as podcasts, blogs, and videos, in this chapter, my mission is to show you the advantages of email marketing for affiliate campaigns.

I will also bring you the most precise tactics to apply the method and tips so that you start structuring your emails on the right foot. Accompany me!

Why should affiliates have an email marketing strategy?

Mailing campaigns represent a powerful process to improve the cost-benefit ratio of your initiatives as an affiliate.

Today, empirical evidence makes it clear that email marketing is the digital channel that generates the highest ROI. Generally, every dollar invested returns between $38 and $42 in profit.

In affiliate marketing strategies, email becomes interesting due to its scalability and recurrence. Over time, you can build your email list with high-converting forms and landing pages.

At the same time, you send them messages of different types to understand their preferences and segment them more and more, automating your email campaigns to obtain more openings, clicks, and future sales.

It is not so easy to measure the ROI of affiliate marketing because the income depends on several factors, such as:

- the level of specialized knowledge you have acquired,
- the commercial and promotional tactics that you apply to share your links;
- and the model of commissions that you receive in different affiliate programs.
- But there is a fundamental difference between email marketing and other media concerning the volume of expenses it requires.

While ad campaigns, for example, depend on a more aggressive initial investment, the mailing structure is cheaper and more organic.

With a multifunctional email marketing platform like GetResponse, you can send up to 2,500 emails monthly and create forms to attract new recipients without paying anything.

To make your mailings more sophisticated over time, you can sign up for a paid plan for more advanced list segmentation and campaign automation features. It is a worthwhile investment because you concentrate all your activity on a single platform.

After putting together your entire operation in it, you have to explore the creativity to write the texts of each email, which will change according to the objective you assign to it.

The process is also speeded up by the ease of using newsletter templates and other emails, which you can customize to suit each campaign.

Finally, there are many opportunities for experimentation in email marketing, which allow you to optimize the results.

In GetResponse, you can, for example, A/B test various mail subjects and messages to see which one generates the most interactions.

Email marketing or social networks: in which channel should we invest more?

Many affiliates put almost all of their efforts into ads and social media posts but could use a balance with email marketing.

The key question you should ask yourself is: what would I do if a social network went down or went bankrupt?

You could continue generating sales only if you were the actual manager of your contact base rather than a big tech like Twitter, Google, or Meta.

Such a scenario makes us reflect on the decision to go fully into social networks and consider email marketing as the foundation of our strategy.

And what to do if one-day GetResponse or another Email Marketing platform ceases? You keep control of your contacts because you can export them to offline files from those tools.

In any case, this does not mean that you cannot or that it is not convenient for you to use the networks because they are channels with a wide audience and are capable of generating new contacts for your email marketing lists with well-targeted ads.

4 interesting types of email marketing for affiliates

Mailing is a fairly flexible communication model. Therefore, you can structure your mailings in different formats, which can be useful if you act as an affiliate.

The idea is to integrate them to expand your possibilities and cover all the conversion funnel stages since some emails will be more informative. Others will be more directed toward a purchase objective.

Let's take a quick look at some types of campaigns you can explore.

1. Invitations, calendars, and promotions

Using emails to send news, launches, or events is a great way to segment your contacts and understand their interests. Thus, you will build a more mature and active audience base, which will generate sales in the long term.

Work as an affiliate of a marketplace like Amazon, for example. You can share links to new products regularly, providing information about their impact on the market and competitive advantages.

Thus, your contacts will always be aware of the news that you share to make a purchase when they feel ready.

You can share specific links to receive direct commissions by building your segmented lead lists.

The interaction rate will depend on the relationship between the contacts' preferences and the offers you share.

2. Newsletter

The newsletter is one of the main email marketing formats. It works as a selection of news and useful content for contacts, helping to form a true community around the brand that sends it.

Affiliates often create newsletters to further their engagement with recipients, especially when they provide them with specialized knowledge.

Consequently, it is a tactic that goes beyond direct sales. By offering emails with relevant insights and advice, you can keep your readers engaged and encourage them to follow your posts.

In addition, it is an excellent channel to educate your contacts and conquer them for your ability. By sharing messages with different levels of depth and topics, you will have much information about the characteristics and needs of those who read you.

Another advantage is the ease of the conversion process to a newsletter. With a simple online contact form, you can capture the email address of your users and grow your list instantly.

At GetResponse, you will find ideal newsletter templates for your strategy; they are all free and work automatically on mobile devices or computers.

3. Lead nurturing

Especially for affiliates, this strategy always stands out for the good results it generates. With the automation of email sequences, you create a flow of messages with high conversion potential.

As its very name suggests, lead nurturing emails are about increasing the level of knowledge and maturity of the contract, thus preparing them to buy at the right time.

In short, you create content such as blog articles, ebooks, podcasts, and videos to show how the solution you are selling helps eliminate a specific problem.

For example, if you offer an online course, you can automate a series of lead-nurturing emails, each containing snippets of the points you present in your classes.

GetResponse has autoresponders to schedule automatic responses on certain dates based on user actions on your website. For example, when they sign up to receive your newsletter or register for one of your webinars.

You can also create lead nurturing flows with customizable templates automatically activated to educate and warm up contacts.

We have the following specific workflows for affiliate campaigns:

- Online course promotion;

- affiliate online course;
- webinar promotion;
- cross-selling for affiliates;
- affiliate welcome message;
- assignment of engagement tags;
- attribution of activity points for contacts.

4. Seasonal Email

These emails are tied to specific dates important to your strategy or the market in general. Today, many content creators consider viral trends and topics to provide relevant insights.

Taking advantage of these windows of opportunity, in which the minds of your contacts are already prepared to receive information on the subject, you can approach them with your instructions, which will be the most precise for the occasion.

It's also a great tactic for online store affiliates because there are many business dates to explore, like Christmas, Black Friday, or Easter.

4 keys to building your email marketing campaign as an affiliate

The process is simple; there are clear steps and good practices that you can follow to improve your email marketing metrics.

However, it should be noted that the results and liquid commissions depend on the closeness you can establish with your contacts, the credibility they see in your communication, and the quality of the segmentation you attribute to your recipient lists.

To overcome such challenges, choosing the right email marketing platform is essential. Let's look at each stage in more detail so you can put your plan into action.

1. Think about every aspect of your campaign.

One of the first steps is defining your person, the ideal contact profile you want to address with your messages.

Put yourself in their shoes to understand their needs and what concepts you have to teach them so they want to buy what you offer, be it a product, service, or material.

You must complete all stages of the conversion funnel because your contacts are at different times in the purchase process, and for each one, there is a more appropriate type of email.

Diversify your strategy, creating informative campaigns with newsletters, others to share more advanced materials and transmit your knowledge, others to promote your launches, and, finally, commercial messages to make your sales.

Integrate them, conditioning the sending of one to the results of another. For example, if one of your newsletter topics generated more opens and clicks than usual, consider doing an event or ebook with a similar proposition to expand performance in the long run.

2. Use GetResponse

GetResponse is the leading email marketing solution on the market and today stands out for its affiliate-specific resources that maximize engagement and sales results.

With a generous free plan and cheap contracting options, our platform stands out for having various solutions to structure your campaigns, such as:

- tool to create landing pages;
- pop-up windows to attract new subscribers;

- artificial intelligence website builder (with affiliate website templates);
- platform to create and present webinars;
- automated conversion funnels, which I just mentioned;
- AI email generator;

and many more.

Indeed, GetResponse also has an attractive affiliate program, offering recurring commissions of 33% per month or one-time payments of $100. Later we will explain it fully. Still pending!

3.   Create a lead capture plan.

Lead generation can be a complex task. Here, you can also create different entry doors for your contacts, taking advantage of the power of content marketing to arouse their interest.

An accurate tactic is to create lead magnets or rich materials that you can offer the user at no cost in exchange for their data on landing pages or forms. Some examples are ebooks, webinars, and spreadsheets.

Then, you wait to consolidate a base or make announcements to push your content to interested profiles.

Try different types of forms to capture information from the users of your website.

Use more than just landing pages with several data fields. Sometimes it is best to start with a form that only asks for the user's email address, adding them as subscribers to your newsletter list and converting them into leads at another time.

Another essential point is compliance with data protection regulations, guaranteeing that all contacts are permitted to receive your messages, preventing your email from being considered spam, and protecting your recipients from malicious emails.

4.   Take the first shot and correct what is necessary.

Email marketing is a strategy you can constantly refine to maximize click-through, open, and conversion rates.

After the first delivery, look for relevant insights by analyzing the map of user interactions in your message, perform A/B tests to discover the best version of your content, experiment with shooting at different times and days of the week, etc.

All these changes depend on permanent monitoring. Therefore, manage your campaigns from a growth hacking perspective, identifying small factors that you can implement in the following ones to obtain better results.

Suppose you are interested in finding reference data for your strategy. In that case, I recommend reading our email marketing benchmark, which provides information on the average performance of emails in different countries and market segments.

What email marketing KPIs should you analyze as an affiliate?

KPIs (Key Performance Indicators) are valuable sources of information for affiliates because they indicate optimization points for future campaigns.

Undoubtedly, such analysis must be part of your email process. But many metrics are available, and some are less important than others. So let's see the ones you must follow to evaluate your performance.

- Open rates

This indicator refers to the percentage of recipients who clicked on the emails you sent to open them.

Today, an email with more than 20% opening is considered efficient, while a regular email usually has between 10% and 20% opening.

The email subject line is crucial in determining your numbers on this metric and the accompanying preview text.

- Click-through rate per email open.

Here we have an excellent resource to measure the engagement in your emails, which varies greatly depending on the objective of the email and its entire composition (content, design, and call to action).

For example, in a newsletter or promotional email, you want the click-through rate higher than in a transactional email because this is generally only sent to inform the user about a completed action.

The number of links you use also greatly influences this indicator. If you include your personalized affiliate link at various points in the message, with texts like "click here" or "buy my products now," you can annoy the reader and hurt your click-through rate.

- Cancellation rate

The unsubscribe rate indicates the number of recipients who no longer want to receive your emails.

It is a metric that is quite susceptible to the strategic changes you make, such as a drastic increase in the number of emails or a reduction in the quality of the content.

For example, if you made template changes without an A/B test to justify them. If contacts aren't very fond of your new version, the rate of requests to cancel shipments can grow significantly.

- Spam Complaint Rate

Email providers frequently ignore spam and complicate your relationship with the contact base. When you get to a very high level of spam, your communication can be invasive.

If this problem happens to you, it is convenient to try some factors to solve it, such as avoiding the excessive use of images or guaranteeing the security of the links you share to avoid the frustration of the contacts.

These metrics are available on GetResponse's email marketing dashboards, which update in real-time and provide a clear view of your performance on each one.

Mega Guide to create a funnel or conversion funnel that does convert

A funnel is the methodology used to define and plan a user's steps to meet one or more objectives.

Following the success of my automation guide, let's talk about what a conversion funnel or funnel is, but above all, to share my experience in recent years creating funnels that do convert. I have always said that if I were to launch my blog again, the first thing I would do would be capture leads, and the second thing would be to create funnels. Both strategies have allowed me to reach more people and increase my conversions.

Are you ready to dive into the fantastic world of funnels?

I will begin with the basics, then I will show you real examples of funnels that you can apply to your business, and I will show you how you can measure the results of your funnels.

A funnel is the methodology used to define and plan a user's steps to meet one or more objectives.

Why do we use conversion funnels?

We use funnels for different reasons, but the most important thing is that you are aware that a funnel is about planning and conversions. Below I will provide you with other reasons why you should use a funnel with your business:

You reduce the steps a user takes to become a lead or customer, which means you will get results quickly.

You turn your website into a conversion system because you optimize everything and generate funnels for recruitment and online sales.

You only communicate with interested (qualified) users and leave out mass marketing.

You can offer unique offers and discounts to users interested in your product or service.

You optimize your investment in content, public relations, paid advertising, and Email Marketing.

With the funnels, we can better understand the needs of our customers and cultivate our relationship with them in a more efficient and personalized way.

Are the funnels only for professionals, or do they also work for companies?

Many professionals like me (bloggers and business people) have been using funnels for years, which may be why this technique is only for professionals. Still, in reality, the funnels or conversion funnels are for any business:

- What attracts new traffic
- What do you need to capture new leads?
- who sells products, who sells services
- You want to sell more to your current customers

With my consultancy Convert, we have worked on automation and funnels for many clients in different areas:

With an events company, we designed and implemented funnels to boost and automate the sales of a face-to-face event aimed at managers. Some funnels were connected to the Call Center to close sales of qualified leads.

With a health client, we designed funnels to convert social media fans into affiliates.

With professionals who sell services and online courses, we have designed funnels to launch products or services and sell on autopilot.

With a Real-State company in the United States, we design funnels to convert attendees of face-to-face events into customers of a digital product and to sell online courses automatically and with webinars.

The reality is that funnels are for any professional or business that wants to convert more into digital media.

Ingredients to create funnels that do convert

To create a good funnel or conversion funnel, you will need the following:

Organic or paid traffic (Facebook Ads, Twitter, Adwords, YouTube, etc.). You must create and optimize content (SEO) or invest in advertising campaigns on search engines and social networks.

Email Marketing automation tools such as ClickFunnels, Benchmark Email, GetResponse, InfusionSoft, or Active Campaign configure the emails of your funnel.

Landing pages of information, sale, recruitment, payment, and thanks. If it is only for landing pages, I recommend Leadpages, although I leave this topic with many powerful tools to create landing pages.

Tools like LeadsBridge to create Facebook audiences automatically; In this way, you will be able to carry out remarketing campaigns and close more sales. Below I show you how it works.

Tools to sell online, such as Thrive Cart, SamCart, SendOwl, Gumroad, or Selz.

Tools to host your content if you sell online courses. You can use WordPress templates, membership sites like Memberpress or Memberium, or free platforms like Hotmart.

Convey your message with the best copy. To create a good copy, you must know the writing techniques my friends Maïder and Lupe teach in their blogs and your audience's needs well. That is why it is always recommended to do mini-surveys in our database to find out what words they use and their problems. We then use that information to create our attraction, cultivation, and sales copy.

Do you want to use a single tool to create funnels instead of 5 or 7?

ClickFunnels is a great option to save money and has several funnel options on a single platform:

Creation of all kinds of landing pages

A payment gateway that connects with your Stripe and Paypal

Email tools for automation

Automated webinars in Evergreen (it is NOT a platform like WebinarJam to broadcast live, but it is for already recorded webinars or to embed a direct video from FB or Youtube).

advanced metrics

Membership sites to host your online courses or info products

You can create your account for FREE and for 14 days to try creating your first funnels.

Types of funnels and examples

We can implement different funnels in our business; I classify them into three categories. However, I confess we have funnels in my business and projects so long that they group the three categories. I will show you an example with the infographic below.

A. Lead capture funnels

Lead capture involves converting a fan, page visitor, or user who views an ad into our lead (potential customer). In this short funnel, we attract users who leave us their data in exchange for a gift that we make. Example: Subscribe and download my book for free.

As you will see in the image below, with this funnel, users of social networks, visitors to our website, and users of ads will enter the funnel when they leave their data on our recruitment landing page. Once they leave their data, they go to a thank you landing page and will receive an email with the download of what we promised them.

B. Lead nurturing funnels

We use the cultivation of leads to improve the relationship with our potential clients, but above all, to educate them, give them gifts, and contribute to them before selling. If the users in this process show interest, we pass them on to the online sale.

I'm tagging the users who show interest in the gifts I'm giving them. In this way, I can group the interested users and avoid trying to sell or doing it the same way to ALL the new leads that entered.

C. Online sales funnels

Online sales funnels should start with users interested during lead nurturing campaigns.

As you will see in the example below, the funnel begins with the users of a certain tag and with a sales email. In this email, you need to offer an interesting offer (discounts, 2×1, etc.).

If the pre-qualified users are interested, they will go to the Sales Page and the payment page to purchase and receive the welcome email and purchase confirmation.

The cool thing about this funnel is that we do automatic remarketing to users who have shown interest and have yet to purchase.

D. Remarketing in Facebook Ads with a sales funnel

To go deeper into remarketing, I have chosen to share the real data of a campaign I did. The first important thing is that we review what you have to do remarketing with a funnel:

A tool to create Facebook custom audiences like LeadsBridge or Zapier.

A Facebook Ads campaign that is set up for the paid product audience and has ads and custom copy. Remember to exclude customers who have your product tag in these campaigns.

I sent a sales email with a Yes, I want to automate my business button. This button brings to a Sales Page to promote my funnels and automation workshop. Users who click on this link will be affected by remarketing in two different ways.

Remarketing in Facebook Ads. It automatically clicks, and an audience is created with LeadBridge, and in this way, these users will see ads on Facebook to buy the product.

Email remarketing. By segmenting users interested in buying, we can send them reminder emails only.

The remarketing action on Facebook generated brutal results for us.

We invest 82.57 euros.

We generated $3,589 selling the course

Net income would be 3506.43 (3589 − 82.57)

Each sale cost us €2.2

As you will see, we must include remarketing actions in our funnels to sell more. If I had not done this campaign, I would have stopped earning 3 thousand dollars.

The overall takeaway from this remarketing campaign is that I have to get more interested leads to close more sales with remarketing because the cost is ridiculous. The funnels' main objective is to have many leads that enter so that our final conversions increase.

E.   Up-sell to new clients

Why limit yourself to one sale if you can generate more income from just one customer?

Up-sell campaigns allow us to sell related products or services to customers. There are two ways to up-sell:

Up-sell with landing pages. Instead of taking customers who have just purchased to a thank you page, we take them to a landing page with an exclusive offer.

Up-sell with emails. We let a few days pass and propose an irresistible offer 3-5 days after a user purchases.

From experience, the first converts more, but in reality, we can use both, and I will show you in the next funnel.

As you will see, we offer an OTO (one-time offer) to users immediately after the purchase, although later by email and after 4 days, we send them the offer again. If they click, we send them a second and final reminder email.

Add an evergreen counter (Deadline Funnel) to put more pressure.

F.   The Mega Funnel: 4 funnels in 1

As I told you before, with my project, I have mega funnels; If we put together the previous examples and add some technical details, the mega funnel would look like the one I show you in the infographic below.

Important metrics for funnels

We can use many metrics to measure our funnels' effectiveness; I recommend the following.

- Lead attraction metrics
- ad reach
- CTR on ads
- Number of ad clicks
- CPA (Cost per action), CPL (Cost per lead), CPV (Cost per sale) through ads
- Number of leads captured
- CTR on the capture page
- Number of confirmed leads

Lead nurturing metrics

Average email open rate

Download lead magnets

CTR in emails

Metrics for online sales

number of sales

Total revenues

Average CPV (cost of each sale)

Number of visits to the sales page

CTR sales page

sales page conversion %

Number of visits to the payment page

Checkout Page Conversion %

% conversions per bump

% returns

EPC

A practical example of how to measure the results of a funnel

I want to share a practical example to help you calculate the results of your funnel.

Imagine that you launch a Facebook Ads campaign to capture leads that will enter a funnel to sell a $97 product.

Your results would be the following:

- Investment in Facebook Ads = 200 dollars
- Number of clicks on the ad (these clicks went to your sales page) = 3000
- Number of leads captured = 800
- Number of visits on the payment page = 400
- Number of sales generated = 65
- Generated revenue = $6,305 Results with powerful formulas and KPIs⇨ CPC (Cost Per Click) | 200 (investment) / 3000 (clicks) = $0.06
- CPL (Cost per lead) | 200 (investment) / 800 (leads) = $0.25
- CPV (Cost Per Sale) |200 (investment) / 65 (sales) = $3.07
- % conversion on checkout page | 65 (sales) / 400 (visits) *100 = 16.25%
- EPC (Earnings Per Click) | 6,305 (revenues) / 3,000 (clicks) = $2.10
- ROI (Return on Investment) | 6305 (revenue) − 200 (investment) * 100 / 200 (investment) = 3052.5% ROI As you will see, these last metrics are decisive for making decisions.

What no one tells you about funnels

To conclude this article, I want to share some anecdotes about funnels and marketing automation.

The first version of your funnel rarely works how you want, and sometimes it only works.

You can NOT limit yourself to a single funnel; if you have several, you can experiment and get results quickly.

Creating funnels requires a triple investment: time, tools, and investment in advertising or SEO.

Funnels are NOT just for paid traffic campaigns. I have been implementing funnels at vilmanunez.com for years, and they only work with organic traffic.

A funnel must have remarketing to be complete. With remarketing, you can close more sales without being aggressive with emails.

The perfect funnel does not exist. If you have a funnel that works, you must optimize it and constantly change it. I have friends who have been selling the same product with a single funnel that they have been optimizing for years.

Chapter 3: Influencer Marketing and Partnerships

"We can do something with influencers" or "How does it work with these influencers?" are just two of many similar statements that were heard particularly frequently in the last year. But what at first glance doesn't seem much different from working with content publishers requires significantly more communication and, in some places, a corresponding instinct. This series presents what influencer marketing in affiliates means, how to acquire potential influencers, and how to work with them.

Mutual respect for people, brands, and goals is a basic requirement for successful cooperation with influencers. Companies like to see influencers as another advertising channel that can be scaled as the mood takes them, like advertising via AdWords. What needs to be remembered, however, is that a lot of effort and strategy has often gone into creating a personal brand for the influencer. Conversely, some influencers, unfortunately, have the attitude that (large) companies are cash cows that you can sell a buzzword without providing any measurable advertising performance. Fortunately, not all parties think that way, and influencer marketing can play a serious role in the affiliate sector.

A natural point of friction is also the difference in the objectives of the affiliate channel and the influencer. While affiliate marketing is traditionally geared towards sales and performance values, influencers tend to act more in the areas of branding and reach. This must be considered when working together, as made clear in the following examples. How this affects contacting and negotiating with influencers is the focus of the second part of the series, "Procedure for Acquisition." The conditional possibility of using tracking links, e.g., on Instagram, difficulties with billing models, or even conflicts of interest between individual marketing channels represent difficult hurdles for the industry,

Therefore we would like to leave the clichés and misconceptions aside and show how meaningful cooperation can succeed. We also discuss how the individual step can look in a specific case with suitable examples.

Influencers = content publishers? Not so almost!

Influencers differ from content publishers primarily in that the operator of the blog or channel is established as a brand. Influencers have an existing group of followers that is constantly expanding. Users follow them because they identify with the person and thus the brand behind them or find the way of communication exciting. In a direct comparison to content publishers, it can be seen that influencers' followers are more likely to be in discovery mode. In contrast, users or visitors of content publishers are already in search mode. Accordingly, influencers are - for the most part - active at an earlier point in the customer journey. However, through the discovery mode, these can also occur at other points in the customer journey and be involved in the purchase.

Where and how does one best start as a merchant?

For a start, it is recommended to find a clear strategic line. First and foremost is the question: Which target group do I want to reach? This does not automatically have to match the entire target group of the shop. For example, do you want to focus on a particular range? Is the focus on positioning in a specific set of topics? Accordingly, it is important to formulate the target group. This is also a first indication of the spheres in which the potential influencer is moving.

Case A: Working with influencers is an option to promote yoga products. Awareness of this range should primarily be strengthened in a female target group aged between 20 and 35, with a middle income, sporting interests, fashion awareness, and a middle to high level of education.

Case B: The merchant's shop has a new section for design items. The range and branding effects of influencers are used to raise awareness. Male and female customers are equally relevant for this shop. The shop's demographics are used to define the target group further.

In the next step, it should be considered how to define a suitable influencer for the collaboration. Starting with the typology and delimitation of the term influencer from personal brands, this approach leads, in the best case, to a list of important KPIs, such as the desired reach, the activity, and last but not least, the proximity of your brand to that of the influencer. This gives you an optimal profile, which can be used to search for the right partner. However, these points should also be handled flexibly because personality is often more important than a key figure. Qualitative key figures and requirements always have to be checked with a certain amount of effort. This starts, for example, with checking the spelling, considers the quality and addressing of individual contributions, and ends with an assessment of the quality of interaction with users. High fan counts alone can often give a good impression, but the conversion rate will not look any better if there is no corresponding engagement. The below list provides a rough overview of the quantitative key figures of the most important networks that can be consulted.

Case A: For the action in this area, the networks are equally relevant when searching for influencers. However, the integration on Instagram is less important due to the need for tracking options. The topic engagement in the defined target group is particularly important as a key figure. Post-interaction also plays a role since the action is designed to promote sales. The growth rate is less important because a long-term branding effect is not the focus.

Case B: To increase awareness of the sales area, influencers with a wide range are primarily in demand. However, there is also the opportunity to work with several micro-influencers with a higher topic commitment than a few large ones. A sufficient range can thus also be achieved. The focus here is on the visual networks Instagram and YouTube. Especially on Instagram, customers are usually still in the exploration phase and can easily be made aware of new segments.

Last but not least, the target projects for cooperation should already be evaluated. In what period should the campaign be carried out? What services are desired? Should it be a blog post, video, Instagram post, editorial content, or using a specific hashtag? This does not have to be a fully planned campaign, but at least there should be a rough idea of what is possible with your brand. For some, visual content fits very well, while products that require explanation can benefit more from descriptive texts in a blog. But here, too, it is important to have the courage to use new media formats and confidence in the influencer's performance, who usually knows his craft best. Of course, possible budgets should also be determined at this point. Where are possible WKZ limits? What could a possible compensation look like? Which products can be made available? Is a fixed sum or commission agreed upon? This should be clear before the first negotiations with potential partners begin.

Case A: In consultation with the merchant, the scope of possible cooperation is now being discussed:

- Product samples for influencers possible
- CC budget of 250€
- The promotion period of one month
- Working with an influencer
- At least two posts with links to the products and images per influencer

Case B: In this case, too, a picture of the scope of the action emerged:

- Product samples for influencers are possible (price limit depends on the size of the influencer)
- CC budget of 2500€
- Campaign period of three months
- Collaboration with up to five influencers
- 1 video with a product in the influencer's living environment (per influencer)
- 1 post with a presentation of the new range (per influencer)

These key points can create clear conditions before the first contact is made. If the goals are clearly defined on both sides, it becomes clear whether cooperation makes sense. In the next part of this chapter, we'll explore how best to design the process of acquiring influencers and what to look out for.

Our assessment

Influencers can also play a role in affiliate marketing. Above all, clear ideas and the courage to try something new are important. Clear communication about goals and remuneration creates a trusting basis.

Research and Acquisition

The acquisition begins when the preparatory measures have been completed, and the goals and framework conditions have been defined. In the meantime, a separate agency landscape has formed around the topic of influencers, which makes direct contact more difficult. Nevertheless, contacting the respective influencer directly is best to ensure long-term and personal cooperation.

It is important to proceed strategically and plan enough time for the acquisition. Experience has shown that addressing and negotiating with the influencer or agency takes much time. The final selection of the right influencer also takes time.

How do you find the right influencers?

When researching influencers, various tools can be used. In principle, it is, of course, advisable to first look at social media itself. Personalities in a similar topic can often be discovered through hashtags you have used. Groups on Facebook are ideal for getting a feel for the influencer scene in a certain milieu. Last but not least, the classic Google search is always a good idea. You can use this to find suitable influencers in all networks with various operators from the subject area you want to cover. There are also portals like influencerDB where companies and influencers can get closer.

However, there is no one-size-fits-all strategy for finding the right influencer. Instead, it helps to follow the path from the user's perspective. Which content might interest the target group? What are your customers still looking for? Where are the people you want to reach located? On which channels are they moving? Social network sites often have suggested functions, making discovering new profiles and fan pages easier. Services like Buzzsumoprovide information about who is ahead on which topics in social media. The search becomes easier when the first influencers are found because you are now in the right subject area and can quickly find similar profiles.

How do I deal with the found influencers?

After intensive research, you are now faced with a list full of different personalities who would come into question. This list should then be prepared and supplemented with all relevant information. Therefore, This step collects all possible information and checks it for compliance with the requirements formulated in advance.

An Excel table in which all influencers and factors are collected makes it easier to evaluate all information about the respective influencers later. There you can see what technical options are available. Where does the influencer have their profiles? Has he made any product or brand-related recommendations in the past? Can tracking links from affiliate networks already be found in the history? How many fans does he have? What about other self-formulated KPIs? Tools like Fanpagekarma also help with the evaluation of social media profiles. In this way, the first insights about an influencer can already be collected, and you get a better insight than if you were only choosing the influencer based on public fan numbers.

Based on this list, it can quickly be seen who is still an option and who is less relevant for the planned cooperation. But - as mentioned - one should not be guided exclusively by these factors but also consider the influencer from a qualitative perspective: Does his approach fit well with his own company despite deviating from KPIs? Does it have a promising, unique content format? Here you should take the time to look closely.

Finally, the time has come, the first contact

Now the moment has come: A suitable selection has been made, and the first inquiries should go out. But there are many different ways of making contact, and they can all have different degrees of success. A cover letter by post can seem strange to some influencers and lengthens the process immensely. On the other hand, it can also stand out from the crowd – but this should primarily be used to address older influencers. The classic way via e-mail or social networks is the most convenient and offers the possibility of a non-binding direct contact. However, the response rates here are sometimes low. These means of communication are, therefore, particularly suitable for follow-up communication. For the first contact, a telephone inquiry is recommended. The attention is guaranteed.

It is necessary to meet the influencers at eye level. With a confident attitude, you show your appreciation for their work on the one hand and make it clear that you are not going into the negotiation naively. In doing so, one should wait to fall into the house and throw wildly around with targets, price expectations, or demands. You should also be careful with particularly technical details - the know-how of tracking links, and Co. is rather low among influencers. The strengthening of the personal relationship must be addressed. Most of the time, these are younger people and not hard-nosed professional business people, so it's important to strike the right note. First, general factors such as the possibilities of cooperation should be inquired about. Of course, providing initial ideas for the cooperation to show the added value right from the start is beneficial. The initiation is not done with a single email. Sufficient time should be allowed for follow-up, relationship building, possible meetings, and choosing the appropriate communication.

The financial aspect is also interesting: Is there agreement on a CPO basis, or is it only possible to work together via WKZ? The requirements defined in advance can serve as a guide here. In this way, it can be clarified whether both parties can meet the needs of the other. You should have these things ready, especially when asked, and not proactively reveal them too early - this is a better way to avoid the image of a mere "sale."

Case A: In this case, the selected influencers (e.g., Fvck Lucky Go Happy or Oh My Yogi)* were contacted directly in the network. Due to the medium range of the pages, direct contact was possible without any problems. Since this is a hobby or leisure sport for many, special emphasis should be placed on personal contact. If the chemistry is right, the first phone call will quickly take place, during which the exact intentions of both sides can then be better explained.

Case B: When contacting possible influencers (e.g., chez_claire or lovelynature.de or svenja_traumzuhause)*, a mix of tools is used. In the case of smaller ranges, inquiries are also made via the networks. For larger influencers, by email or directly by phone. Since branding is the focus here, particular importance was attached to a suitable image for the influencers and identification with the brand.

*The examples are only possible results of research based on our model. The projector and the channels presented have no business relationship with each other.

Now that all relevant influencers have been requested and, in the best case, further information is available, the next step is to select the right partner.

The last steps to start a campaign

The various options are once again precisely matched to your wishes and requirements. This may seem tedious, but a clear strategy is still an important cornerstone of an influencer campaign.

Now that all doubts have been removed, the cooperation with the chosen influencer can be sealed. The defined goals and services should be recorded jointly so that both parties know what to expect. We have already answered whether contracts make sense at this point in ours. In principle, it can be said that there is nothing wrong with recording obligations and expectations in this way. However, the principle "whoever overregulates loses" applies.

From the technical side, it is still important that all the necessary content and advertising materials are available for the partner. Then nothing stands in the way of starting the campaign.

Case A: After we agreed on a suitable period for the campaign with the selected influencer, she was allowed to choose suitable products from the collection to be advertised as part of the cooperation. Since she knew her target group best, she quickly found what she sought. She received the products promptly and suitable image material to enhance the articles. The appropriate deep links to the product were also made available. After the first post had already brought good traffic, but few conversions, more information was provided for the second post. With more specific information, the influencer was able to convince her fans of the product better.

Case B: At this point, we decided to work with several influencers. When choosing the products, care was taken to ensure they reflect a certain aspect of the range. While smaller influencers were already satisfied with higher-priced products alone, we agreed with the influencers with larger reach on an additional 500€ to cover their video creation costs. While the influencers were free to create the video to remain true to their style, a brief was formulated in a post to present the range. Since many questions from followers followed the individual videos, it was important to maintain close communication to provide suitable information constantly.

It is advisable to evaluate the performance of the influencer during the campaign. This way, flexible adjustments can still be made, for example, to the content. This way, the influencer can receive new materials and respond differently to his audience. Is one aspect going less well? Then the necessary steps can be taken here to ensure improvement. Is something going particularly well? Then there is the possibility of intensifying this aspect.

Our assessment

Acquiring and making contact is difficult to pour into a uniform process. There may be differences depending on the company, product range, and requirements. However, with the help of our guide, it is possible to find the right strategy for yourself. It is always important to look at your own goals. You should also always remember what performance you ultimately get for what. With the individual steps presented here, the procedure can be structured, and the process can be designed clearly.

Furthermore, the evaluation of a campaign provides information about where the process can still be optimized and what was already going well.

In the next part of this series, we will go into more detail about the possibilities of concrete cooperation with influencers and present various strategies and levers with which a campaign can be designed.

Variables of the Partnership

In the last part of our topic on influencer marketing in affiliates, we take a closer look at the eventualities of a collaboration. The cooperation design seems almost endless, so we provide an overview of the relevant parameters and possibilities in the ongoing partnership.

Collaboration variables

A partnership can be attractive for both parties with the right billing model. The classic CPO cooperation is the hobby horse of the affiliate channel. Influencers can thus benefit directly from the success of the campaign. The more successful their content leads to sales, the more they earn. This can be a further incentive to promote the content in a high-quality manner. It is also conceivable to set up an action-related performance relay. A particularly strong sale is rewarded with additional profit opportunities. But this classic billing arrangement also offers many advantages for the merchant. Costs are only incurred when a transaction occurs.

Especially with particularly complex campaigns, however, the influencer makes creative and sometimes financial advance payments. This effort should be paid fairly in advance. Hybrid models are best suited for this. The sales are regularly compensated via a CPO. The influencer receives an appropriate promotional tool or a product sample for the effort.

Product samples also generally play an important role. Choosing the right product has already been covered earlier in this topic. But the lever should be mentioned again at this point. On the one hand, the product can serve as an advertising item, but it can also be part of the remuneration above a certain value. The right fit between brand and influencer rises and falls with the product.

Ultimately, the principle of supply and demand also prevails in influencer marketing. An advantageous pricing strategy can emerge depending on the company's industry and the influencers' niche. Here the idea should not prevail that a performance service is bought but that cooperation takes place in the spirit of affiliate marketing.

It can also be interesting for influencers to benefit from a brand's reach or target group. Companies can connect influencers with relevant interlocutors or enable networking. These things can also provide incentives and non-monetary value. We recommend creativity when designing compensation and looking beyond the classic "CPO box."

If all of these billing options are outside the influencer's interests, direct collaboration is still available outside the networks.

The development of a long-term partnership

Once a good working relationship has been established, it is in the interests of both parties to continue and maintain it. In this way, a one-time cooperation can also become a permanent cooperation. The influencer thus becomes a permanent brand ambassador. In the same way, an ongoing business relationship can develop that is only activated at the right opportunity.

A long-term partnership can have many advantages for the online shop. So it is conceivable to extend an influencer campaign into the shop. With good cooperation, the shop is offered to the influencer as a platform, and products with joint branding may even be offered. The reach of the online shop and influencer complement each other seamlessly and merge into one another. If you go one step further and offer the influencer your sub-shop or category, you usually save at the WKZ with a particularly wide range of influencers. In this way, both brands can benefit from their reputation and authenticity. It is also possible to share content and play on the respective channels.

In a long-term partnership, the influencer often enjoys the company's trust and creative freedom. In addition, it can be interesting for him to continue receiving products from the shop that he uses daily in the future. He might be able to sponsor his hobby through this channel, for example, in extreme athletes. The reliability advantage and lower risk in a well-established partnership should be addressed. Worrying about outstanding payments or agreements is a thing of the past. With an increasing wealth of experience in performance values, fair conditions can be discussed together and further developed with good cooperation.

Influencer events are a special tool. With attractive events, contacts can be made without obligation, and good partnerships can be rewarded. Influencers are thus allowed to get to know the brand and product world better and to get a first impression of the company. Those who have been there for a long time experience a special appreciation.

What else is there to consider?

A principle of reciprocity should always apply to whatever variable or action is taken. Even if many of the measures contribute primarily to the branding of one's brand, cost-effectiveness should not be neglected. Depending on the product offered, the contribution margin can be quickly exceeded if large events must be co-financed, etc.

In addition to all these soft factors, tracking is often one of the biggest challenges. As mentioned in the previous parts, it should find its place again here. Influencers or social media stars often come from a completely different direction than the classic niche site operator and are primarily active on social networks. Especially in the case of Instagram, the tracking options are limited. That is why empathy and sometimes patience are required here if the influencers are to be tracked via one of the well-known networks.

And finally, there is the big philosophical question: influencers and affiliate marketing? Really? Admittedly, everyone would like to have a big piece of the influencer marketing pie, and now affiliate marketing too? The answer is definitely yes! As has become clear in this series, the cooperative character is clearly in the foreground. Managing cooperation is something that every affiliate manager experiences and implements daily. As a result, there is no better area of online marketing to locate this type of collaboration. In addition, the technical possibilities of the area offer the best and fairest remuneration models.

Nevertheless, we agree that interdisciplinary work on "influencers" only makes sense. The trusted social media manager will certainly have a better view of the correct placement on the social web at one point or another and can provide valuable input when designing an influencer campaign. Nevertheless, influencer cooperation can offer a strong added value for every partner program, but you should at least partially say goodbye to the idea of performance.

How influencers and affiliates provide different strengths to your affiliate revenue growth strategy

While influencers and affiliate marketing are fundamentally quite similar, there are clear differences between them that you should understand to get the most out of both types of partnerships. In the following topic, we look at what differentiates influencers from affiliates, what they have in common, and how you can develop a strategy that uses both channels effectively.

In the world of partnerships, affiliates, and influencers belong together like Beyoncé and Jay-Z. Both, on their own, can do great things in terms of sales - but if you let them shine side by side, they will work wonders for your marketing strategy.

However, just like the popular hip-hop couple, influencers and affiliates come with unique strengths that set them apart from each other and other sales channels. When you get your goals and metrics right, the dynamic duo can be a real hit regarding revenue growth.

What are affiliate partnerships?

Affiliate partnerships are revenue-generating machinery that directs consumers to branded products through dedicated links. When one of those consumers purchases through an affiliate link, the affiliate earns a commission—that is, they make money through revenue sharing.

What are influencer partnerships?

Influencer partnerships increase the trust and authenticity of social media personalities, trendsetters, subject matter experts, and content creators. These people have a community of followers behind them who trust them, their content, suggestions, and recommendations.

Unlike affiliates, influencers are in direct contact with their followers. Therefore, followers are far more likely to buy their products or services when influencers recommend a brand they like. Successful influencers can act like affiliates and earn royalties on the products they promote – but not all affiliates enjoy that level of trust from their audience; Conversely, they cannot act like influencers.

How can you measure the goals for influencers and affiliates in your partner program?

Like the rest of your marketing strategy, finding the right partnerships starts with identifying your end goal. How your brand defines, and does measure success can drive how you differentiate between affiliate and influencer partnerships—while also considering how to use their similarities to your advantage.

How affiliate metrics help you spot growth opportunities

To better understand the performance of your program, you should always keep an eye on all the important affiliate marketing KPIs. These metrics will support you to identify growth opportunities and take immediate action if things don't go your way.

Affiliate marketing goals and metrics often include:

- converting sales/leads
- incremental sales growth
- Increase in product acceptance or conversions
- Traffic increase or new customer acquisition

How can you develop effective influencer performance measurement strategies?

The key here is to set clear (and sometimes different) strategies for each campaign. Each campaign should only focus on one or two goals.

Influencer marketing goals do often include brand exposure goals such as:

- Hiring influencers to create user-generated content

- the launch of a new product/service
- the creation of brand awareness
- entering new markets

Metrics quantify the success of influencer campaigns, but there are no proven standard benchmarks for this - the metrics you measure always depend on the specific goals of the respective influencer campaign.

Influencer metrics often include:

- Total reach (follows/web traffic)
- engagement rates
- sentiment ratings
- impressions
- saves

How do you acquire influencers for your affiliate program?

Finding partners who can act as affiliates and influencers allows you to expand successful partnerships. First, look at your existing affiliates and influencers before investing in new partnerships. You may already have good relationships with key influencers interested in acting as affiliates.

When influencers become affiliates, it opens up new avenues for you to promote your products. In a campaign, for example, you could recruit an influencer and pay them for a specific post to increase your reach or engagement. After the campaign ends, you create an affiliate link for the influencer's posts, creating an ongoing income channel for you and them.

Bloggers, media companies, trendsetters, idea brokers, or knowledge leaders who act as brand affiliates can also act as influencers. Affiliates can provide brand exposure through brand awareness campaigns, although the ultimate goal of an affiliate program is to generate revenue.

Influencer partners may also use affiliate tactics, such as posting branded content links. Some influencers are already making a good chunk of their revenue from affiliate link commissions—others have not explored the revenue potential of affiliate marketing but are open to tapping into it.

How to best structure compensation for influencers who act as affiliates

Flexible remuneration conditions allow you to set up individual partnerships individually. Brands can use hybrid models such as pay-per-post or pay-for-creation. Later, these posts can be turned into posts with affiliate links.

Traditional affiliates rely on vouchers, discount codes, bonuses, cashback, or loyalty programs that track last-click interactions. However, influencers are sometimes the last click in the conversion funnel - so if you only pay via the last click via affiliate links, influencers could invest much work for nothing.

Influencers can present your brand to their audience, get them excited about your products and generate engagement. Influencers can also push purchases of products their audience is already familiar with. Bonuses are an additional incentive when influencers regularly do a lot to generate interest or engagement for your brand among their followers.

You can reward influencers for the awareness and interest they create, even if they're not the last click along the customer journey.

Develop an engaging influencer and affiliate marketing strategy

Influencers invite your brand into trust, and you can benefit greatly from building good relationships with affiliates and influencers as part of your successful affiliate strategy. Get the most out of your partner relationships by becoming familiar with what each type of partnership can contribute and how to measure that contribution.

Chapter 4: Automation and Tools for Affiliate Marketing

Talking about your product is arguably the most important and challenging aspect of digital marketing. Although there are, it can seem overwhelming to keep up.

Perhaps one of the most overlooked marketing techniques is. Not only can you get consistent income from your affiliate program, but you can also produce much excitement about the products you offer.

Do you run a SaaS company?

Rewarding offers the easiest tools for businesses to create their affiliate program using the Stripe payment gateway.

The platform does automate everything from commission management to payments and refunds. And to top it off, Rewardful has one of the easiest setup processes of any affiliate program platform.

- Have a Stripe account ready.
- Create Account
- Connect your Stripe account with Rewardful
- Copy and paste a simple JavaScript snippet
- Create your campaigns from the panel

Once the above steps are complete, the snippet you added to your website will grant affiliate management for your product. Rewarding provides a dedicated dashboard for any affiliate who signs up for their program.

This dashboard includes link management, banner ads, payments, and more. Since it integrates with Stripe natively, all payments are automatically tracked and managed.

Pricing does start at $29 per month for the basic plan, with the option to upgrade to Enterprise for about $299 monthly.

PartnerStack

Partner Stack is a well-established, all-in-one partnership platform designed for B2B SaaS companies to build, manage, and scale their affiliate, reseller, and customer referral programs.

With more than 100 integrations and a vast, high-quality affiliate network, Partner Stack makes it easy to grow your program and increase your income. Their platform offers a wide range of benefits, including:

- Integrations with SFDC, Stripes, and many more
- Unique ability to manage affiliate, reseller, and referral associations in one place
- More than 80,000 XNUMX partners in your market
- An easy-to-use dashboard
- Ability to host training resources for partners
- A complete support system

Get to partner stack to get started

Tapfiliate

Tapfiliate is also a snippet-based affiliate program platform. However, his emphasis leans towards a jack-of-all-trades approach. In other words, Tapfiliate explicitly targets various website content and systems. Their affiliate program software can be integrated with Shopify, WordPress, Wix, and other popular platforms.

Here are the key features:

- Automated integration with the most popular content management systems.
- Customizable dashboard with pre-built workflows, triggers, and affiliate management features.
- Affiliates can bookmark your board.
- Custom rules for commissions, including external ones like bonuses and rewards.
- It works with the main payment gateways.

Plans start at $69 per month, with 0% transaction fees.

Post Affiliate Pro

Post affiliate pro is a custom affiliate tracking tool for managing affiliate sales, payments, and users. It includes an all-in-one panel to maintain your personal affiliate program. Also, you can use this platform without prior technical experience. Almost all of the installation steps are completely code-free and explained in detail.

The platform covers sales tracking, individual product support, coupons, and commission management. In addition, Post Affiliate Pro helps avoid dissatisfied customers by monitoring potentially faulty transactions; fraud protection.

Each affiliate who signs up to promote their products will have a designated board. This dashboard includes the tools to build affiliate links, manage payments, and track new leads.

Kiflo

Kiflo specializes in helping brands like yours execute a partner relationship management strategy. In essence, it targets growing companies that want to take the next step in promoting their product.

Once your sales follow a linear curve, you can use Kiflo's extensive PRM tools to increase your long-term exposure. Everything from the affiliate dashboard and custom link management is at your disposal.

Plus, you can use Kiflo's unified dashboard to connect with your partners and build long-lasting relationships. Your partners are likely to be the users of your product themselves.

WP Affiliate Manager

WordPress is a powerhouse of a content management system. Initially famous for the best blogging functionality – WordPress is now considered to power media sites, SaaS startups, business platforms, and eCommerce stores. WP Affiliate Manager will be a good news if you run your business or startup from WordPress.

This plugin is designed to integrate with your existing product management software and then allow you to invite affiliates to become part of your program. Existing supported platforms include WooCommerce, Easy Digital Downloads, WP eStore, S2Member, and others.

And because it's based on WordPress, you get that easy-to-follow traditional workflow environment. This tool uses your existing WordPress data to generate user dashboards and provide convenient affiliate management features.

CJ Affiliate

In the early 2000s, Commission Junction was known for its notorious reputation in the affiliate marketing arena. Almost every digital marketer at the time used Commission Junction specifically, as it had the largest available pool of products to promote. These days, CJ Affiliate is focusing on helping Advertisers and Publishers.

Unlike standalone affiliate software, CJ provides exciting benefits to get your affiliate program off the ground. First, the advertiser feature lets you list all your products in a single panel. From there, you can specify the smallest details about the product or service you are trying to market.

And secondly, CJ is also a platform for publishers. This results in a convenient way to immediately attract new affiliate partners. The CJ Publisher Dashboard lists all the products available for promotion. And the audience is diverse enough that someone is always looking for a product in a specific category.

ShareASale

Shareasale also dates back to the early 2000s. The platform has survived many different changes in the field of marketing, but it is still a solid option for anyone looking to promote their product using an affiliate system.

The main advantage of ShareASale is that it is a well-known platform. Even famous brands like Motif Awesome use ShareASale to manage their affiliate needs.

Part of this concerns the fact that ShareASale makes it easy for publishers. Anyone can promote a product and earn affiliate commission very efficiently. Its payment history is solid, making it an easy choice for affiliate marketers.

Impact

Affiliate marketing is not just about the bottom line. It's also about partnerships: the people who earn you more income in the long run. Impacto Engage is a platform designed to help you keep an open line with all your partners.

You'll see which partners are performing exceptionally well by having access to detailed reports. And, if you're satisfied enough, you can offer them special offers and better commission rates for their hard work.

Generally, you would do this out of instinct or a good heart. Instead, Impact helps you make data-driven decisions. You could even.

Volume

Volume is an all-in-one advertising tracker for your business. With this tool, you can do more than manage your affiliate programs.

As an example:

- You can track your ad campaigns on Facebook, Instagram, and Twitter.
- Put your data to the test by analyzing it for patterns and other insights.
- Get actionable tips to improve the overall performance of your next campaign.
- Track your affiliate purchases and their origins. Find out who has the most significant impact on your sales and take advantage of it.

If you already have an established midsize business, Voluum is a tool that will give you a statistical advantage over your competition.

Tarta

TARTA is a performance-based marketing tool for managing leads, optimizing multi-channel strategy, and nurturing partner relationships. It is better to use it for an internal existing affiliate system. And it will be beneficial to collect quantitative data to optimize your affiliate performance.

Although it may initially seem complex, learning CAKE is easy since its functions are intuitive. You can run reports, track specific partners, or send promotions using nothing more than the tools provided within your dashboard.

Refersion

Refersion is an all-inclusive affiliate marketing platform that helps you build an affiliate system for your product. But it also lends a hand in attracting new members. All Refersion clients access a special marketplace where more than 5,000 publishers seek new products to promote.

Besides that, you will find many informative guides and videos.

This affiliate platform tool will work great with e-commerce store owners. For example, you have a Shopify store and want to expand your business. Refersion has seamless integrations for Shopify, WooCommerce, and other popular eCommerce platforms.

AffiliateWP

WordPress is undoubtedly one of the easiest website management platforms to use. And for many, switching to another solution is out of the question. We have good news if you love WordPress and want to manage your affiliates from the main panel.

AffiliateWP is WordPress's first affiliate marketing management plugin to help you earn more. Since you already publish your products using WordPress, using AffiliateWP will be extremely easy.

Start with a basic setup and specify specific rules for your affiliate program. You can then add an Affiliate Program page to your website. This page will serve as a means for your new members to sign up and receive their affiliate links.

Similarly, your partners can track your progress and request payment withdrawals once you pass a certain threshold. As the administrator of your affiliate program, you may choose to provide custom banners or other advertising options. Your partners will then have direct access to those resources.

If you already know how easy WordPress is, then the AffiliateWP plugin is no exception to the same trend. It's easy to understand, very flexible, and allows you to do as much customization as you want.

EasyAffiliate

EasyAffiliate is an all-in-one plugin for WordPress that helps you create a self-hosted affiliate program for eCommerce stores or WordPress sites in minutes.

Grow your revenues with an Affiliate Dashboard, real-time reporting, fraud detection, eCommerce integrations, email marketing, one-click payments, and no transaction fees. The setup is easy - no need to fiddle with the database or any special scripts.

WordPress Customizer helps to tweak the pre-built dashboard to fit the brand. In addition, the panel provides easy access for your affiliates to edit account information, monitor status, view payment history, and download your banners and links.

Everything is there in the WordPress admin to run the affiliate program more conveniently and securely. It is a secure plugin you can trust to track every commission accurately and protect you from attacks. Easy Affiliate also helps create custom tracking links. With Pretty Links support, your links look great and short.

Easy Affiliate integrates with email marketing services providers like ConvertKit and MailChimp to enhance your. It gives a fully featured platform for managing banners and links so you know your affiliate marketing strategy is on point.

For secure payments, it is compatible with PayPal. You'll also find it easy to upgrade to AffiliateRoyale's Easy Affiliate with just one click and access all information quickly.

Its pricing starts from $99.50/year for a single site.

Starting an affiliate program is relatively easy. If you have a strong product to sell, chances are there is someone who would like to help you promote that product. And the benefits of doing so are invaluable.

Depending on your product/business size, you must consider your chances for the best affiliate marketing platform.

This guide to affiliate marketing tools should have enough diversity to cover your small business and enterprise needs.

Top 15 Best Affiliate Marketing Tools and Platforms

Affiliate networks are a series of platforms that combine many websites to promote products through advertisements. These systems act as intermediaries between the affiliates (in this case, the content creators) and the advertisers (the brands that need promotion).

Advertisers are in charge of establishing their parameters within the affiliate network. At the same time, content creators have the task of finding those programs that want to serve as a window to promote what the advertiser offers on their websites.

An advertising brand can choose the websites it wants based on its interest in seeing its brand related to those websites. Once both the advertisers and the web portals agree, these websites will place the ad in the form of a link, banner, or any other format, and each time an action is generated with that ad, the advertising brand will pay a commission.

What are the best affiliate tools and networks?

Different tools help to promote the affiliate marketing of a brand, thus allowing it to achieve a greater reach and contributing to more customers becoming interested in the brand and in all the products or services it offers. The tools we have selected are the following:

- admit
- pump
- Affiliate
- Awin
- cake
- city ads
- Easy Affiliate
- Grow (Trade doubler)
- Kiflo
- LinkMink
- Post Affiliate Pro
- Rakuten Advertising
- reference
- send owl
- trade tracker

admit

Admitad is a platform that serves as an intermediary between brands that want to advertise on the Internet and websites that may be part of their affiliate network and allow the brand to monetize. It does so by offering different very specific affiliate programs, which can be applied by the users themselves and whose ultimate goal is to achieve the ideal web traffic to generate conversion.

The campaigns can be adapted according to the needs of the client. Currently, Admitad has more than 800,000 publishers and around 2,000 clients worldwide.

pump

Adpump is an affiliate network that specializes in CPA affiliate marketing. The vision of Adpump is to provide improvements for advertisers and platforms that are part of an affiliate network.

This marketing network operates in 14 countries around the world. Its objective is to provide services and technologies that allow associates to achieve their different objectives efficiently and timely, with current and unique technological solutions that improve traffic control, customer orientation to integrate multiple web systems, and web statistics to monitor their traffic internally. Among the service areas that Adpump covers are: e-commerce, travel, finance, online games, education, apps for mobile devices, finance, binary & forex, etc.

Affiliate

Affiliate is a platform that provides brands with affiliate networks that allow them to connect and collaborate with the right influencers and affiliates. This platform is especially an online tool, easy and fast to install and with modules to work with Prestashop, Woocommerce, or others.

Likewise, you can fully customize your campaigns with a complete set of SaaS tools; In addition, you can define clear conditions for remuneration, distribution, and attribution, which builds trust between brands and affiliate networks. With this tool, you can even determine the weight of affiliates, create groups, grant different remunerations to affiliates or groups of affiliates, and remunerate clicks and sales, individually or jointly.

Awin

It is a specialized affiliate marketing platform that seeks to position itself as a mediator between the advertiser and the affiliate, thus allowing it to help in program management, strategy, and technology. Awin has a set of tools for managing and generating affiliate reports that are easy to use, flexible, and with a wide variety of information and functionalities with which clients and affiliates can make the most of the affiliate channel. In 2017 Awin merged with Affilinet, another reference company in affiliate marketing, to create a giant in the sector.

Cake

This company has affiliate marketing software that helps its clients measure, manage, and optimize their campaigns to get the most out of them. From Cake, they strive to make their services comfortable and easy to use and understand, democratizing access to digital marketing.

A solution that grants companies of all sizes to measure the level of their marketing actions and make the most of their digital investment. Marketing solutions that are driven by creativity and innovation. 500 advertisers, networks, and publishers trust Cake in over 50 countries and a team of business thinking and technology development experts.

City ads

Cityads is one of the most prominent affiliate networks internationally, with active campaigns in almost all existing niches. In addition to offering the classic advantages of affiliate network marketing, Cityads provides unique and patented solutions based on big data.

It is the only affiliate program network that uses its proprietary DMP to target advertising as precisely as possible. Such a system is responsible for collecting and processing data from many websites, which allows you to attract the attention of your target audience and motivate them to take specific actions. The information included is operational data (purchases, trips, financial services), interests (preferences, lifestyle), and geographic and demographic data.

Easy Affiliate

Easy Affiliate is a plugin that will help you create a self-hosted affiliate program for your WordPress website. It is designed so that its handling is simple and easy; it is unnecessary to be an expert to take advantage of this tool.

It has a personalized affiliate board that will adapt to the needs of your website and with which you can monitor statistics, edit your account information, make downloads, and check your payment history. It is also possible to set commission rates, customize them per user, and ensure security that a fraud detector is included.

Grow (Trade doubler)

Grow is the platform of another of the leaders in the sector, Tradedoubler, which offers a system that takes care of all the tasks, handling the payment of commissions and all the corresponding financial processes so that small businesses and startups focus solely on establishing their affiliate networks. In addition, Grow provides its users with dedicated plug-and-play tracking integration to major eCommerce platforms such as Woocommerce, Prestashop, and Shopify.

Kiflo

With its affiliate partner program, you can organize workflows and designs easily, expand your reach and add new leads faster. Content management becomes equally intuitive, facilitating the exchange of information with partners.

In addition, Kiflo also allows the integration of Stripe, making it easier to automate the rewards system for your partners, managing commissions and payments without the need to resort to spreadsheets, and increasing the trust they place in you.

LinkMink

LinkMink is a membership tracking and management tool that helps SaaS companies increase revenue by sharing it with partners who help promote them. With this tool, you can keep track of leads, referrals, and commissions from your partner's promotions.

Similarly, it offers integration in 15 minutes and accurate tracking of commissions to real income through Stripe to its clients.

Post Affiliate Pro

Post Affiliate Pro is an intuitive, fast, efficient, infinitely expandable, and scalable affiliate network software that can run an entire affiliate program.

Their system gives you access to both the merchant panel and the affiliate panel, depending on who uses it, and in which they can see their statistics and thus allow them to manage their promotional materials. The program will take care of completely automating the affiliate program of a client.

Rakuten Advertising

Considered one of the largest pay-for-performance affiliate networks in the world, Rakuten Advertising is a system responsible for offering a marketing solution that helps clients optimize their campaigns across all communication channels, thus seeking to connect with their target audience and help publishers monetize their content.

Reference

Start boosting the growth of your business thanks to the affiliate marketing solution that Refersion presents. Thanks to its adaptability, this platform with proven ROI will allow you to recruit, manage and track the results of your affiliates, influencers, and ambassadors.

Refersion guarantees a perfect match between brands and creators, matching the most suitable candidates. In addition, the number of affiliates that can be incorporated is unlimited. The payment options are automatic, direct, and multiple, and the commissions can be customized. This solution makes integration easy, enabling you to connect your eCommerce platform with popular marketing applications.

Send owl

It is a platform that helps customers host, distribute and collect all digital products they offer (ebooks, courses, videos, audio, etc.). But also, you can use SendOwl as a payment platform for the client's services or physical products; it doesn't matter if you use WordPress or woocommerce.

Trade tracker

Tradetracker is an affiliate marketing platform where both advertisers and publishers come into contact. In addition, this service offers all the necessary tools with which users can promote advertisers' products and services within the platform.

In Tradetracker, the websites have the different brands and retailers segmented into 28 categories: fashion and jewelry, gifts and gadgets, home and garden, household appliances, office, toys, etc.

10 free tools to use in your affiliate campaigns

I want to tell you about my 10 favorite free tools for that market.

Ultimately, we all like free, so I want to inspire you to start your campaigns with these recommendations. Remember that this list is for those who have just made their first membership moves.

Another point that should be emphasized is that you get what you pay for. Therefore, these tools may seem very limited in terms of their functionalities. However, they are still useful for getting your releases going.

Manage to grow and generate a constant flow of income. You will be able to become fully familiar with this category of tools and invest more, even acquiring a paid version of each of them to expand your results.

Without further ado, let's get started.

Affiliate Productivity Tools

- Buffer

A great alternative to programs like Hootsuite. Hootsuite would have gotten a spot here if they still had a free version.

As powerful or even better in some areas, I believe Buffer offers great resources for managing social media posts.

If you want to grow your fan base and improve your reputation, you must focus much on the content you create. You need to keep a regular schedule with high-quality posts, and Buffer is great at keeping you consistent.

This tool allows you to produce content for Facebook, Linkedin, and other platforms. You can schedule them to leave on certain dates, so you will always have something new prepared for those accompanying you.

You can link to 3 networks with the free version, and Buffer also gives you an AI content generator and landing page maker.

- Evernote

You will notice that it takes work to find the ideal activity rhythm. You will try to associate with affiliate programs of different brands and products, requiring good organizational skills. That's why I recommend it.

Testing various types of products means monitoring endless links and promotional codes. Evernote will be a great tool to collect and follow all the links, even if they are already available on affiliate platforms like CJ or Impact Radius.

You should have the Evernote app popups on your cell phone and copy your link instead of entering several times and navigating the platform until you reach what you need. Evernote promises to help you do the following:

- Clipping — articles, recipes, pages, images — monitors everything useful you discover online.
- Tasks — capture checklists with related notes so you're always up to date.
- Searches — find any text in any note. The tool even detects errors and provides suggestions.
- Organization — Use notebooks to a structure to your content. Add tags to simplify the process of finding your notes.
- Bitwarden

A directory for managing passwords, like 1Password (no longer has a free plan).

Bitwarden offers a generous no-cost option, which includes all its top features, unlimited devices, and as many passwords as you want.

You don't get much more than that for their fair $10/year plan. But it's worth buying if you want to use two-factor authentication, a Bitwarden-specific authenticator, Emergency access, and security reporting.

If you're already experienced in marketing, you already know the sheer number of programs and tools you accumulate, so a password directory like Bitwarden becomes essential.

The best Affiliate Email tool

- GetResponse

With all the honesty in the world, we take the gold medal for free tools. It's amazing how many benefits you get on GetResponse's free plan; check out:

- Email Marketing — we are referring to our newsletter tools, which allow you to send multiple emails to promote products and exclusive offers. It is a super efficient method to generate affiliate marketing sales, clicks, and conversions.
- Website Builder — everyone who wants to build an Internet audience will inevitably need a well-structured website at some point. As an affiliate, you can use that space to share content about

your niche, include forms to capture leads, and promote your brand. GetResponse has free, with customizable templates.

- Tool to build email lists — this point is linked to the first one. GetResponse helps you get contacts for your lists at no cost, with online conversion forms for all models. You should develop a genuine and faithful contact base to communicate with an audience that values your credibility as an affiliate.

Tools to manage and send files

- WeTransfer

A program that will solve many problems for you. How many times have you been unable to send a file by email, text, or other methods because it was too large or had an incompatible format? This unusual situation has touched me.

You can also download content, monitor your downloads and use the version for the iPhone in its free version. One small drawback is that your transfers expire after 7 days, but it's a great free tool overall.

- Google Drive

We all know Google and its great resources, most of them free, but the quality of Google Drive to manage documents is worth noting.

If you have a low budget, you can replace Word with Google Docs, Excel with Google Sheets, and Powerpoint with Google Slides. Google Drive is a great tool because it makes it easy to manage all those formats on one platform.

Its 15 GB memory limit is not that generous, but it will be enough to get you started on your affiliate marketing adventures. It is a very useful resource for saving files, images, and other documents you will need in your affiliate activities.

The best image editing tool

- Canva

I still seek a better one with free video, images, and other file modification programs. Let's look at just a few of the benefits your free plan includes:

- more than 250 thousand templates;
- 100+ layout types for social media posts, presentations, and letters;
- more than 1 million images;
- 5 GB of space in the cloud;
- and much more.

You can also use their services for free to collaborate with others, which is a great bonus. Canva gives you everything you need to create visual materials, a must in affiliate marketing.

An excellent proofreading tool

- Grammarly

If you don't have writing experience yet or haven't written for a blog in a while, Grammarly will be necessary and fascinating for you. I was an average student in high school and would have LOVED to use that tool back then.

My current writing skills aren't spectacular either, so Grammarly is extremely helpful to me. Surely you can count on her when producing your next article.

Its powerful artificial intelligence identifies any spelling or grammatical errors to correct your texts. If you have not tried it, sign up for its free version today and explore its mechanism. It's so worth it!

In addition to the resources I just mentioned, the free version of Grammarly offers conciseness suggestions for your texts and discovers the tone of voice for your message. I don't know how they do it, but I always find their recommendations valuable.

A tool to make video calls

- Zoom

This was a challenge because I have always had a strong opinion about that product. With the popularity of the home office, it was inevitable to explore different video-calling tools to see which one was the best.

At some point, I was an ambassador for Google Chat and even tried to convince some friends to use it. That program had a video call feature, but then Google released the Meet tool and discontinued Chat.

I am still determining exactly what happened at that stage of Google, but in recent research, I found that Google Chat is still an option for text messages, and Meet is still the go-to tool for video calls. Two seemed interesting because I wanted to discover more alternatives for those times.

Microsoft Teams made a good marketing strategy, especially during the pandemic, so I started using it with other Microsoft programs.

But Zoom was the one that won me over from day one, and to this day, I see it as the best on the list.

Your free package includes calls of up to 40 minutes, up to 100 invitees per call, integration with digital calendars and email providers, a whiteboard, and a team chat feature. However, I can say that if you use any of those platforms, you will have a good experience.

Chapter 5: Diversifying Your Affiliate Income Streams

The cruel truth about affiliate marketing: 95% of people who get into it fail!

And by failing, I mean they can't make a living out of it.

Certainly, they earn 100 200 € from time to time.

But more is needed to earn a good living.

Fortunately, There's a different way to affiliate that makes it easy to earn money.

It is possible to make around 10,000 euros per month, or even more, with this other way of doing things.

Here's how it works. Why affiliation is the easiest way to make money on the Internet?

Affiliation is the fact that a person (an affiliate) promotes the products of someone else (a seller) and earns a commission for each sale he succeeds in making. These products can be sold in affiliation and are generally found on an affiliation platform.

And sales are tracked through affiliate links promoted by the affiliate. Links, usually to a website, contain within them, in the form of code, a tracking cookie.

Beyond the theory, the beauty of this system is its simplicity. And because it's simple, it can get anyone started on the internet and start making money online.

Because what keeps people from getting started on the web in general?

What most often blocks beginners

It has to create their products, for example, or sell coaching to earn money. However, starting can be challenging because you must gain the skills to start. Because we feel like we need to be more legitimate. Whereas with affiliation, the advantage is that there is nothing to create. Nothing scary. It is enough to promote a simple link to a website. And with affiliation, there's nothing to manage either. Because since it's not its products, there's no customer support, updates, etc., to worry about. It is, therefore, an excellent way to start a business on the Internet.

The concern is that there is only an extreme minority who manage to earn a good living with affiliation.

Here are why most people who get into affiliate marketing fail to make money.

At best, they get a little extra income from it at the end of the month.

But nothing resembling real business turnover.

However, some entrepreneurs that Antoine BM, the creator of this blog, met earn more than 10,000 euros per month simply with affiliate income, despite having a small audience.

And what these entrepreneurs are doing is that they have done almost the opposite of what everyone else does in affiliate marketing.

Unlike them, which, unfortunately, most people do, it is these 3 errors that I will detail for you now.

- Combine affiliate programs that do not pay much.

For those who fail in affiliate marketing, what they usually do is sign up for a whole bunch of low-commission affiliate programs.

And then they throw themselves into the flower in the gun to promote all their links.

They share them right to the left, desperately trying to collect a few clicks.

And at best, they manage to earn enough to make ends meet.

But not real income.

An example of a low-commission affiliate program is the Amazon Affiliate Program.

Depending on the product, Amazon is no more than 5 or even 10% commission.

Nothing spectacular!

Especially if you sell low-priced products, like books.

- Not working on your relationship with your audience

Contrary to what one might think, those who earn the most in affiliation do not have the biggest audience.

Far from there!

On the other hand, they have an extremely strong relationship of trust with their audience.

So when they promote something, people jump on it.

- Not having a real strategy.

You also need to understand that those who succeed in affiliation do more than share their links with their friends, family, and acquaintances on social networks.

No, they don't just do things haphazardly.

But they follow a real strategy that allows them, in the long term, to generate real affiliate income.

How to start in affiliation with this strategy?

You will find out now.

The 3-step method to affiliate success

You will see that it consists of doing the opposite of what people who start affiliate marketing traditionally do.

Step 1: Identify the affiliate programs that make the most money

To succeed in affiliate marketing, you must first identify 2-3 consistently profitable programs and focus on them.

So the first thing to do is to identify the most profitable affiliate programs.

And these programs are only found in some themes.

Some themes pay off a lot in affiliation. Others earn almost nothing.

In general, physical products pay little. And so with these products, you have to make many sales, at the risk of running out, to start earning interesting sums.

On the other hand, there are niches in which you can earn nice commissions.

In these niches, sellers make many margins, so they can afford to pay high commissions.

And they also do it because, with the increasing advertising costs, it is all the more interesting for them to find affiliates.

So, in which themes are these programs?

Well, for your information, the most profitable affiliate programs are in the following categories:

Internet Marketing

This theme has interesting affiliation commissions, particularly for everything related to online marketing software (autoresponders).

Examples:

- ClickFunnels
- Shopify
- Leadpages
- Vimeo
- Podia

Online training

- You can earn great recurring commissions by promoting online courses created by someone else.
- You can find training courses promoting many themes: cooking, personal development, raising children, investing, etc.
- Some of them have already proven themselves and sometimes enjoy a good reputation.
- For example, you can find interesting training courses for sale in French on the ClickBank platform.
- On this platform, it is possible to find sellers who offer commissions of almost 80%.
- And we can see a whole series of statistics that tell us about the sales performance of the products.

Banks and insurance

- Most people don't know that...
- But in this area, too, there are good commissions, especially because the value of a customer (customer lifetime value) is very high.
- To find interesting affiliate programs in this area, you can register on the Awin platform.
- These products can be found in the "Savings and Investments" section.

Health/beauty/fitness products

- Some sellers in these themes offer generous commissions, particularly for selling protein powders and slimming creams.
- You can also find these products on Awin in the "Health and Beauty" section.

Another possibility: negotiation on a case-by-case basis

- Some content creators (bloggers, YouTubers) or even some brands you know may offer products you want to sell.
- But which are not available on affiliate platforms.
- You can contact them, offer to become their business partner and negotiate your commissions directly.

Step 2: Become an "ambassador" affiliate

Once you have chosen 2 – 3 high-value products, becoming their ambassador will be a question.

Not a representative among others, but the number 1…

The main trusted advisor.

How to do that?

The best way is through content creation.

You will have to create relevant and interesting content for each product you have identified that will position you as a reference on the subject and thus increase your chances of earning commissions.

The idea is to invade the Internet with your content so that you end up becoming essential.

You will therefore avoid diluting yourself by offering much content but on extremely few products rather than the opposite.

This is what Antoine BM calls the "tree method."

It consists of planting dozens and dozens of seeds to create an ecosystem that will bring you good fruits for years and years.

Because if some of your seeds will not bring you anything, others will grow and give centenarian trees.

Where to plant your seeds?

Well, you can create content that highlights your products on YouTube or even on Google, thanks to articles optimized for SEO.

You can also create a reference Facebook group for each product.

Why not create a dedicated forum and banner ads with your affiliate links?

You can also directly advertise your products on social networks, provided you calculate well if it is profitable.

What to say in your content?

Don't come off as a vulgar rug dealer, but try to bring value to people.

For example, you can give your opinion about your product.

You can also explain how it works by creating tutorials and user guides.

You can also make announcements in a journalistic style to give news about it, such as discounts or updates or how it is a solution to this problem or an effective alternative to another product.

In short, become a mine of interesting and useful information on the products you have chosen to sell.

An important tip: be careful with your calls to action

This is essential for the people who follow you to pass through your links.

The best thing to do is to be completely transparent that you are part of an affiliate program and will receive a commission for each click.

Honesty always pays.

Feel free to communicate the advantage for the customer of going through your link, particularly if you succeeded in obtaining a reduction from the seller.

" I was able to get X% off for you! »

And finally, to increase your conversion rates, mark the path of your visitors by clearly displaying your link and explaining to them what they must do.

" Click this link to activate the 10% discount on X: [your link]. "

Diversify your income

Even though affiliate marketing has many advantages, you are ultimately still dependent on the success and development of another company. If this company is doing badly, you will inevitably earn less. We have often had to witness the closure of partner programs.

Spread your income over several affiliate programs. Consider developing your products or services or running classic display ads.

There are a large number of different options. Although this topic is intended to educate about affiliate marketing strategies, one of those strategies for us is to diversify our income.

How to Increase Revenue with Travel Affiliate Marketing?

The travel industry, or as affiliate program participants call it, the travel niche, has retained its popularity even in the era of covid restrictions and quarantine measures. This topic will tell you who and how to increase travel income by participating in tourism affiliate programs.

A certain category of people find it difficult to sit still. They will always travel, which means they will consume the services of travel agencies and companies and buy travel products and related products.

Even pandemic restrictions have not forced travel enthusiasts to give up their hobbies. The only difference is that in 2021, for example, the number of trips abroad decreased, but the demand for domestic tourism increased.

Travel Niche Features

Large capacity and huge possibilities

Even if we assume all external directions will be closed for some time, internal ones will remain. If we talk about such a huge country as Russia, in each region, be it the south, the middle lane, Siberia, or the Far East, there is where to go and what to see.

Ukraine, the CIS countries will also be forced to develop domestic tourism, faced with restrictions on external tourism. It's unavoidable. Those who quickly create a travel affiliate program and place it on a suitable online platform will win. Oddly enough, with the large capacity of the travel niche and fierce competition within it, travel affiliate programs can still be counted on the fingers.

Suppose you are planning to launch a travel affiliate program very shortly. In that case, we recommend the Alanbase SaaS platform for its placement as a tool with a very convenient statistics system and affordable tariff plans.

High average bill

The cost of air travel and hotel accommodation is constantly rising. In foreign tourism, this is due to fluctuations in the exchange rate. In the interior - with underdeveloped infrastructure and relatively few modern hotels. All this is a fat minus for the tourism industry, but it is a plus for the affiliate program participant since the partner can count on high payments.

Wide range of travel products

For some reason, many web admins have a strange stereotype that a well-known affiliate program can provide the main income from travel for the sale of air tickets. But upon closer examination, there are indeed a lot of worthy products in the tourism niche that can also be recommended to end users. Even those who are not going to fly anywhere at all.

the possibility of earning on a small traffic

In the travel niche, you can earn on small traffic. A web admin can earn income from the travel of other citizens, having a site that receives 500-1000 unique visitors per month, but with the right offers for targeted traffic.

Wide target audience

Tourists and travelers can be divided into different segments: lovers of beach holidays, hiking, rafting, or kayaking; fans of educational tourism, etc. All this allows you to find your direction already inside the niche, concentrate on it and receive income from the travel of the selected segment.

Industry digitalization

Book flights, hotels, and tours pay for excursions - all this can be easily done online. Therefore, it is also relatively easy for an advertiser to make an affiliate program in tourism to consider conversions and share part of their income with partners. Or you can choose a SaaS platform with a ready-made solution, where your affiliate program is set up within a day.

How can a partner start earning income from other people's travels?

The algorithm of actions is very simple; only the partner needs to be aware that participation in any tourism affiliate program is a game for a long time. There will be no result tomorrow, and classic arbitrage schemes work a little worse than betting on your resources.

By the way, many travel affiliate programs, as one of the requirements for future partners, put forward the presence of a website of the relevant subject.

Life hack. You can be someone other than the owner of a content site about tourist attractions in a city or country. Everything that happens in the field of tourism can and should be looked at more broadly.

For example, you have an online store where you sell equipment and things for winter leisure. Such a resource can also be used to receive additional income from your customers' travel. Yes, you sell them skis or snowboards, but is there anything stopping you from offering these people discount bus tickets to the nearest ski resort or the opportunity to book a hotel room at that resort? So offer!

Now back to the algorithm

First, you need to create and work on developing your resource, but rather a small bundle of such resources.

Your site should occupy the central place in this system. It can be either a very broad topic - about tourism "in general," or aimed at a specific country or even a city - a site about Italy or a site about the sights of St. Petersburg; you can even make a microsite about a specific railway or bus station or even a specific train. It all depends on the imagination of the webmaster.

In addition to the site, you can develop thematic groups in social networks and instant messengers, constantly transferring traffic from there to the site, where you place interesting offers to the target audience.

Offers are selected in a suitable affiliate program, and the webmaster starts to receive income from the travel of his site visitors because he recommends the travel products they need.

What else should a web admin who works with travel offers know?

In this niche, there is very high competition and pronounced seasonality.

The pent-up demand is at work here, and therefore you will need patience and perseverance if you want to achieve real success and start making good money on people's passion for traveling.

The fact that you will constantly have to test different ideas and show creativity, as well as look for non-standard solutions.

All of this is worth doing because the output can be passive income, as much as possible, in affiliate marketing.

FAQ

How do I travel with affiliate marketing?

You can travel, blog about your travels in parallel, and make money in affiliate marketing by finding profitable travel affiliate programs.

How much do travel partners earn?

Depends on the partner, his perseverance, resources, and profitable connections found. You can earn up to $300. per month, and it is possible and $10000.

How do travel partners make money?

They make money by promoting travel products and related services. For example, travel life insurance.

Is the travel partner profitable?

Profitable with a competent approach and the ability of a webmaster to be creative.

Increase your CFD affiliate income by keeping up with the trends

Financial markets are volatile, but this can benefit anyone who understands market trends and asset performance. Any CFD affiliate who does understand the basics of affiliate marketing can quickly grow their CFD affiliate income by keeping up with current trends.

In this topic, we explain how to identify market trends and how these trends affect potential CFD traders. Learn how to tailor your content and marketing strategies to grow your profits as a successful CFD affiliate. If you can look past the clickbait headlines and understand your traders, you can make money as a broker affiliate in any market condition!

How Do Market Trends Affect CFD Affiliate Earnings?

Market trends, e.g., the Bitcoin boom in 2021 or the commodity crisis in 2022, increase public attention to financial assets and their specific markets. A popular asset trending up and increasing in value can easily attract new traders. When potential traders see an opportunity to make money quickly, they will urgently look for online brokers.

Negative market trends tend to attract fewer new traders. Not only is there a need for positive hype in the news and on social media, but many newbies assume they will inevitably lose money by investing in down-trending assets. Your job as an affiliate is to explain how experienced traders adapt their trading strategies to volatile markets, try to profit from the latest trends, and anticipate future trends.

When you become a CFD affiliate, you make money through commissions. Your affiliate program pays this when you recruit new traders who register with the online broker. When an asset like Bitcoin, Zoom stocks, Gold, or Oil suddenly starts trending up, it will draw media attention. If the underlying asset has novelty value or is spectacular in any way, it can generate viral interest on social media platforms.

With effective affiliate marketing, you can expect increased traffic during current market trends. Your commissions will increase for the duration of the trend. If you're smart, you'll analyze your campaigns and traffic. The goal is to determine what strategies and content worked best and build on that next time.

5 CFD Affiliate Strategies for Market Trends

Too many people fail to increase their CFD affiliate earnings because they fail to capitalize on new trends. There's a good analogy with surfing: you have to be in the water to catch a wave. You also need to understand where the wave is coming from and position yourself to catch it, i.e., you need the ability to ride it and the awareness to be ready for the next wave. Trends work like big waves.

1. Stay up to date and find out about current market news. You don't need to delve into the financial press. Get a general overview of the markets and subscribe to quality financial alerts and analysis. AvaTrade offers traders eight broad asset classes. Are any of these markets trending?

2. Find out about the factors that motivate potential traders. Crypto and forex traders are usually motivated to make large profits quickly. Like many traders, these are often afraid of missing out on a sudden rally or bull market. Other traders are more risk-averse, while others are more interested in specific assets. You need to know how to target a wide variety of visitors.

3. Work closely with your affiliate program when marketing trending markets. When an asset or market moves significantly or over some time, brokers may add additional financial instruments to their asset index. Some brokers may launch special promotions or offer better trading conditions, higher leverage, reduced spreads, changes in a rollover, or other advantages for traders. This free marketing should be the focus of your CFD affiliate campaigns.

4. Always be able to post interesting content at short notice – trends can change very quickly. A large crash can accelerate within hours. When that happens, you need to comment in real-time on social media. Your affiliate business is a bit like a media company; You should take precautions to produce high-converting marketing materials in the short term. Consider hiring designers and editors.

5. Find and promote the positive in every downtrend. Simple words like PUT or SELL can be persuasive with the right images. Get the message across that CFD traders can potentially profit in all market conditions, including downtrends. If one asset falls suddenly, another may rise. For example, if the US dollar is falling, you may need to promote gold or the CHF.

CFD affiliates must be extremely cautious when making specific predictions about the financial markets. When you promote a regulated broker like AvaTrade, you get clear rules about what you can say in your affiliate marketing content and campaigns. These regulations give you a useful edge in attracting quality traders and building your brand as a trusted CFD affiliate.

Reporting on the opinions of expert financial analysts and major investors is permitted and encouraged. You can add your interpretations and invite your blog readers and website visitors to comment. Aside from creating valuable online interaction, you also have the opportunity to increase your SEO value by linking to quality websites.

Assets and markets that could develop

If you want to increase your CFD affiliate earnings by keeping up with the trends in Q3 & Q4 2023, the following assets and markets are worth monitoring:

cryptocurrencies

Bitcoin (along with Bitcoin Gold and Cash) still has the potential to surprise investors and make headlines. All broker affiliates should watch Bitcoin and be prepared for a sudden bounce. It is a highly volatile asset that has historically made strong comebacks.

raw materials

Precious metals, energy, and agricultural products could change in Q3 and Q4 2023. We are in a new market area, and global events can affect the oil, gas, and staple foods supply.

shares

If inflation peaks now, we could see an autumn and winter rally in stock markets 2023. Based on performance over the past few years, there is potential -- and investor desire -- for significant wins. When the stock market trend is positive, CFD affiliates could increase their commissions by promoting trading CFD indices simultaneously.

Invest in your core affiliate marketing.

Promoting trending assets is an excellent way to increase your CFD affiliate earnings. However, you should pay attention to your core affiliate marketing. Investing in your key SEO content and increasing your reach through blogging and guest posting is important. Since the rise of cryptocurrencies, markets have been in motion every day of the year.

The highest-earning CFD affiliates tend to be the ones who think long-term and are willing to put the time and effort - and a portion of their profits - into their websites and social media accounts. Regularly adding new, quality content will get results in both SERPs and conversions.

If you focus too much on keeping up with market trends, you could be paying attention to the fundamentals. It is worth investing in teaching materials to earn a lucrative basic income. Add more trading tutorials to your website, videos to your YouTube channel, start webinars and podcasts, etc. Your goal is to generate higher traffic volume and convert high-quality traders who will continue to earn for you through RevShare trades.

Other ways CFD affiliates can benefit from trends

Most CFD affiliates start as online affiliates. Anyone with a basic website or above-average social media profile can earn large commissions as a CFD affiliate. If you're already making money during uneventful periods in the market, a sudden bull market could allow you to diversify. A spike in traffic could give you the impetus to start a trading academy or become an introducing broker.

You might renegotiate your commission plan as you diversify your affiliate business and find other ways to attract traders. Any good affiliate program will always be interested in making lucrative offers to business school owners, Ibs, and master affiliates who refer sub-affiliates to the affiliate program. You could create a commission plan covering any income stream and maximizing your profits as a CFD affiliate.

You must join an affiliate program to profit from the next market trends. It's the perfect time to launch and position yourself for the next market move. The potential gains for Expert Affiliates are extremely high in both bull and bear markets.

How to diversify your affiliate strategy in times of economic uncertainty?

Build a strong revenue base through diverse affiliate strategies

Current economic conditions remain uncertain despite the optimism of some marketers. A situation to which we have become accustomed for a few years.

However, affiliate marketing has played an important role in helping advertisers weather this economic uncertainty. Thanks to its performance-based objectives, affiliation has confirmed its place in advertisers' marketing strategies as a driver of commercial results.

Most advertisers see what affiliate strategies they can consider tried and tested. If these strategies continue to bring profits, the next logical and essential step is to build a broader base to generate higher incomes. That's why advertisers are looking to employ more diverse affiliate marketing strategies to help them stay ahead of the market.

While diversification is different for every brand, there are avenues every advertiser should explore.

New markets, new income (and learning) opportunities

Growing into new markets is a logical way to tap into new revenue streams, but it can take time to get started. You have to be careful with the different cultures and sensitivities of consumers. There is sometimes a fine line between approaches that will resonate and those that will miss the intended target.

Affiliate marketing is the ideal channel to try out for the first time. Knowledge of the local market is crucial, and the first step is to partner with publishers in the market who can reach relevant consumers. Close collaboration thus allows the alignment of customer knowledge with the local vision of the publisher established on the market and the possibility of identifying the most effective strategies.

The international expansion brings additional benefits. Traditional affiliation strategies such as couponing and cashback are still relevant in Europe. They are increasingly challenged by new players such as deferred payment solutions, Buy Now Pay Later, loyalty offers linked to bank data, and card linking offers.

Influence, or influence strategies, because this lever cannot be summed up in a word given the various ways of working with Influencers, are taking more and more place in affiliation strategies because consumption behaviors are changing, and influencers are increasingly controlling the profitability of their audiences thanks to affiliation.

All these developments show that it is essential to actively monitor and test new growing partners in markets to maximize the effectiveness of your affiliate strategies.

Build on publisher loyalty and diversification.

Affiliate marketing has reached a level of maturity such that publishers have created very strong bonds of trust with their customers. Loyal consumers often turn to their favorite cashback or coupon sites for product inspiration or to discover new brands.

Faced with a growing and engaged customer base, publishers also see the opportunity to diversify and expand their offerings. We are witnessing the emergence of "super-publishers," which bring together affiliate models to support consumers throughout their buying journey, from interest and inspiration to activation, conversion, and loyalty.

Working with these super publishers can be a way for advertisers to leverage a wider range of affiliate strategies while continuing to build relationships with publishers who already understand their business and goals.

Understand consumer sentiment

In recent years, consumers have become more aware of sustainability and want to make purchasing decisions that reduce their environmental impact. Recycled, refurbished, and second-hand products all saw significant sales growth. The "responsible consumer" is, therefore, here to stay.

Today, many consumers are suffering the effects of financial instability. Therefore, the established concept of the responsible consumer has taken on a new dimension. The sensitivity to ecological questions was added to the general awareness of the financial costs. And it is indeed an addition. Despite broader cost-of-living pressures, consumers will maintain their values. Advertisers must therefore be empathetic to the pressures exerted on consumers and agile in their affiliate activities to guarantee long-term commercial success.

Considering cashback as an approach to reducing consumer spending can pave the way for new ways of shopping. The Goal Bonus can reward publishers with specific, sustainable channels that align a brand's values with the consumer's (but only if they're authentic). Now is the time to listen to consumer needs and feelings.

A larger affiliate base is the key to success.

Lessons learned in Affiliate Value over the past few years will be useful to advertisers over the coming months. However, relying solely on already proven activities could be limiting. It's time to be bold and explore how new affiliate strategies can branch out to ensure continued success for businesses and brands.

Chapter 6: Case Study: Advanced Affiliate Marketing Techniques in Action

Study of the customer journey via affiliation

An analysis of customer journey data through affiliation involving single or multiple publishers.

Introduction

In CJ Affiliate's white paper on Incremental Affiliate Value, we found that having the Affiliate Leverage present in a consumer's path to purchase generated 88% more revenue per buyer than a path to purchase without an affiliation. This white paper investigates the relationship between publishers and their position in a consumer's buying journey based on this finding. Using data from our "Affiliate Customer Journey" solution, we compared the performance of journeys with a single publisher and those with several publishers.

Key lessons

17%

customer journeys via implicit affiliation

more than one editor, which results in

higher average order values,

regardless of the type of publisher or its position

in the purchase journey.

83%

of customer journeys via affiliation do not involve

only one editor.

These insights show that allocating investment to publishers that have been part of the customer journey before the last click can generate incremental revenue while keeping to invest in the unique reach offered by journeys involving a single publisher. This white paper presents these lessons practically so you can apply them to your program. Through the success stories of a leading international brand in the consumer electronics market and a renowned brand in the network services vertical, you will be able to appreciate the value of these lessons.

methodology

We leverage our proprietary "Affiliate Customer Journey" solution, which uses data from across the CJ Affiliate network, to examine where publishers are positioned in the buyer's journey and their impact on the revenue generated. For commission-generating events, we selected an observation window of 45 days to provide readability on how interactions with publishers affect key performance indicators (KPIs), regardless of the compensation terms reference period. Data for this study were collected from May 2019 through August 2020 and included aggregate data from over 143 million transactions and over $18 billion in revenue from over 3,000 advertisers.

Different players in the affiliate channel

Past Affiliate Customer:

A consumer who purchased through an affiliate link.

Contributing Publisher:

A publisher that is part of the customer journey before conversion.

Last Publisher:

The publisher was the last point of contact before the conversion and was rewarded for the resulting transaction.

What does this mean?

1. For most customer journeys via affiliation, there is only one editor in the buying journey. Publishers are generally not in competition for a conversion.
2. Publishers attract loyal and diverse audiences through various models that meet consumers' needs, inform them, and build confidence in purchasing decisions.

3. Continuous recruiting and diversification of publishers in terms of business model or size allow advertisers to reach unique and new audiences through publishers that meet consumer needs. This leads to sustainable growth.

How should it be done?

1. Feel free to call on many publishers through different business models. A more diverse program will provide a wider unique reach.
2. Recruitment efforts must be continuous to maximize and sustain development over the long term.
3. Avoid using one-size-fits-all compensation models. Structure your offers using Scripted Commissioning to reward publishers for their specific strengths and maximize consumer engagement to drive them to conversion.
4. Take advantage of the incredible incremental potential of the affiliate channel (88% incremental revenue per buyer compared to other channels) to optimize your omnichannel marketing strategy and benefit from higher conversion rates and greater revenue.

Examples of strategies to increase reach

1. Work with Search editors. Cost-effectively reach more consumers by allowing search publishers to target long-tail queries through Trademark Plus auctions (brand name + additional term, such as "free shipping"). It's a complementary approach to direct traffic efforts (direct traffic brings together all internet users who typed a website's URL directly into their browser's search bar), freeing up time for internal teams to focus on key brand terms while building competitive advantage through a risk-free, performance-based model.
2. Look for placement opportunities in publisher newsletters. Strengthen your email campaigns by using an affiliate partner to maintain brand awareness. Look for placement opportunities in publisher newsletters after you run an email campaign. This additional touchpoint does improve conversion rates with target consumers looking for another "voice" to help them decide to purchase your product.
3. Leverage a laddered acquisition channel. These recommendations, reviews, or testimonials give consumers the confidence to buy from you. Partner with content publishers and influencers for a genuine third party to help customers who are hesitant or need to learn you convert.
4. Partner with publishers offering geo-targeting. Reach consumers who prefer to buy or collect their purchases on the spot. Work with publishers who can geotarget online consumers with in-store offers to ensure you create a diverse shopping experience that accommodates regional differences in shopping habits and preferences.

Grow through recruitment and activation.

An advertiser selling consumer electronics, recently using Affiliate, selects CJ Affiliate to recruit and activate publishers to grow its revenue internationally, demonstrating the importance of recruiting publishers in building a diverse portfolio.

BACKGROUND

Focusing on recruiting, activating, and diversifying its publisher base, the advertiser turned to CJ Affiliate to sell its products and increase its revenue.

STRATEGY

*   CJ's recruiting solutions and networking expertise helped the team identify, recruit and activate a diverse set of publishers to reach key demographics within international markets.
*   CJ's Account Managers and Global Publisher Development teams have leveraged their data science insights and strong relationships with overseas publishers to activate and quickly optimize new partnerships.

- The Account Managers CJ team also conducted adaptability testing, tested regional offerings in new international markets, and developed an automated MEA tracker to identify ideal placement opportunities by region, publisher vertical, rate, and period.
- Scripted Commissioning has allowed the brand to offer flexible, premium, and exclusive rates on specific products at specific times to support successful launches and sell-off inventory.
- POINT TO REMEMBER ABOUT RECRUITMENT AND ACTIVATION
- 93% of publishers recruited in 2018 generated revenue in the last 12 months. And editors newly recruited in 2019 generated 22% of the program's revenue that year.
- Publishers recruited and activated 2018 generated 78% of program revenue in 2019.
- The program's revenue-generating publisher base grew by 61% from Q3 to Q4 and an additional 31% for the same period in 2019.
- 77% of publishers hired and activated in 2018 continued to generate revenue through Q4 2019.
- In 2019, the program increased the distribution of content from small/micro-influencers by 60% and 30% for medium-sized publishers, while the revenue concentration risk between major publishers decreased by 20%.

17% of customer journeys through affiliates involve multiple publishers, resulting in higher average order values regardless of publisher type or position in the purchase journey.

What does this mean?

1. Our data shows that all publisher models do play a role in both helping conversions and completing them.
2. Affiliate customer journeys are as complex and endless as the buyers who use them. Customer journeys involving multiple publishers drive more value, and publishers should be seen as complementary.
3. Customer journeys involving multiple publishers should be encouraged and rewarded.

While the majority of affiliate customer journeys involve a single publisher, those involving multiple publishers offer a staggered acquisition channel, resulting in higher-value purchases (as demonstrated by the higher average order values below). How should it be done?

1. Break down compensation to account for how often publishers are involved in customer journeys with multiple publishers. Program terms and conditions should be easy to understand: overly complex compensation terms can hurt results.
2. Make recruitment an ongoing priority. Recruiting a diverse group of publishers, and reaching unique audiences, allows you to reach unique audiences for long-lasting results.
3. Use customer journey data to grasp which publishers are reaching consumers ahead of conversion and invest in growing your media coverage or content with those publishers.
4. Be sure to invest in different types of exposure across various business models (cashback, offers, content, influencers, search, etc.) to increase the number of affiliate touchpoints in the consumer's buying journey to increase your average order value. Each type of publisher model both contributes to and converts consumers.

Examples of Strategies to Increase Average Order Value

1. Partner with a group of content publishers and influencers. Compensate these partners with fixed fees for content creation, reviews of your product, and sponsored posts. These partners value authenticity, which results in increased consumer confidence wherever they are in their buying journey, from product discovery to conversion.
2. Optimize or add cashback publishers. These partners play a key role in helping shoppers explore and discover products and brands, giving your brand additional reach. Offer more cashback and invest in premium placement opportunities to get more visibility on a cashback publisher's site.

This will help consumers discover your brand and increase their chances of converting through you rather than a competitor.

3. Use the services of Search editors specialized in Trademark Plus (TM+) strategies. It's a cost-effective way to expand your search scope. These publishers offer great performance-based growth opportunities and complement your direct traffic efforts. TM+ partners provide a competitive advantage by ensuring that your brand does appear in search results for long-tail queries when consumers are in their product discovery or research phase (for example: when they search for "CJ Affiliate Platform").

Grow by investing in influencer marketing.

Leading Service Provider Increases Efficiency and Efficiency with CJ's Affiliate Customer Journey **Solution**

A global consumer and enterprise brand has leveraged CJ's Affiliate Customer Journey report to diversify its media partners, resulting in increased return on advertising spend (ROAS) and the development of new customer contracts.

BACKGROUND

- The advertiser, a longtime affiliate partner, has consistently outperformed its competitors in the telecommunications category.
- The CJ Account Managers team sought to optimize return on advertising spend (ROAS) with active media partners. It recommended investing differently, based on Affiliate Customer Journey data, to bring in publishers that influenced consumers first.

STRATEGY

- Leveraging the Affiliate Customer Journey solution, the CJ team analyzed customer journeys through the advertiser program and identified a group of publishers whose influence on customer conversion was impossible to identify under the last-click attribution model.
- The CJ Account Managers team proposed to increase investments in other strategic partners, influencing the beginning of the customer journey (the starting point for research and reflection), but also in publishers who are the last point of contact before conversion.
- Account Managers' CJ team recommended testing investments with 7 new media partners that demonstrated critical influence early in the customer journey.
- After analyzing the results, the strategy benefited all publishers participating in the customer journey, regardless of their consumer touchpoint. This resulted in increased conversions in the program and return on ad spend.

17 Affiliate Marketing Statistics for 2023

Let's break down some affiliate marketing statistics for this year.

1. The Global Affiliate Marketing Market Is Worth Over $17 Billion

The current global affiliate marketing market size is over $ 17 billion. This is an increase from $13 billion in 2016. The US affiliate marketing market alone is worth over $6 billion.

To remember

Affiliate marketing is huge.

There's much money changing hands in affiliate marketing; you can take advantage of that if you have a website with an audience.

2. Affiliate marketing is a top source of income for 31% of publishers

31% of publishers say affiliate marketing is one of their top three sources of income. For 9% of them, it is their main source of income.

To remember

3. Affiliate marketing is the most important channel for 20% of brand marketers.

It is the most important customer acquisition channel for 20% of brand marketers. 54% rank it between their top three channels.

That's more than organic/paid search (16%) and ads (15%).

To remember

Affiliate marketing is a mutually beneficial relationship. This is an important source of income for publishers and brands whose products are promoted.

4. Google searches for "Affiliate Marketing" did double between 2015 and 2023

Google Trends shows us that monthly affiliate marketing searches are on the rise.

To remember

Affiliate marketing is a growing popular way for publishers to monetize.

It's not the only one, however.

5. "How to create content for affiliate marketing" is one of the top searches on Google

"How to create content for affiliate marketing" is one of Google's top 20 content marketing questions.

To remember

Content creators want to know how to make money from affiliate marketing.

The strengths are:

- Adding links and banners in the footer and sidebar of your website
- Write reviews or share existing reviews
- Email and social media leverage
- Writing a list-style blog and including the product in it
- Update your old blog posts (if any) to include the product

6. 56% of affiliate programs increased revenue during the Covid-19 lockdown

56% of affiliate advertisers and agencies increased their affiliate channel revenue as of the end of March 2020.

To remember

eCommerce has seen important growth during the pandemic. In 2019, online sales did account for 16% of total retail sales. In 2020, this figure has increased to 19%.

Affiliate marketing is no exception – more than half of affiliate marketing programs increased their revenue during lockdown.

Many shifts in consumer behavior are likely to continue beyond the pandemic. This is the perfect time to grow your following and earn from affiliate marketing.

7. 19% of affiliate programs are in the fashion industry

The fashion industry dominates affiliate marketing, accounting for 19% of programs. In second place are sports and outdoor products with 15% and health and well-being with 11%.

To remember

If you run a popular fashion website, you're spoiled for choice regarding affiliate programs.

But that doesn't mean you can't be an affiliate marketer in a more obscure niche. All types of brands are looking for affiliates to advertise their products.

The easiest way to find affiliate programs in your chosen industry is to search Google for affiliate programs for [product type].

Here's another tip: spy on your competitors. Look at sites like yours and see if they have posted affiliate links.

8. The toy industry saw 109% growth in affiliate marketing last year

The fastest-growing product category in affiliate marketing is toys, growing 109% last year. It is followed by software (103%) and DIY (86%).

To remember

Still, looking for your niche?

A few industries, like toys and software, are rising in affiliate marketing. These industries offer great opportunities to increase your income.

9. The retail industry generates 43% of affiliate marketing revenue

The largest share of affiliate marketing revenue comes from the retail industry at 43%. Next, come telecoms and media with 24% and travel with 16%.

To remember

Most of the big opportunities in affiliate marketing come from the retail industry.

Some websites, like fashion blogs, have a clear connection to retail. Other times the connection could be clearer. But you can still find retail products to promote on your site.

Think about your typical audience and the type of products they might buy.

10. 59% of businesses use influencers for affiliate marketing

Influencer marketing and affiliate marketing are different. Many influencer marketing campaigns aim to promote brand awareness rather than just sales.

But 59% of brands and marketing agencies also use influencers as affiliates.

To remember

Companies with affiliate programs are looking for affiliates who have already earned the trust of a big audience. Occasionally that means influencers.

Being an influencer in the traditional sense of the word isn't a requirement for affiliate, but you can pick up some sales tips from successful influencers in your niche.

Take a look :

- The type of content they create
- How they engage with their followers
- The keywords or hashtags they use on their website or social media

11. 88% of customers have been inspired to purchase something by an influencer

88% of consumers say they decided to buy an item based on what they saw from an influencer. Most men (83%) and women (89%) have experienced it.

To remember

You, too, can encourage your subscribers to buy a product.

Many consumers are open to product recommendations. Build a group of buyers who trust you, and you can successfully promote affiliate links.

12. 64% of consumers prefer videos when engaging with influencer content

When engaging with influencer content, 64% of consumers prefer watching videos. Only 38% of consumers prefer written content. 61% of consumers say they prefer pictures.

To remember

People love videos. Here's another supporting stat: the average person spends 2.5 hours daily watching videos online.

Consider promoting your affiliate links with videos. For example, you can embed them in your blogs or landing pages or post them on social media.

13. 77% of consumers make buying decisions based on reviews

77% of consumers consider customer reviews to be a deciding factor in purchasing a product.

To remember

Today's customers are savvy. They don't only read an ad or product description and they assume the product is great – they want to hear from real people who have tried it.

This is why product reviews are one of the most efficient ways to promote affiliate links.

Your review must be genuine. You're promoting a product and building trust with your audience.

In addition to writing your review for your website, you can use third-party reviews to add weight to your recommendation. You can link to these reviews or get permission to embed or screenshot them.

You can link to our review landing page if you are part of Kinsta's affiliate program. This way, you can still use your affiliate link.

14. Amazon Associates holds 43% of the affiliate market share

The Amazon Associate program does dominate the affiliate marketing space with a 43% market share.

To remember

Amazon is the best player in the game.

Fortunately, the Amazon Associate program is also lucrative for many affiliates. What's great is that you can promote any of the millions of products Amazon offers.

So you can decide products that fit your niche and that your audience will love.

15. 99% of affiliate programs do offer a CPA payment model

There are many ways to get paid as an affiliate marketer, but 99% of programs do offer a CPA model.

CPA stands for "cost per action." This means you get paid for each customer who performs a particular action, almost always a sale.

To remember

If you become an affiliate marketer, you will gain an affiliate commission every time someone purchases following your affiliate link.

However, some programs also offer other payment models.

For example, you might get paid for clicks on your link (CPC or cost per click) rather than sales made.

16. Some Affiliates Earn Millions

Publishers who released their earnings reports include Pat Flynn, who grew his business from $ 8,000 to $100,000 monthly, and Adam Enfroy, who earns $200,000 monthly.

To remember

Some affiliate marketers have really top careers. Will you be the next affiliate marketing billionaire?

17. 81.2% of affiliate marketers say they earn more than $20,000 per year

According to a survey of STM forum visitors, 81.2% of affiliate marketers earn more than $20,000 per year.

A good number of them claim to earn millions.

To remember

STM Forum is a famous online community of affiliate marketers that requires a paid membership.

In other words, the majority of people on the forum are experienced affiliates serious about making money from affiliate marketing.

This will slightly distort the results of this survey.

Still, plenty of people earn a decent income by becoming affiliate marketers. As affiliate marketing grows, you can be a part of it.

Conclusion

Remember, the little things often set your site apart from other affiliate marketers. In the future, SEO measures must be taken from the viewer's perspective. Even if SEO is still important today, it is all about the content. Gone are the days when SEO tricks catapulted pages to the top. Top Tip: Go beyond the ordinary!

Keeping up with every single update to Google's algorithm is nearly impossible. Therefore, the most important SEO tactic to remember is optimizing content for users and technology for bots.

Writing content for the search engine was a thing of the past. People and their experiences are at the heart of all SEO tactics this year. So, focus your time and energy on creating quality content that engages and informs the target audience.

This is the foundation of any good SEO strategy. Then use a few key SEO tactics to refine and optimize your efforts.

As you can see, the advanced SEO techniques of the future are similar to what has been done. The user and his preferences are still in the center. We recommend that, before implementing some of these techniques, you do an SEO audit to find out what the weaknesses and strengths of your site are in this regard.

SEO affiliate marketing can be a way for businesses to increase online sales. By focusing on SEO best practices and harnessing the power of targeted keywords, affiliates can bring more qualified traffic to their links and increase the likelihood of conversions. However, it is important to remember that SEO is an ever-evolving field, and staying up to date with the latest strategies and techniques is crucial to succeed. You can maximize your affiliate marketing revenues and build a successful online business by staying engaged and committed to improving your SEO skills.

So now you thoroughly understand an affiliate marketing funnel and how to use it for your online business.

Now it's time to put it into practice and create your sales funnel, set up email marketing sequences, and drive traffic into your funnel.

And if you still need help, you can boost your affiliate funnel with email swipes and many strategies for promoting your affiliate marketing products in our top affiliate marketing training.

As you can see, it's not as difficult as it might seem at first glance.

Ready to choose the right email marketing tool for your business? This guide explains everything you need to know and introduces the top candidates. Everyone has something to offer. It is up to you to decide what is most important to you.

My recommendation? For me, there is a clear winner. The best email marketing solution in this field is GetResponse. Openly welcomes affiliated companies. Offers clear advice and assistance. There are no restrictions on the type of affiliate promotions allowed. And it has a good set of advanced capabilities perfect for helping grow an affiliate business.

Affiliate marketing is one of the best ways to reach and influence consumers worldwide at every stage of their buying journey.

With the right tools, you can achieve mind-blowing results. Look at the tools we have selected and use the ones that make the most sense for you.

Affiliate customer journeys are as complex and endless as the buyers who use them, and all publisher models play a crucial role in these customer journeys. The ideal positioning for an advertiser is to be present in as many customer journeys as possible. Focus on creating opportune moments because there is no optimal customer journey.

Single-publisher customer journeys reach unique customers and offer strong growth potential and increased reach. Journeys involving multiple publishers are as important and yield even more fruitful results. A diversified portfolio that prioritizes and invests in customer journeys involving multiple publishers introduces brands to new audiences. With a staggered acquisition channel, these publishers convert potential buyers into customers.

Given the ability of this marketing channel to generate 88% more revenue per buyer than other channels, continued publisher recruitment, activation, and diversification are key to sustaining long-term sustainable growth. A strategy that encourages single-publisher and multi-publisher customer journeys is essential for brands to gain a competitive advantage and improve their bottom line.

Now that you know how to use ClickFunnels for affiliate marketing, it's time to take your business to the next level.

With its powerful features and easy-to-use interface, ClickFunnels can help you increase your conversion rate and sales.

An affiliate marketing funnel is one of the best ways to increase sales. Depending on the platform you are using, you will have different options:

Track your affiliate funnel

Analyze your funnel

Optimize your funnel

With split testing, conversion and pixel tracking, and landing page design, you can increase sales with the same amount of traffic you have today.

References

The Complete Guide to Affiliate Marketing on the Web By Bruce C. Brown

https://ahrefs.com/blog/affiliate-marketing/

https://neilpatel.com/what-is-affiliate-marketing/

https://www.hostinger.com/tutorials/how-to-start-affiliate-marketing

https://leverinteractive.com/blog/affiliate-marketing-how-to-choose-the-right-network/

https://www.awin.com/ca/how-to-use-awin/affiliate-marketing-programs-that-work

https://www.analyticsinsight.net/how-to-find-a-profitable-affiliate-marketing-niche/

https://getaawp.com/blog/finding-a-profitable-niche-affiliate-marketing/

https://adsterra.com/blog/how-to-build-an-affiliate-website/

https://wpastra.com/guides-and-tutorials/how-to-create-affiliate-marketing-website/

https://seochatter.com/affiliate-marketing-case-studies/

https://www.contentellect.com/affiliate-marketing-case-study/

https://digitalmarketingskill.com/affiliate-marketing-mistakes-to-avoid/

https://statusbrew.com/insights/social-media-for-affiliate-marketing/

https://socialbarrel.com/5-tips-to-use-social-media-affiliate-marketing-to-drive-sales/141538/

https://www.mailmunch.com/blog/affiliate-email-marketing

https://sleeknote.com/advanced/ecommerce-glossary/what-is-affiliate-marketing-email

https://geniuslink.com/blog/podcast-affiliate-marketing/

https://chrisstarkhagen.com/blog/affiliate-marketing-checklist

https://econsultancy.com/seven-steps-to-plan-manage-your-affiliate-marketing-campaigns/

https://settingpoints.com/diversifying-income-streams-exploring-affiliate-marketing/

https://impact.com/affiliate/how-are-influencers-different-from-affiliates/

https://blog.uniqodo.com/influencer-marketing-enhances-affiliate-marketing

Affiliate Marketing For Dummies by Ted Sudol and Paul Mladjenovic

https://influencermarketinghub.com/affiliate-marketing-strategies/

https://influencermarketinghub.com/affiliate-marketing-automation-software/

Printed in Great Britain
by Amazon

40105997R00097